Cover

Amid the cacophony of
"No, don't, why, wait"
many unknown warriors
struggle through mazes of terror
to change the future
for a better world.

Swallowed Tears

A Memoir

Freya Anderson Rivers

authorHOUSE®

AuthorHouse™
1663 Liberty Drive
Bloomington, IN 47403
www.authorhouse.com
Phone: 1-800-839-8640

Published by AuthorHouse 6/7/2012

ISBN: 978-1-4772-1222-6 (e)
ISBN: 978-1-4772-1223-3 (hc)
ISBN: 978-1-4772-1224-0 (sc)

Library of Congress Control Number: 2012909393

This book is printed on acid-free paper.

Published by
Freya Anderson-Rivers
3863 Waverly Hills
Lansing, MI 48917

1. African American families-Non-Fiction. 2. Louisiana-Non Fiction. 3. Racism-Non-Fiction. 4. Desegregation-Non-Fiction.

Cover design by Freya Anderson-Rivers
A collage of several paintings from an unknown Nigerian artist

Cover photos:
Baton Rouge State Capitol by Freya Anderson Rivers

For my beautiful and beloved mother,
Inez Smith Anderson,
who insisted I tell the story

For my children and grandchildren
Monica, Shariba, Sanford, Assata and Angie
Asha, Ausar, Kasi, Nyah and Assata
to learn their heritage

For my Southern High Classmates
who are always here to
nurture, inspire and love me

For all children,
to understand the effects of
hatred, racism, discrimination and violence

For all people
who want a future of harmony and peace.

Acknowledgements

I want to acknowledge and thank my husband, Griffin Rivers, who has been so patient and helpful during the time I spent writing this book. Without his support this book would have been almost impossible to complete. I would also like to thank my mother for pushing and thereby forcing me to write about my father and his work for our children and grands to understand his legacy. Thanks to my daughter, Shariba for taking time from her busy schedule to edit even when it's been at the last minute. Finally, to all my friends and family for your love, I thank you.

TABLE OF CONTENTS

PHOTOGRAPHS

Prologue

November 22nd another anniversary of the assassination of President John Fitzgerald Kennedy. As usual I find myself crying, not for Kennedy, but for myself because I could not cry for so many years. 1963 forced me to become stoic, holding back the tears that burned inside. Tears were a sign of weakness and they had no part in my survival plan. As I watched the replay of Mrs. Kennedy in her pink suit and pink pillbox hat waving at the crowd smiling, the President, John, next to her with his auburn hair blowing in the wind and the motorcade moving along the streets of Dallas with the joyous, waving crowds, shock suddenly broke through the sunshine and smiles as Mrs. Kennedy began crawling across the back of the convertible onto the trunk of the car in panic to get help for her beautiful husband. That instant.... that day... turned me into a different person. That was my senior year of high school. I was full of hate, bitterness and revenge, but at some point the memory blocked until a tragic current event brought back flashes of horror. Freud says we repress things that hurt. I guess I'm fortunate because I was able to suppress the pain for 25 years and go on with my life, or so I thought, but even now remembering is agonizing.

I generally begin by recalling the first time I saw JFK with his top-heavy frock of hair falling on his face in the humidity-laden breeze of New Orleans. The sun caught the reddish highlights on his hair and gave it golden sparkles while his smile brighter than even the sun's rays acknowledged everyone who had come to see him. He touched, nodded or waved to each person. I remember Daddy holding me up and stretching me close to Kennedy's car. I touched President John F. Kennedy! I heard him speak. I was there in New Orleans with my Daddy who insisted that I miss a day of school to see the presidential candidate. Daddy believed in providing us with living, hands-on experiences and this was one of the best. I thought the world was going to change if we elected this young president, but most of all, I knew that he could change the plight of Negroes in the United States.

"Ask not what your country can do for you; ask what you can do for your country," was what JFK required of us in his inaugural address. Daddy had been doing for his country a long time and he already had me committed to follow in his footsteps, but the more he did for his country, the more this country did him in. We were immediate advocates for Kennedy. Even though Daddy didn't quote the Constitution "for a more perfect union," he always felt that this country could be a better place for all citizens if we struggled together and worked hard for respect and equality. He tried to believe that Kennedy, a brilliant man, a man of dreams, a man of change, could be a man of hope.

JFK was a young, vibrant, dynamic president who inspired the youth of this country to join the Peace Corps to give back to their country and the world. He was a president who did not retreat from the Civil Rights Movement but encouraged equality and freedom, the same principles of Daddy's beliefs. Kennedy loved the United States of America and was loved in return by the world—that is, the entire world except for Baton Rouge, Louisiana.

That city ignited the cancerous pain of hatred that was enveloping me and destroying my life. At some point I had to face this pain and the people of Baton Rouge to exorcise that demon. So, in 1988 I took a step forward or ….. maybe backward. The Black Alumni of Louisiana State University had a reunion to honor the African American pioneers who desegregated LSU. I was invited because in 1964 I became a pioneer by filing suit to desegregate the undergraduate division.

I did not attend all of the activities for the weekend because my legs would not walk on that campus. Every step across each blade of grass was stressful. Every look and sideways glance brought flashbacks and a tenseness of my senses that caused me to be alert. I could not recall the summer of desegregation without clenching my teeth and tightening my jaws, which caused a severe sharp lightning strike in my head that started a feeling of nausea. My soul was still not ready to open up and talk about what I felt and how I survived. I fought back these emotions with deep breaths and swallowed tears.

After some friendly persuasion from my father, I agreed to go to the alumni dinner because all I had to do was receive an award; I did not have to speak publicly. I was afraid that seeing old faces and hearing the old stories would leave me vulnerable. Only recently have I begun to talk about my feelings. First, talking to very close friends, later, my family and now I can finally speak to audiences.

During the dinner I heard that A. P. Tureaud, Jr., who filed suit to integrate LSU in 1953, spoke during the morning session and cried, as did many others. However, I remained stoic thinking to myself, "I am aggressive, strong, determined and successful. I will not only survive but thrive without anyone's help and I will not cry!" That was my survival mantra. Every November 22nd when I see John-John saluting his father as the caisson passes on TV reruns, I find myself crying privately and thinking, "Damn you Kennedy for dying. Damn you for leaving me all alone."

Negro Society

For anyone to understand my pain, they need to know my history, my family, my friends and my life. Just telling a desegregation story would be almost meaningless unless you could understand the reasons behind my agony. So, I'm starting from the beginning of me, of my city, my parents, my family, my schools and friends. Then, you can walk with me through the most horrific year of my life.

I grew up in Baton Rouge, which means "Red Stick," but Blacks called it "Red Neck," because that is what they called racist whites. Baton Rouge is the capital of Louisiana and sits on the east bank of the Mississippi River. The weather is almost tropical year round with high temperatures and humidity that make your hair curl. You can see the steam rising from the blacktopped road looking like steaming tar. The sun is so hot that the black top melts and an egg can be fried on the sidewalk, but po white trash can walk with bare feet and not get blisters. Great oak trees line the streets, pecan trees in backyards, azalea bushes in spring, heavy rainstorms that flood and lightning and thunder that scare everyone to sleep in the same bed.

For whites there are three important things in the city: LSU Tigers football team, the State Capitol and the LSU Tigers football team. Blacks have one important claim to fame and that is Southern University. Baton Rouge's claims to fame are the LSU Tigers football team and Billy Cannon, LSU's 1959 Heisman Trophy winner, along with its infamous political scandals.

LSU is revered. Even in a predominately Catholic city, it is The Vatican for Baton Rouge. Exceptions are made for Holy Days because of an LSU football game. On a Saturday night when LSU is playing football, all traffic becomes one-way to the LSU stadium before the game and then one-way from the stadium after the game. Pray that you never get caught in the traffic flow because whether you planned to go to the game or not, you will be directed to do so and not allowed to go in any other direction until the second quarter. LSU's colors, purple and gold, are everywhere in the city. Houses are purple and gold. Cars are purple and gold. Flags and clothes during football season are purple and gold. Stores are purple and gold. Even people are purple and gold.

LSU is at the southern end of the city on the Mississippi River. Southern is at the northern end on the Mississippi. The State Capitol is in the middle of the city, downtown. Southern sits at one of the highest points on the river called "The Bluff" which is one of the best sites on the river. It has the most beautiful view of the entire Mississippi in Baton Rouge as the river bends at that point looking across and down the river to the old and new river bridges. Most whites probably don't know this because few come on Southern's campus. They don't know that the bluff, looking out over the river, is probably the most peaceful place in the city. That's about the only advantage that Southern has over LSU.

Most of the state university funding goes to LSU with Southern as an afterthought. LSU is the pride and joy of Baton Rouge. From the richest person to the pick-up truck driver with loaded guns in the gun rack, a confederate flag on the back window, a six pack in the cooler behind the driver's seat and a 9th grade education, if that, they all love the LSU tigers and will kill and die for them while bleeding purple and gold. That's the white of Baton Rouge.

Blacks' claim to fame in Baton Rouge is Southern University, the Jaguars, blue and gold. Southern University was across railroad tracks that frequently had railroad traffic that prevented students from getting to class or visitors to a game. Who cared if Negro students missed class? On any Saturday night when the Jaguars were in town, traffic was backed up for miles and hours trying to get to the game and back home after the game had ended. Who cared if Negroes missed a game? Still, sitting on hard bleachers on only one side of the field (because there was only one side to view the game from)—the opposing side had to stand or join us—watching the Jaguars play all Negro SWAC (South Western Athletic Conference) teams was a great treat and a reason to party no matter who won the game.

There was and is a white Baton Rouge and a Black one. Whites did not know what Negroes did or did not do and did not care unless the doing infringed upon them and white rights. Whites did not know that Negroes ate, drank, slept, went to church and died just like whites …. but better. Negroes lived like all humans. We still do with a little extra flavor. Our food is spicier. Our drinks are sweeter. Just try our Kool-Aid and sweet tea. We have been known to not only snore in our sleep, but we talk, walk, dance, sing, and I know someone who even played basketball while sleeping. Our churches are interactive and frequently humorous, and we second line home from our funerals to a party of waiting relatives who eat and drink and toast the departed. Leaving the graveyard, there is a brass band parade to celebrate the joyful rising of the departed into heaven. The "main line" is made up of family members and relatives, but the people who follow the parade to hear the music or enjoy the band and dance are called the "second line," a dance with handkerchiefs and umbrellas keeping beat with the music. However, the second line dance can stand on its own without a funeral. Given the right beat, handkerchiefs start waving and people just start dancing.

Black folks enjoyed each other and we could have taken care of ourselves if we were allowed to do so. I believe that if government had played fair and unequivocally had "separate but equal," we would have been satisfied for a long time in our own world, but eventually our society would have crumbled in on itself because we were too busy trying to mimic whites even to the point of discrimination.

We discriminated against each other because we were taught to discriminate, dislike and even hate ourselves, our physical attributes, culture and social characteristics. It began with the kidnapping of Africans and enslavement. Divide and conquer was part of the "seasoning" of enslaved Africans to dissuade unity that may have led to uprisings. Slave owners constantly created dissension by discriminating between groups of people. Enslaved people who worked in the "big house" were thought to be better than the ones who worked in the fields. Those who had light complexions were better than those who were darker because they had white blood. Strong young men and women were worth more than the old and young because they could harvest more. Men were worth more than women but women could breed. Children were taken from their families and husbands were sold away from their wives if they were even permitted to marry. The "Black Codes" even used religion to teach that whites were the angels and masters and the Blacks were their slaves. The 200 years of divide and conquer failed to prohibit slave uprisings, but unfortunately, much of the discrimination remains within Black society.

Negroes established stratification ranks. The criteria were based on the color of one's skin, hair, eyes, speech and more. Just as Negroes were taught during enslavement, lighter skin was better than darker skin. Black was described and defined as bad, ugly, scary, threatening, and even dumb. There were "Brown Bag" parties where a brown bag was hung at the door and if you were darker than the bag, you were not welcome. Louisiana had to be the worst state with the color stigma because of its population that divided Negroes into octoroons, quadroons and other classifications depending upon the amount of white and black blood you had in your family due to miscegenation.

Another important group of mixed people in Baton Rouge were the Creoles who were of African, French and Spanish heritage. Generally, Creoles had light complexions with "good" hair, but caramel colored people were accepted if they had the "good" hair. These traits should have given them a step up in Negro culture, but the Creoles did not consider themselves Negroes, so they did not participate in Negro culture. Creoles in Baton Rouge sent their children to St. Francis Xavier Catholic School (the Negro Catholic School) for an elementary education, but by high school many of their children were taken out of school especially the boys. These Creole children were sent to work in their families' businesses. The Creoles of Baton Rouge almost had a monopoly in the building industry with brick masons, ironworkers and carpenters and were looked upon as a separate race. Whites as well as Negroes used them for building and it became a very lucrative family business that was passed from generation to generation. Many became quite wealthy but they were never fully accepted as part of either the white or Negro society.

Facing this conundrum, Creoles and some light skinned Negroes, passed for white to attain white privileges and merge into white society. Passing for white was called, "Passé Blanc." The Creoles and the passé blanc were different societies in the city and I know little about either because they usually stayed together and did not let others into their world for fear of being recognized as Negroes. Those fair skinned Negroes who did not pass were often ostracized by both Negroes and whites in many ways, but generally in a Negro school lighter children were considered the smartest and the darker students were often not given a chance to participate. This also held true for jobs with light skinned Negroes getting hired first and darker ones relegated to menial positions in both Negro and white society. There were many contradictions in Negro society, but if you lived in it, you knew the criteria and rules and you played the game to survive.

Another status symbol was/is hair. I hated to hear "good" hair, but I heard it all my life. "You have 'good' hair. It's so pretty and long." Then someone would proceed to put their hand in my hair. I hated it. Hair is another standard for discrimination in Negro society. Good hair was straight hair, wavy hair, curly hair and long hair, but unlike what the theme of the present-day book *Happy to be Nappy* suggests, tightly curled "nappy hair" was not "happy" during that time. Women and girls were hard enough on themselves about their hair, but Negro men were the ultimate judges. They wanted Negro women with long, straight hair—like they saw on white women—that they could run their fingers through. So, Negro women hot combed, permed, dyed and bought wigs and pieces to look pretty. Braids, naturals, twists and cornrows were all too "African" and that was a curse word for most Negroes. Africa was the land of Tarzan and illiterate black skinned people of the jungle, according to all our authorities on the matter, i.e., teachers, the news and the movies. Negroes did not want to be associated with Africa even though we were African.

Yet another status symbol was eyes. Light brown eyes, grey eyes, hazel eyes were also a sign of being "mixed" (white and Negro) which earned someone a notch up in the Negro rating. Blue or green eyes even made up for dark skin or nappy hair. Funny that Negroes had all these elements in their criteria to discriminate but whites did not care what color you were or what your hair or eyes looked like. The only thing that mattered to them was if you had a drop of Negro blood, then you were a Negro. That meant you were three-fifths of a citizen according to the Constitution and relegated to all things marked "Colored." Nothing else mattered to whites—not a Ph.D.,

M.D., J.D., Reverend D., money, age, color, eyes, hair or who you knew. However, Negro society had its own rules of acceptance and all of these attributes counted toward your status in the community.

If one were regarded as a "higher up" because of skin or eye color or hair texture, the other critical attribute was to not "act colored." Not acting colored meant talking correctly and properly. *Ebonics* was not a word in that time period. Speaking Ebonics was not acceptable even though everyone spoke it whether they knew it or not. The best examples of Ebonics speakers not claiming Ebonics were always the Negro ministers preaching and singing in a call and response. Their usage of all the elements of Ebonics was, and still is, quite colorful.

Black folks stretched words and used different intonations that gave multiple meanings to words defined by circumstance like "bad, baaad, BAD!" or "My sssweeeet Jesus" which was not the same as "sweet tea." Profane words like "shit," "MF" and the "N" word could be any and all parts of speech depending on inflection. Blacks didn't know that the reason they didn't add an "s" for plurals was that two or more automatically denotes more than one in African languages, and "I be" is the now of what I'm doing. They also did not know that there were no digraphs and double consonant ending sounds in African languages and that's why Blacks said "nof" instead of "north," "do" instead of "door," and "cole" instead of "cold." We had no knowledge of linguistics or our history, but we did know that speaking this way would be taken as an indication of our lack of intelligence, and it was embarrassing. Ebonics was considered "colored" and not to be used by "intelligent" Blacks. All of us "educated" Blacks tried to speak the "King's English."

Other criteria that would get you the colored label were being loud, using profanity in public, lack of manners and respect, eating watermelon in the front yard, men wearing hats backwards, and women not wearing hat and gloves when dressed. It goes without saying that anyone going barefoot was just plain colored and countrified. Coloreds had their own time called "CP Time" (Colored People's Time) where Negroes were always fashionably late. There were other issues with hair like sitting on the front porch combing hair, hair not combed in public, lint in hair, hair that had "gone back" (not straight any longer from sweat or humidity) and nappy "kitchens" (hair at the base of the neck). Then there was fried chicken. Many Negroes tried not to be associated with fried chicken but that was impossible, so the rules required making sure you did not leave grease on your hands or face and that the grease was not transferred to working papers, programs, furniture, sheets, etc. Ashy skin (dry black skin has a gray or "ashy" look) was definitely frowned upon and Vaseline was the cure. Some babies were so greased down with Vaseline that they could literally slip out of your hands. Grinning and shuffling, bowing and scraping were unacceptable even though Negro men were still lynched for looking whites in the eyes, walking on the same side of the sidewalk, not tipping one's hat or talking back to a white person. There were many requirements to being Negro and not colored, and most of us failed at one time or another because a lot of it was just our nature. Too bad we were embarrassed of who we were, why we were, and what we were when we should have been glad to be alive and, for the most part, thriving because of our culture.

Negro society was and is a completely separate society in which whites still know very little about us and how we live. We had our own newspapers, magazines, businesses, professionals, social and civic organizations and even secret societies just like white folks. Negro society included schools, restaurants, stores, theaters, nightclubs, churches, funeral homes, graveyards, motels or rooms to rent and in some cities, banks. There were Greek fraternities and sororities, social and civic clubs, church organizations, insurance companies and much more. Negroes were doctors, dentists, lawyers, teachers, preachers, entrepreneurs and the list goes on. The Negro community mimicked the white community in every way unless prohibited by the whites, the law or the klan. Growing up in the segregated south left Negroes really wanting for little that they could not get in their own communities, but they paid taxes and felt that they deserved equality.

The inequities of segregation and Jim Crow revealed that the public facilities and schools were atrocious. Negroes paid more than their fair share but received few services. White water fountains had cold water and colored fountains were hot. White restrooms were clean and if there was one for coloreds, it was dirty, without paper and usually not in working order. Negroes could not try on clothes and shoes in stores, but rather had to trace their foot on cardboard and hope the shoe fit at home. Negroes could cook the food in restaurants but had to stand outside to order and eat. Negroes could clean the hotels but were not allowed to stay, regardless of who they were, famous or infamous. In theaters and entertainment venues Negroes were relegated to the balconies, the back of events or end zones. Jobs were limited and when hired in the same position as a white the salary was never equal. Negroes were given inferior service, attitude and gratitude even though they were paying the same as everybody else. Hospitals did not permit Negro physicians to practice. They had to turn over their patients to white doctors when admitted to the hospital. City and state jobs were not open to Negroes. Bank loans, insurance policies and investing were prohibited. Inter-racial marriages were forbidden. In spite of the humiliation and degradation that accompanied trying to go to white events, places and services, some Negroes continued to support white businesses and professionals because Negroes had been trained to think that,

"White ice is colder than Black ice," or in other words white is better. "If you're white you're right; yellow you're mellow; brown stick around; Black get back." However, there were a few Blacks who fought back, not only for themselves but for a more perfect union. One of these fighters was my father, Dr. Dupuy H. Anderson.

PART I

Segregation

Revolutionary

Malcolm X took the letter "X" as his last name to signify the African name he never knew and to rid himself of the slave master's name. Denouncing his last name was a protest against having to carry the name of the slave masters and their violence against enslaved African American women. Most African American genealogy began with enslavement followed by rape. Yes, RAPE! When someone owns you, there is no consent involved. You do as you are told or you die. That is the significance of the surname and a part of the African American heritage that we would prefer to forget.

Dupuy Henry Anderson, my father, kept the slave master's names but researched genealogical archives his entire life mailing his last computer printed copies to me on August 1998, ten months before his death. He was determined to find the family history to try to find the families of the perpetrators of injustice. He felt that knowing the past is critical to the future because the past is the foundation for the future. His past, or as much as documentation allows, began in 1806 at a "Public sale of 18 slaves imported from Africa" (ship name: Success). Unnamed: black "Brut" female; age 8; sold to Charles Duval in 1806 in Baton Rouge.

I'm still doing the research and so far I've found Duvall and Devall listed on both sides of Daddy's mother's family: Frozine Duval Cobbs (1859-1923), whose mother Creshy Henesboisn was raped by a white Duvall in West Baton Rouge Parish, and Charles Dupuy's grandmother, who was raped by a Devall in West Feliciana Parish. I don't know if they were related but I'm also scared to find out. Frozine and Charles Dupuy gave birth to Lillie Dupuy (Grandmother, January 18, 1896), Daddy's mother.

Daddy's father, Henry Andrew Anderson (Paw Paw) was listed as mulatto in the 1910 census, which means that he was of mixed heritage, born March 8, 1895. His mother Julia Bockel was the daughter of a white Prussian, Conrad Bockel, who raped his black servant, Margaret Bockel (1870 census). Julia married Henry R. Anderson, Paw Paw's father. His parents John Anderson and Sophy Washington listed themselves in the 1880 census as Black farmers in St. Francisville, West Feliciana Parish, Louisiana. Those Black Andersons in St. Francisville were well respected, not only as entrepreneurs but also for operating the power plant. One brother was the only operator of the plant. He would turn the power on and off daily for the entire area. Henry R. Anderson divorced or left Julia Bockel shortly after Paw Paw was two years old and married Emma George. He remained in contact with Paw Paw and left him his house and car when he died. So, my paternal great grandparents were mixed with whites and were considered mulattoes.

Henry Andrew Anderson (Paw Paw) and Lillie Dupuy (Grandmother) were married April 28, 1917 and had five children: Dupuy Henry Anderson (4/30/1918), my father, was the oldest of Lilburne (Lulu), Uncle Bobby, Uncle Cliff and Aunt Phrozine. Grandmother and Paw Paw lived with her father, Charlie Dupuy, until Lulu was born. After becoming a postman, which was considered a very good job for Blacks at that time because it was a federal job with a pension and benefits, Paw Paw moved his family to North Street in a white neighborhood close to downtown Baton Rouge.

Mixed neighborhoods were strange to other southern cities because most of the south had defined separate housing areas for whites and Blacks, but many of the Baton Rouge neighborhoods were mixed. The Anderson-Dupuy families desegregated North Street. There was Paw Paw and Grandmother's house facing North Street and behind them was Charlie Dupuy, Jr. (Grandmother's brother), who we called "Son." Behind him were NinNee (Grandmother's sister), her husband, Charles Washington and their family, and around the corner lived Aunt Francis Duval Gardette. She was grandmother and NinNee's aunt who lived with her husband, Willie Gardette. We called him Uncle Doo Doo. I don't know how he got that name, but he was one of the best stonemasons in the city who was often drunk because of the humiliation he had to endure. Recognition for his work and salary often went to his white supervisor as did any accomplishments of Negroes at that time. Black men rarely received credit for their work, which caused them to drink or seek other refuge to escape reality. That was the explanation given to us, the children, to explain his drinking.

NinNee's children were George, Sis, Margaret, Eunice, Corrine and Tutti who, living directly behind Grandmother, made up the Anderson-Dupuy-Washington extended family. Daddy played with his siblings and cousins. From eight to ten years of age Daddy and his cousin George also played with some of the white kids in the neighborhood who grew up to become influential political leaders. Daddy was the self-appointed head of the children in the family, and they all attest to the fact that he came into the world as a leader and dictator, albeit a benevolent one, with strong ethics and beliefs wanting everyone to be the best that they could in every situation to make the world a better place. He never let any of them settle for less than their maximum potential.

His siblings described him as headstrong, bull-headed and outright bossy. He knew what he wanted and set out early in life to try to right the wrongs. As a child Daddy wanted to join the Boy Scouts but there were no troops for Blacks. In his junior year of high school he was finally able to join Black Troop 547 organized and chartered by Mount Zion First Baptist Church. J. L. Kraft, football coach for McKinley, Baton Rouge's Black high school, was

Troop 547's first Scout Master, but the Black troop could not buy uniforms or go to camp or any of the general gatherings. Daddy always talked about how disappointed he was in the Scouts for their discrimination and how denigrated he felt because of color.

Later, as a young adult working with other local leaders, he organized a fundraiser at the Temple Roof. The Temple was a Black theater downstairs and a social hall upstairs. The money was to purchase uniforms for all the boys in the troop, but even after the money was raised, they were still denied the privilege of purchasing the uniforms. At the time Daddy was working in the stock room at the downtown store, Welsh and Levy, where the uniforms were sold, but that made no difference. The store refused to sell uniforms to Black children. Despite the obstacles, the young men persevered. Daddy said their troop trained from the *Boy Scout Handbook*, went hiking and camping on their own and "Nigger-Rigged" (the term used when Blacks were inventive enough to find solutions to problems presented by segregation) the supplies they needed to accomplish their medals. He remained a Boy Scout until his 18th birthday and then served as an assistant Scout Master, Scout Master, and eventually, Commissioner. Daddy didn't let anything stop him from achieving his dreams. Every time whites thought they had won, Blacks found the barriers as just one more hurdle to cross. The Boy Scouts became one of Daddy's lifetime revolutionary fights.

At the same time as his fight with the Boy Scouts, Daddy became aware of the inequities in the school system. He was one in a group of boys selected to pick up textbooks at a white school for the Black McKinley High School. What they picked up were raggedy, old, outdated books that the white school was discarding. Without backs, pages torn, names written in all the lines, writing on pages, lines blacked out, these books became the texts for Black students after the white students had thrown them away and were receiving new ones. He also noticed the differences in the whites' buildings as compared to those of the Black schools. The white schools were painted and well-kept with no broken windows or torn screens or peeling paint. The white schools offered more courses, were well supplied and had a longer school year. Blacks had a shorter year since many children worked on farms to help their families harvest sugar cane and cotton or other work in the fields. Supplies in Black schools were non-existent. Black teachers paid for supplies out of their one-third-less-than-white-teachers' salary. Anger, with hatred for a system of inequality, began brewing in my father who refused to accept second-class citizenship. Educational equality became another revolutionary fight for the rest of his life.

When not fighting for equality, he tried to be an ordinary teen, but then maybe not so ordinary because he occasionally had problems trying to "fit in." One day he and his cousin George, who was called "Brother," had Paw Paw's car on blocks working on it. Daddy told George, "You get under and check it because I don't know anything about cars. All I know is how to turn the key and put in gas." George agreed, "Ok, see if it will turn over." George was under the car when Daddy started the car, with his foot on the gas! The car jerked forward rolling off the blocks and rolling over George. Daddy was scared and immediately got out of the car. He started shaking George and yelling, "Bro, are you dead? Bro, are you dead? Speak to me Bro!" Fortunately, George was all right but the cacophony of screams and hollering of all the children at the house brought everyone running and eventually laughing after they found out that Brother was not harmed. The family still laughs about it at every gathering.

Another Daddy teen moment was the night Grandmother heard someone at the back door and saw the handle shaking. With Grandmother and the other children standing at the door, Daddy got Grandmother's brother Uncle Jim's gun and shot through the door barely missing Grandmother and the person trying to get in the house, but whoever it was ran for his life. Aunt Phrozine said the man tripped over the clothesline, and then fell over the fence before he finally escaped. Daddy was a take-charge kind of person. Act now and think about consequences later as a bullet might whiz by your ear.

Another of those times of not thinking about consequences was when a white police officer came up to a car that Daddy was sitting in and told him to get out. He told the policeman, "No!" The policeman replied, "Nigger, you know I'll shoot you," but Daddy said that he looked that white man straight in the eye and told him, "You're not going to shoot me." To be that bold during the Jim Crow era, Daddy could definitely be called a crazy man, but he never thought of himself as unequal to anyone and he refused to be mistreated.

He was quite smart and did well in school, graduating from McKinley High School in 1935, but he knew he wanted and needed a higher degree to succeed. At 18 he registered to vote by correctly reciting the Preamble and answering questions relating to the Constitution and state government to pass the required registration examination. He told the registrars that he wanted to be registered as a Democrat but they stamped his card as Republican, which meant that he could only vote in the general election for governor every four years and not any of the primary elections because Louisiana was a one party state, Democrat. This just added fuel to the fire in him to go to college and become the first person in his family to have a college degree. He felt a degree would demand respect. With the little money that Paw Paw had saved for him and Lulu, Daddy began studying at Southern University. He worked part time and summers to get him through. Paw Paw's white mentor, a Mr. Kaufmann, the Postmaster, advised him on financial issues that enabled Paw

Paw to eventually accumulate a savings account that paid for most of the tuition needed for Daddy and Lulu to attend college. After graduation from Southern University in 1940, Daddy still wanted more education, a higher degree. He wanted to become a dentist.

Accepted at Meharry Medical College, a Black medical college in Nashville, Tennessee, Daddy left Baton Rouge. Without all the money he needed to attend, he begged for any job on campus to help him pay for books, housing, food and other necessities. When he inquired at the library about the possibility of a job, he was asked if he had any training in the Dewey Decimal System; he responded that he did. Daddy told the story to us grinning because he said, "I didn't know anything about Dewey Decimal. I had been to libraries and knew how to check out books but I didn't know how they were filed. So, I lied to get the job. I spent the next few days in the library finding out all that I could and I got the job." That job helped him remain at Meharry. In his many speeches that he gave me as a child, he often told me that he never went out to parties or peer activities on weekends because he was always in the library working. He was determined to get his dental degree. I later found out that Daddy could also be the life of a party. He didn't spend every weekend in the library. He just did not let anything deter him from the degree because his Aunt Dell instilled in him that education was paramount to attaining your dreams. The family believed in education and Daddy's generation became the first to achieve higher degrees. Armed with determination, Daddy continued to work odd jobs during the summers to pay for college.

Digging ditches at Ryan Airport in Baton Rouge was one of those jobs and the only job he could find as a Black, even **with** a college degree. He took the job even though he had never done manual labor before. He talked of his hands and back being in constant pain, but he always said, "Be the best at whatever you do even if it's a ditch digger." Daddy never failed to practice his beliefs and he was a great ditch digger, which gave him an opportunity to talk to the supervisor who, after hearing Daddy's qualifications (including being the teacher assistant in an engineering course at Fisk with Jimmy Lawson who later became President of Fisk), promoted Daddy to supervisor of the ditch diggers.

Not wanting to be a ditch digger for the rest of his life, Daddy pressed on in his studies and community involvement while at Meharry. A community involvement incident at Meharry landed him in jail. His instructor who taught dental jurist prudence ran for an elected office in Nashville, Tennessee. Someone paid the poll tax for students at Meharry who had been in the state for more than six months to permit them to register. The students did register. The professor won the election. The city threw the election out and put the students in jail when they tried to vote again in the second election. Daddy went to jail. They didn't remain jail, but it was supposed to be a lesson on staying in one's place. In spite of politics Dupuy H. Anderson completed his Doctor of Dental Surgery from Meharry in 1944 and received his Commission as First Lieutenant Dental Corps, Army of the United States. He served in the Medical Administrative Corps.

While studying for the board exam in Baton Rouge, Daddy went to the library for resource materials. The librarian informed him that he could not stay there and read but that there was a room for "coloreds." He told the librarian that the room was too small and dark and he could not read in that room. The compassionate librarian showed him a secluded, large, bright room that no one else used and hid Daddy in the room so that he could study. Eventually, he led the fight to break down the barriers in the public library. The city agreed to let Blacks in the library but only certain people. However, the night that the council agreed, Daddy called every principal in the city to let them know that the library was open.

On February 21, 1945 the Louisiana State Board of Dentistry sent congratulations on the successful completion of the State Board Examinations for Dentistry just days after Daddy had been issued his Army ID on February 9th. He was now a licensed dentist but could not set up office until his tour of duty was over. During the time he was in medical school, Lulu (Lilburne) went to college, graduated in Home Economics, began working and sent money to Daddy to help him with finances in college. Phrozine was in nursing school. His brothers Bobby and Cliff joined the service during World War II and never completed their college degrees. Bobby followed in Paw Paw's footsteps by working with the postal service and Cliff became a master carpenter.

September 5, 1946, First Lieutenant Dupuy H. Anderson was promoted to Captain in the Air Force at Ft. Sam Houston, Texas and his military life became a living hell. The hatred of another institutionalized system of racism, the Army and its people, carried the burden of inhumanity without any means of rebuttal, revenge, retribution, or reward for Black people. Daddy gave an extensive interview with Maxine Crump for LSU's Oral History Project in 1994 where he described his experiences in the Army.

With the bombing of Pearl Harbor, all males at Tuskegee had to sign up to join the army. "After we signed up, it was about two or three months before we had army training. We all left and went to Fort Benning, Georgia, for our exam, to be issued clothing and everything. The next thing that struck me was, after being examined, we sat out in the bleachers in the hot sun. A colonel got up and made this remark, 'Well, I'll be damned. Here's a bunch of niggers without syphilis or gonorrhea.' That was one thing that stayed on my mind."

Then, "I was sent to Ryan Army Airfield as a First Lieutenant, Medical

Corps. I went in and had my physical. I went over to the hospital and every typewriter stopped typing, every head turned toward me. A gray-haired colonel walked out. The captain gave him my papers. He threw them back to me. He said, 'They must have made a mistake.' I took my papers and went home and took off my uniform. I felt like burning it. I stayed around here (Baton Rouge) and received my pay until I got orders to move. When I got orders to move, about a year after, I got a letter from the Air Force Surgeon General wanting to know where I had been. Where I had been! I was burning up, furious. I wrote a letter. It had to go through command, and they wouldn't send the letter that I had written. They wrote it over because at that time I was out in the secular world, and I used some bad language telling them the reason why you don't have a record of me at Ryan Airfield is that they denied me signing-in because I was Negro."

Daddy described Fort Huachuca in Arizona in the middle of the desert with few recreational facilities for Blacks who were in a separate area from the whites. Whites had a nice club and swimming pool and much more, but Blacks weren't allowed up there. So, "a group of us decided we were going up there. And we went up there." The Blacks that defied the rules were given written reprimands for their actions. These were the type of things that made Daddy say, "If you send me overseas, you may as well send a brick overseas. You'll send a dead weight."

Daddy's love of softball and having the ability to play saved him from being sent overseas. He tells how he got out of going and felt sorry for the guy that had to go in his place. Daddy recounted, "We had a softball game. Our commanding officer said the first one to hit a home run will get a forty-eight hour pass. I hit it inside the park and stretched it into a home run, and then I laid out in the field. I had a bad knee. I went to the hospital. It did hurt, but I complained and complained. They sent a boy by the name of Wells overseas in my place."

Daddy's next assignment was Tuskegee Airfield. On the way he had a stop in Atlanta and was hit in the head by a policeman for going through the front door and not the back door for "Colored." He said there was nothing that he could do about it. "I saw a black soldier killed in cold blooded murder. We went over to Atlanta and a black soldier was backing up to park in a space. A policeman drove up and started questioning him. And the soldier spoke back to him and said he was 'just going to park here.' He had seen this space and was pulling in. The officer said, 'Oh, you're a smart nigger!' and shot him…. Nothing happened. He was just another dead Black person. The army wouldn't take up your cause hardly at all." So, when the officer hit Daddy in the head for entering the wrong door, he decided not to buck the system thinking he might be the next to be killed.

While stationed at Tuskegee, Black soldiers had to go to movies during the day if they had time off and not at night with the whites. There were separate water fountains and restrooms for "colored" and whites. Blacks had to sit at the back of the bus. Black pilots had Master's Degrees and Ph.D.'s, but they had to endure "head" white officers with inferior qualifications. Black divisions were supervised by white officers who were generally less educated. Blacks also had to fly the older planes while whites flew the newer ones. Daddy knew that Blacks had to always be better than whites to get ahead. One of his mottos became, "Not as good as, but better than." He learned this from the army.

Daddy met Charles Drew while stationed at Tuskegee. Drew was the scientist who created blood plasma and the blood bank during World War II that helped save lives on both sides of the ocean and continues to save lives to this very day. After Daddy left Tuskegee Drew was injured in a car accident on his way to Tuskegee in 1950. Word circulated that Drew was transported to a white hospital after the accident and the hospital denied him a blood transfusion—the very blood plasma he created—because he was a Negro. As a result of not receiving the proper treatment, Dr. Drew died. Every time Daddy told this story it brought tears to his eyes.

Daddy told a story about driving the dusty road to Tuskegee. "There were only a few Blacks officers that had automobiles and when the Black sharecroppers living in the falling down shacks would see a car and us driving, they'd come out and wave at us and holler like we were celebrities. It was probably the first time many of them had even seen an automobile or Black men in uniform. When we'd stop and talk to them they were so proud of us, which made us proud, too. You have to live through those things to appreciate what happened to us. They knew nothing, but they were happy. I remember a very pretty little girl on our way back to camp. She came out and brought us a piece of watermelon asking, 'Can I touch your suit?' Then she went out and looked at the car. They didn't know anything about different makes of automobiles. They just knew it was something strange. It wasn't a mule or a wagon. You think about those things. You think about schooling, how many miles they had to walk in the dust and the rain to go to school. You see, those are things that make your heart bleed."

Memphis, Tennessee was another hot bed of discrimination. White editors from *Stars and Stripes*, the army newspaper, came down to get some information on Black soldiers and met with Swindler who was the editor of a Black newspaper in Memphis. He was also editor of the Sphinx, Alpha Phi Alpha fraternity's magazine. Swindler was a frat brother and Daddy remembers, "I happened to be over there. We went out that night to visit a black club, with the editors, trying to give them information. We were arrested. Blacks and whites are not supposed to be together." Another time Daddy witnessed the wife of the President of Lemoyne College being arrested when she was escorting a group of young Black ladies from the college to a dance at the YMCA.

Daddy affirmed a story of returning from Memphis with a first class reservation when he brought an ambulatory patient to the hospital. "The captain carried me over to this reservation desk, first-class reservation, and I got in line. A policeman walked up behind me and hit me in the head saying, 'Niggers don't ride first class.' I rode on a cart that was, must have been made in 1916, opened windows. It looked like a cattle car, cinders blowing in all over you. I got to the base and I went to the adjutant general and told him how I was treated. Nothing was said or done. After I was discharged I came here to practice. **This** (Baton Rouge) is my home when I say I'm going back home. I had other places that, some had enticed me to try to come, some of my classmates, but I said, 'I'm going home.'"

After the war, Bobby and Cliff moved to Chicago during the great migration and Daddy came home to Baton Rouge where he began to tell his biggest lifelong tale. He loved to tell this story and we'd know he was getting ready to tell it when he'd start looking around to see who was listening, and then a big grin would spread across his face as he began. Just pour a drink and his army adventure began. He'd tell how he had flown with the Tuskegee Airmen, and then one time they flew under a bridge. With his arms outstretched as if he were flying then ducking as they flew under the bridge, he was in seventh heaven in his dream of being an airman, but even this tall tale couldn't begin to equate with the real adventures of his life. Moreover, the revolutionary's revolution had only just begun.

Dupuy (Daddy) Anderson
McKinley High School Graduation

Dr. Dupuy (Daddy) Anderson
Meharry Medical School Graduation

Dupuy H. Anderson's Graduations

Lili and Henry Anderson
Grandmother and Paw Paw

Grandmother, Phrozine Duvall

Lilburne (Lulu) Thompson

Bobby and Cliff Anderson

Phrozine McCoy

Nen Nee and Aunt Francis

The Andersons

Daddy at Tuskegee.

Tuskegee

Descendants Of Charles Dupuy
Family Gathering
July 28 and 29 2000

Charles Dupuy Family

Trouble Was Her Name

She was born in Bunkie, Louisiana in 1924, a poor child of an African Creole heritage mother and a father of mixed white heritage. She was small, very fair skinned with blue-grey eyes and blonde hair. Her mother called her the "Sassy One." She was the eighth generation descendant in the United States from Africans who were enslaved in what is now known as Natchitoches Parish, Louisiana. With her heritage, her genes spelled trouble.

In 1736 Francois, not his birth name but his enslaved name, became the property of St. Denis, the Commandant in Natchitoches. Francois married Marie and they gave birth to Marie Therese Coincoin (Coincoin is the African name her father gave her that she kept her entire life) who was later purchased by Claude Thomas Pierre Metoyer with whom Marie Therese Coincoin had ten children.

Claude Thomas tried to marry Coincoin on several different occasions but the Catholic Church refused to marry them because she was African. Inter-racial marriage was forbidden, but Metoyer and Coincoin continued to stay together with their children. On October 23, 1777, Coincoin was convicted by a Catholic priest of being a concubine of a white man. The sentence for the crime was a shaved head, sackcloth thrown over her body, and a forced ride in a cart to be paraded publicly with the word "fornicator" on the cart. She had to be driven through the streets, then kneel at the church and beg for forgiveness, put in a public square until evening and beaten with twenty lashes. At that time this took place, she was pregnant. (Elizabeth Mills. *Isle of Canes*.) Coincoin was beaten for a crime of being born African. She was enslaved and had no voice in her life. And this punishment was carried out by the Catholic Church. The church refused to let Coincoin and Metoyer marry, so he eventually freed her and gave her property in Cane River that she developed into a fortune and a great plantation.

Once freed Marie Therese signed documents using the name her African father gave her, Coincoin. She was able to convince Metoyer to free all of his children and she later purchased the manumission of her four previous children and some of the spouses of her children.

This is the family of the Melrose Plantation in Natchitoches, Louisiana. They became the wealthiest family in the area giving them power in the Black and white communities. Coincoin's eldest child, Augustin, built the first Catholic Church in the Natchitoches area and the whites sat behind him at a time when Blacks were required to sit behind whites. He became the godfather of the Metoyers and grew to become a respected landowner. Coincoin and her descendants owned most of the Cane River area and were very rich people who traveled internationally, were well educated and trained to play the piano. Augustin's son, Francois Gassion, owned over $38,000 of improved property in the 1860 census but after the Civil War there is no further record of what happened to his property. In the 1870 census his wife Perine Metoyer and his son Theodore are listed, but by this time Francois is dead. Perine has remarried and all the wealth is gone.

Theodore was the fifth generation of Metoyers and the first generation to leave Cane River and the Melrose Plantation. Breaking horses and training his son Frank to do the same, they changed the course of the next generations of Metoyers. Frank married Emma Vignes and they had 11 children, including seven girls who Frank fought for all his life. As a horse trainer, he wore a gun and threatened both Black and white men with their lives if they ever touched one of his daughters. Black women were an open invitation for white men for rape and Frank was determined that no one was going to rape his girls. Agnes was one of those girls who he defended. She grew up and married Lester Smith.

Lester was the son of Emma Wells of mixed heritage. A white man raped her mother and Schmidt, a white German entrepreneur raped Emma. Schmidt came to Louisiana by way of Canada, owned a store in Morrows, Louisiana and took any Black woman he wanted in the area. He was the owner of the local store and was financially secure. This is the heritage of Lester and Agnes, who married and became the parents of Gertrude, Almease, Jeannie and Trouble.

She was a little girl who didn't fit the criteria of Negro society. She was very fair with white skin, blonde hair and hazel eyes. Yet, she did not pass. Rather she went to Black schools and attended not only the Catholic Church but also the Baptist Church down the street from their home in Beaumont, Texas. Black children often picked on her and called her names. Her sister Almease had to fight to protect her because she was so small and because of her big sassy mouth. Someone was always threatening to beat her "white ass." Mease kept threatening to let Trouble fight her own fights if she didn't watch her mouth. Needless to say neither of them changed and Mease kept protecting her younger sister.

Agnes and Lester moved to Beaumont from Bunkie, Louisiana and Lester worked as a long distance truck driver. Eventually the entire related clan followed for extended family support. The family depended on Lester to provide for all of them and he drove long hours to support them. Trouble told how she would take her father's boots off when he came in late with feet so swollen that his socks were literally stuck to his skin. Tears well in her eyes as she describes how his feet were blistered and bleeding when she peeled off the socks. She remembers that during the Depression when families were hungry and in need of food, Lester and other Black drivers intentionally broke sacks of food that they were hauling. Broken sacks could not be delivered and were given to the drivers. So, Lester took those broken sacks home and distributed the contents to his family and the other families in the neighborhood.

After several years, Lester and Agnes had to move again and this time to Los Angeles because life became too dangerous for them in Beaumont. Lester applied for a new job but was denied when he was accused of having a colored family even though he said from the outset that he was a Black. Word of mouth had it that the whites were coming after him. Without a choice, he and Agnes packed up in the middle of the night and left the next day for California. They did not have enough money to own or rent their own home so they were forced to live with relatives who generously took them in and helped him get back on his feet.

In 1943 Trouble's family moved into a cousin's house on 33rd Street in Los Angeles, California and rented there. Her father got a job at Fiberboard and stayed until he retired. He went to Los Angeles because there were jobs in defense, but he got a peacetime job. Trouble, her sisters and their husbands and their seven children all lived together. Lester and Agnes became Papou and Mamou to the grandchildren and almost everyone else in California began to call them the same. At one point Mamou had to remind everyone that she did have a name, and it was Agnes.

Trouble's mother, Mamou, sewed and made all the clothes for the grandchildren. Sometimes Mamou would get so tired working the pedal on the sewing machine that Trouble would sit on the back of the machine and turn the pedals manually. She would help the family by taking the children to the park or the beach while their Mamas were working. Rarely complaining, she stepped up and became responsible and began to help the family—without a sassy mouth. All the sister's children began calling her Nanny and still do.

Regardless of money or the hard times the family valued education. It was always stressed and excelling in school was expected. The family sent all the children to Catholic school. They were reared in the church. The family sacrificed to give extras like private schooling and music lessons. Trouble who said that her mother and father kept preaching about education said she was going to school and nothing was going to stop her. Even though neither of her parents had been able to finish school, they wanted their children to go and they would work as long and hard as necessary to accomplish their goal.

As a young girl Trouble loved to read, hated housework and cooking and washing dishes. She often hid under the house to read her books to escape doing her chores, but when pushed she would help out as needed or at least when they could find her. She was a very smart child with a smart mouth that never knew when enough was enough. She had to say her piece regardless of the consequences, but her talents outshined her mouth allowing her to graduate from high school, play the piano and garner praise for her looks and talents. Upon graduation her Taunte (Aunt in Creole) Vic in Beaumont, Texas convinced her to try Southern University in Baton Rouge, Louisiana.

With little persuasion Trouble was eager to try a new venture. She planned to attend Southern in Baton Rouge while the family stayed in California. Working to earn enough money while taking care of her sister's children and helping the family in any way that she could, Trouble and her parents were able to send her to college in Baton Rouge. She didn't know what was waiting for her there.

While Trouble was planning her travels to Southern, her aunt, Taunte Vic, was arranging an engagement. Taunte Vic was an African American entrepreneur who should have been studied because she never missed an opportunity for success. She directed everyone's life and behavior. She bought her house in Beaumont and worked as a schoolteacher. She helped her family's nieces and cousins get houses and jobs. She bought big houses and rented them out to boarders. She was a great businesswoman, always busy and always in somebody else's business. Her daughter, Lillian Ruby, was dating Jimmy Lawson who was teaching at Southern and Jimmy brought a friend with him, Dupuy Anderson, when he came to visit Lillian in Beaumont. When Taunte Vic found out that Dupuy was in medical school, she arranged for Trouble to meet him.

Driving his father's car, Dupuy had driven Jimmy to Taunte Vic's house. Knowing that Dupuy had a car at his disposal, Taunte Vic asked if he would pick her great niece up from the train station in Baton Rouge with all her luggage and trunk and take her to Southern University when she arrived from California. When Dupuy saw the picture of her niece, he gladly volunteered. He picked up the niece from the train station and told her on the ride to Southern, "I'm going to marry you little girl!" Little did he know that he was planning to marry Trouble.

Determined to make his statement come true, Dupuy saw Trouble off and on for over two years, but he did not want to get married until he completed his degree. Then she did not want to marry him until he completed his required Air Force duty. They eventually became separated when Trouble had to return to Los Angeles and give up her dream of a degree from Southern University because or finances. She didn't leave Southern without creating quite a stir as the blonde majorette that many girls were hoping would pledge a sorority so they could "Beat her white ass." They never got that chance. Trouble went home to Los Angeles with her family.

Dupuy did not let distance stop his relationship. One weekend, he sent for

Trouble to visit him in Tuskegee. She stayed at the home of an older couple who were friends. That weekend, Dupuy and Trouble went to a party on base. Quickly, the place became surrounded by police. The older couple assumed why the police were there and hurriedly sneaked Trouble out of the club. They realized that the police thought she was white in this Black establishment. Later, after the police finished their search and did not find her, they left. Trouble was sent back to Los Angeles the next morning.

Undeterred, Dupuy continued to pursue Trouble. It wasn't easy though. Mamou and Taunte Vic had to convince her that Dupuy was a "good catch." Trouble was dating two other guys in Los Angeles and she asked her mother what she should do after Dupuy proposed. Her mother said, "It's better to marry someone who is going somewhere, who can take care of you and your future children and who shares your same values and beliefs about family. Love grows as you get to know the person especially when they love you." Something her mother said must have worked and for once in her life Trouble listened without talking back.

As soon as Dupuy was discharged, he went to California to marry, and trouble began for them that very day. Dupuy, wearing his army uniform, tried to get a marriage license, but he was denied. Again, the clerk thought Trouble was white. She did not have a birth certificate, only a Baptismal Certificate, which the clerk would not accept for a license because it did not prove she was Black. In 1946 in Los Angeles, California the law still prohibited mixed marriages. Fortunately, Trouble spotted a Black police officer who knew her from the church where she was the organist for the choir. He verified that she was Black and the clerk accepted his word allowing them to get married. That should have been a sign for Dupuy to run as fast as he could or at least begin practicing his run, but instead he married Trouble, Inez Smith Anderson, my mother.

Inez Smith

Wedding Day

Inez
Southern Majorette

Inez Smith Anderson

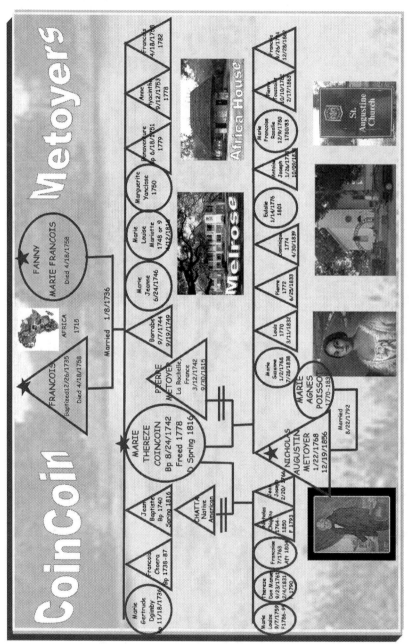

Genealogy Beginnings

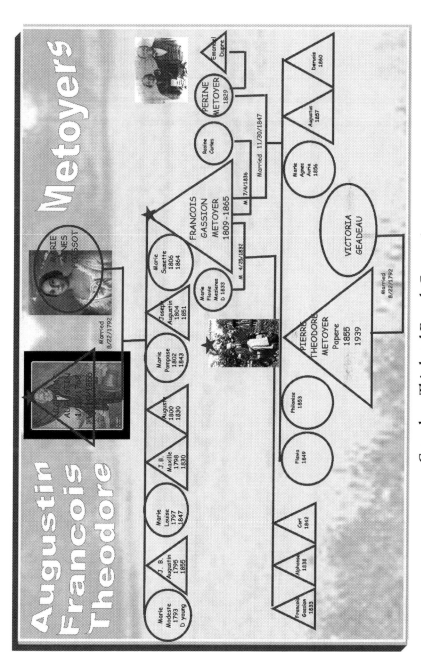

Genealogy Third and Fourth Generations

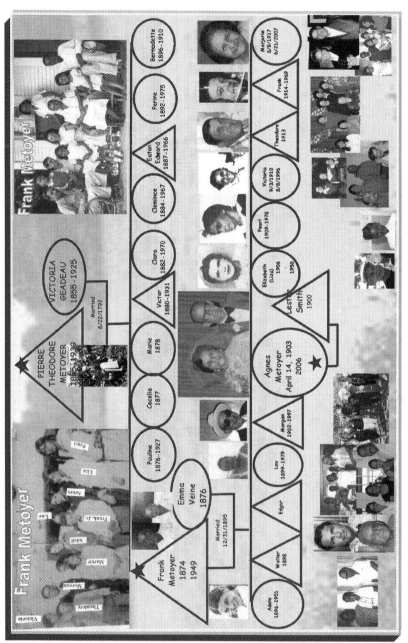

Genealogy Fifth and Sixth Generations

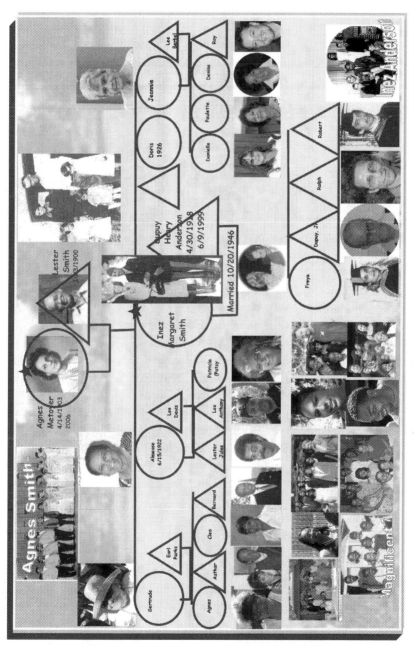

Genealogy Seventh, Eighth & Ninth Generations

The Family

Dupuy and Inez were married on October 20, 1946 in Los Angeles and then moved to Baton Rouge. Newly married with little money, Daddy and Mama stayed with Grandmother and PawPaw (Daddy's parents) on North Street among whites. Arriving in Baton Rouge Daddy took Mama to meet his dearest friends, Aunt Wilma and Uncle Bernie. They weren't really related to him or us but just very close friends. (Black etiquette demanded that children always "put a handle on an adult's name," which meant that you called them by their title or if you knew them well you could call them aunt and uncle). Daddy did not have a car yet so they used public transportation, the city bus, which was segregated. He told Mama to sit in the vacant seat on the front of the bus and she did. The bus driver did not say anything but some of the whites stood up rather than sit by her. Whether they knew she was a Black or not, she was with a Black man and that was enough for whites to move. Mama felt relieved when they arrived without incident and they laughed at how foolish the whites were to stand rather than sit. Daddy thought that since they were in a Black neighborhood and there were so many Blacks on the bus that the bus driver was afraid to say anything.

If he thought the bus driver was afraid, it was nothing compared to his friends. When they arrived at Aunt Wilma and Uncle Bernie's home, Wilma opened the door and then slammed it immediately in Daddy and Mama's faces. Wilma yelled, "Bernie come quick! That goddamn Dupuy has lost his natural mind. He has gone and married a white woman!" By this time Daddy is banging on the door for them to let him in as a few of the neighbors are beginning to come out to investigate the commotion. Finally, Bernie let them in after Daddy explained that she was not white. Once Aunt Wilma and Mama started talking Wilma exclaimed, "Oh no! She's not white and Dupuy if anyone ever doubts it, just let her start running her mouth." Mama was a talker and she knew Black protocol and history, and she had always been sassy. Once she began to talk, all questions about her ethnicity were answered and she never denied it.

Returning to Grandmother's house, Daddy and Mama found out that the police had visited while they were gone. Someone in the neighborhood reported,"A white woman was visiting a Nigger in their home." Grandmother was really upset and called her brother Jim because PawPaw was at work and Daddy and Mama weren't home. Jim waited until Daddy and Mama returned. Then, carrying his gun, Jim took both of them down to the police station. He knew Sherriff Petit, the father of the basketball player Bob Petit. Jim told the Sherriff that Daddy and Mama were Blacks and that he "didn't want this to happen again or somebody is going to pay for it." As they were leaving, Jim gave Daddy the gun, and told Daddy, "If anyone bothers you, shoot them!" Fortunately, Daddy never shot anyone as he worked to build his dental practice, find a home and participate in community and political activities.

On July 30, 1947, the Dupuy and Inez Anderson family was begun. I was born, Freya Sandra Anderson, a beautiful fuzzy peach of a girl with curly black hair. I was born in Beaumont, Texas at Sprott's Clinic because Mama wanted to be with her grandmother, Mamena (Emma Metoyer), and the rest of her family in Beaumont for the delivery of her first child and because the clinic was Black owned and operated—something that did not exist in Baton Rouge. Mama went to Beaumont the week before the scheduled delivery but Mamena proclaimed that I would be born with the full moon, and I was.

When Daddy arrived to see me at the clinic, a nurse told him, "I know who you came to see because she looks just like you." That was it! I became Daddy's spoiled rotten little girl, a lovely child who always managed to get into a little mischief and trouble. It's funny that my parents had the nerve to wonder where I inherited those traits. Do tell!

Mother tells, "We were visiting Dr. and Mrs. Smith on New Year's Day in Beaumont to watch the football games, when I missed Freya. After a brief search of the house, we found her on top of Mrs. Smith's bathroom counter mixing her French powders and make-up and spraying expensive perfumes. I was overly embarrassed and apologized, but graciously Mrs. Smith said that it was nothing and children would be children. Needless to say, we left immediately, apologizing all the way out of the door and asking them to let us pay to replenish the make-up." I was really too young to know what I had done. All I could think was that they should have kept a closer watch on a child of my age. I was just trying to have some fun when adults were enjoying their conversations and not paying any attention to me.

When I was two, Mama was pregnant with Dupuy, Jr. She had morning sickness and general pre-natal malaise. So, she needed to get rid of me to rest and recuperate. I was sent to St. Michael's Nursery School at the young age of two where Miss Frisbie was the teacher. The building was an old church that could have stood a little paint with a large yard and no fence. There were some pews downstairs and a small room upstairs going up to the belfry with a window that overlooked the street. All of the children loved the school and Miss Frisbie loved all of us in return. I don't remember the daily activities, but I do remember specific incidents like trying to pull my cocker spaniel, Boop, out of the car to go to school with me.

He and I would ride in the back window together lying on the ledge above the back seat. Cars today don't have the ledge behind the back seat in the window, but it was fun to lay in it and wave to the cars behind. After I'd get out of the car to go to school, Boop would jump in the front of the car with Daddy and ride in the passenger seat, but this particular morning he would not come out of the window to say good-bye. I started pulling him, but I slipped and fell in the ditch and cut my knee on a broken bottle. After falling I had to go to the doctor for stitches and a shot since the open sewerage ditch contained debris and broken glass and possibly feces. The South maintained dual standards in everything and Black areas of the city did not have sidewalks, curbs or sewerage drainage.

I remember good times at Ms. Frisbie's too, like playing the blocks in the rhythm band. In the middle of a performance for parents I stopped and went out in the audience to ask Daddy if he heard me when I played. He replied that I was great and ushered me back to the stage with the rest of the children. After the rhythm band we sang:

"Sweetly says the donkey as he goes to pray. If you do not feed him you will hear him say, 'hee haw, hee haw, hee haw, hee haw, hee haw.'"

While we were singing hee haw, our thumbs were in our ears and our fingers were waving back and forth like donkey ears. Also, I think the word was bray instead of pray but children rarely get songs or memorized scripts correct at that age.

The other reason I was in school was because my mother said I was a terror and she hoped that socializing with other children might help. At Miss Frisbie's I did take a frozen bottle of coke and put it on the upstairs window ceil at the school and it exploded. Fortunately, no one got hurt. The glass just popped a little. I don't know why I didn't go back to Ms. Frisbie's because I really did like it there. I had a picture of the class standing in front of the church-school. Some of those same boys and girls were in high school with me.

Dupuy Jr. was born a month before I turned three and Ralph came three months after I turned four. This was too much, not only for me, but also for Mama who didn't know what to do with two babies at one time, and one of them who cried incessantly, Ralph. He had colic and cried for three straight months permitting sleep to no one and driving us all insane. Daddy got help.

Joella Malveaux came to live with us to go to school and to help Mama with the boys. Joella lived in Opelousas. Taunte Vic knew the family. She was always trying to help people just like she planned for Daddy to meet Mama. She arranged for Jo to live with us since Jo's mother was ill and couldn't take care of their family. I could not stand Jo. She tried to tell me what to do and I was not having it. She and I butted heads constantly and I'd tell her that she was here for the boys and not me. No one could tell me what to do but my father.

She was in high school and tried to be nice but she overstepped her boundaries trying to control me. I was queen of the Anderson castle. I gave the orders, and people moved when I said so. Most of the time, Jo did stay out of my way and I out of hers but sometimes there were problems. We did not spend much time together since she and I were in school during the day and only encountered each other in the evenings. After school it was time for dinner, bath and bed for me. Jo completed her homework and helped Mama with the boys. She loved Ralph. He was a big, fat, rotund baby with blonde curly hair, hazel eyes and a large precious grin. He was a beautiful baby. She always had Ralph in her arms. Maybe I resented her for giving attention to someone other than me.

My new school was Ms. Doody's Nursery School and I'm guessing on the spelling of these names but if you are Black and grew up in Baton Rouge during the '50's, you know who I'm talking about. Ms. Doody was a big woman and kind of stout. She looked like a military sergeant. Her school was a prison that looked like Stalag 13 consisting of a single story wooden building built off the ground. When facing the building there was a large room on the right that held naptime cots. Ms. Doody's desk was on the left side of the room facing the cots with the restroom behind her desk and tables for lunch on the side of her desk toward the back. The front yard was the playground surrounded by a wooden fence. In spite of these bleak surroundings, we still had fun—especially when Ms. Doody wasn't around because the other workers were so very nice and pleasant. They made up for her mean demeanor.

We sang songs, colored papers, played in the yard, created arts and crafts, ate lunch and snacks and took naps. I can remember songs from two years old so easily and when and where I learned them. One of the songs we sang at Ms. Doody's was:

> "Good morning to you, good morning to you,
> We're all in our places with sunshiny faces,
> and this is the way to start a new day."

I still sing this to my grown children on Saturday morning as they crawl deeper and deeper under their sheets when they hear me coming, but my favorite song at Ms. Doody's was Thumbkin. A real nice little bitty lady named Ms. Doris worked there. Ms. Doris would sing it so cutely with her tiny fingers that hid behind her back and come out front for each name, then wave good-bye as it left to go behind her back and hide until the next finger's name was sung. Ms. Doris's fingers looked like miniature people hiding from you as she sang,

> "Where is Thumbkin?
> Where is Thumbkin?
> Here I am, here I am

How are you today sir?
Very well and thank you,
Run away, run away."

That song would proceed all the way from Thumbkin to Pointer, to Middle Man, to Ring Man until Pinky. Then the whole family of five fingers would emerge. She'd sit in the front of the class looking so cute and nice while Ms. Doody was sitting at her desk looking all mean and evil like a stuffed bullfrog.

My cousins Tony and Bobby, Lulu's boys, went to Ms. Doody's with me and that helped me to get by day after day. Tony was the oldest of the three of us by a year; I was next, and Bobby was a few months younger than me. We did everything together. We visited relatives, our parents' friends, Joe Bernard's Restaurant (that was PawPaw's hang-out) and church, and we played daily. In the early years, we spent most of our time at Grandmother's house while Tony and Bobby's house was being built on Christian Street. I loved Tony and Bobby. To me, they were my real brothers. We were the ones who played together and had fun but Tony got spanked almost every day at Ms. Doody's because he wet the bed during naptime. That was why I really disliked her.

Ms. Doody would not let you go to the bathroom when you needed and she spoke very roughly. Everything was regimented. You could only go to the restroom during prescribed times, which were before and after nap but not during. If you didn't go before, then you had to wait until naptime was over. Tony could never hold for long, but I learned then to use the restroom at home before I left and to hold it until I got back home. Holding my urine all day was important, not only at Ms. Doody's, but to prevent having to use nasty colored public restrooms that were nasty because they were never cleaned or stocked with toilet paper, soap or hand towels.

One day I had to use the restroom during naptime. I had never asked before but I wasn't feeling well and Ms. Doody told me I couldn't go to the restroom. I just stood there. I did not move one inch from her desk and proceeded to Tee Tee down my legs, into my shoes and socks, all over the floor, and a puddle formed under her feet and chair. Then I looked her straight in the face and said, "I'm going to tell my Daddy you wouldn't let me go and he's going to get you for treating me this way." All the children on their cots were peeping at Ms. Doody and me but scared to be caught looking or laughing. If Ms. Doody could have choked me to death and not gone to jail, I think I would have been one dead child. She had Ms. Doris clean and redress me. Then I sat on my cot and waited to tell my Daddy. That was the end of Ms. Doody's for me. Daddy was very upset and he told her that we would not be back. Tony and Bobby stayed.

My next nursery school was Ms. Payne's. The school was in her house, which was a two-story rambling stucco faced building. I begged and pleaded to go there because my best friends in the whole world were there, Judy and Nan James. I had known Judy and Nan since I can remember knowing anyone other than Tony and Bobby. Mama and Daddy belonged to a bridge club with a group of close friends (who remained lifelong friends). The ladies met each month playing bridge while the men played poker. They had parties and dances during football season, Christmas, and Mardi Gras in particular and any other time that they felt like getting together besides the monthly bridge/poker club meetings. Most of them belonged to the same clubs and because there were few things to do and places to go for Blacks, this group provided their own entertainment for themselves and their families. All of these families became our extended families. Some of the members of the club were Dr. and Mrs. Pierson; Judy and Nan's parents, Dr. Louis and Mrs. Geraldine (Aunt Jerry) James; Dr. Waldo, everyone called him Bernard, and Mrs. Wilma Bernard; Dr. Bernard's brother, Dr. Jimmy and Mrs. Bobby Bernard; Mr. Victor and Mrs. Johnetta Baham; Mr. Moses and Mrs. Bootsy McDonald; and Dr. William (Daddy's office partner) and Mrs. Dorothy (Dot) Yates. There were also invited guests each month. The children I grew up with were Judy and Nan James, Victor Baham, Nancy Bernard, Betty Carlene McDonald, and Billy and Michael Yates, who were also our neighbors. That group was a riot to be around. They enjoyed life and each other with no bickering, just good old plain wholesome fun. All adults in the group were addressed as aunts and uncles by the children.

This made Judy and Nan and I cousins by way of close parental friendships. After leaving Tony and Bobby at Ms. Doody's, I didn't mind too much going to Ms. Payne's because I wanted to be with Judy and Nan, my play sisters. If only I could have swapped them for my brothers, the world would have been fine. However, after a few weeks at Ms. Payne's, I didn't like it. Maybe that's when I started blocking out un-pleasantries. I don't remember why I didn't like it but I remember thinking Ms. Doody's was more fun. How can that be? I don't even remember a playground at Ms. Payne's, but I do remember a fix-it shop across the street from the school that was owned by a Black businessman and Daddy knew him. I thought Daddy knew every Black person in Baton Rouge and most of the important whites.

This man at the fix-it shop would repair my radio/record player. It was a white console stand with red and green trim and flowers. I was the only child that I knew that had her own record player—my very own—but it would always break. The owner was a nice man who would smile and say, "What, broken again?" With all of the broken stuff he had to repair, he always took time for me and tried to get my record player back to me as soon as possible.

He gave me a lollipop with each repair. I liked going to his junky shop, but I didn't like Ms. Payne's.

Maybe I didn't like Ms. Payne's because I think I remember Joella working there. I seem to remember Jo arguing with Mama and Daddy that she needed her own money and Daddy saying he gave her money and what else did she need. Even though Jo failed to have an answer her reply was that she just needed her own money. Jo started working at Ms. Payne's and that's why I was there. The rest of that time and space is a blank, but I do think it had something to do with Jo because I remember complaining to Judy and Nan about Ms. Payne's, and they told me how nice it was and how much they liked it. If they liked it, it couldn't have been all that bad. I do remember having time for arts and crafts activities and enjoying them, but that's all I remember. I left Ms. Payne's.

My next school was back with Tony and Bobby again. We went to a real school, Berean Seventh Day Adventist School. It was a one-room schoolhouse divided by a curtain. Pre-primary through sixth was on one side, and seventh to 12th was on the other. Bobby and I were in pre-primary and Tony was in first grade, but we could all do the same work. Sister Sterling was our teacher, and I learned everything! I could compete in spelling bees with fifth and sixth graders. I could read just about anything and I had a crush on Donald Oxley who was in the fifth grade. He was handsome with black hair, dark eyes, tall, thin and smart. He didn't notice me. I was much too young. Berean school was the back of Berean Seventh Day Adventist Church (Grandmother and Lulu's church). It faced South 14th Street and the railroad track.

Sister Thompson (Lulu) taught seventh through 12th grades on the other side of the curtain. I had to remember to call her Sister Thompson instead of Lulu, because that's all I ever knew until Tony, Bobby and I started school at Berean. Even Tony and Bobby had to call her Sister Thompson and not Mama. We didn't like this and most of the time we'd forget.

Tony and Bobby had now moved to Christian Street where I lived. We'd make up games or sayings. One was when we were given good food or treats to eat that we liked, we'd say, "Ummmm boy, Almond Joy," but we figured out later that what we probably meant to say was "I'm going to enjoy." Another nonsense game was to stick one leg in a hanger, hold the hanger in one hand and hop around saying, "Help me anyone." I have no clue as to why we played it or why we thought it was fun. We just did it. Don't ask. We always had to say something while we were doing things. Never was there a dull moment. We'd invent toys like a pop gun made of bamboo that shot china-balls and create plays sort of like the "Little Rascals," or "The Three Musketeers." We were inseparable!

Our favorite place was grandmother's house. Her food was wonderful and that was the first thing we'd do when we arrived, attack the ice box and stove. Grandmother fussed about us opening the ice box and letting in hot air that made the ice melt. We were amazed when the ice man delivered the large block of ice with huge tongs and slid it in the bottom. We could watch him as long as we didn't get in the way. I don't know how Grandmother found the time to do all that she did as she washed clothes on a scrub board and hung them on a line to dry outside. She ironed the clothes with a heavy iron that she had to put on the stove to heat. Yet, she managed to make tea cakes that melted in your mouth. She'd toast bread for us in the oven with butter, sugar and cinnamon. Her Kool Aid was the best. There was always a cake or pie for the Sabbath. I don't remember the real food, just desserts. Delicious smells were always coming from the kitchen.

Grandmother was the treasurer of Berean Church and she also sold vegetarian products to members of the church. Uncle Cliff called it "Not meat, not coffee," but grandmother could make the best "Not meat" around. If you didn't know it was a soy product, you'd think it was real meat. Grandmother drank Postum for coffee and that was another treat for us. We couldn't drink real coffee and no one else drank Postum but Grandmother. Since it didn't have caffeine, she'd let us drink with her and Daddy didn't object. We'd sit at the table pretending we were grown drinking coffee while drinking our Postum with the most fantastic pound cake ever. If we had gone to Grandmother's every day we would have been fat except that we played so hard that we worked off the calories.

Grandmother's was so much fun. We played firemen, sliding down her four-poster bed, which was often broken by our hitting the bed so hard the springs would dislodge and the mattress and springs would fall on the floor. We'd promise never to do it again—until the next time. Daddy or Lulu would have to put it back together when they came to pick us up and we'd sleep on the mattress on the floor until they did. Grandmother also had a high chair that converted to a table with two seats that pushed back and forth with pedals. Tony, Bobby and I fought over the two seats. We touched feet underneath and pushed ourselves back and forth saying "DeeDee DeeDee. Let's play DeeDee." The problem was that it only seated two people and there were three of us. Most of the time the two people sitting in the chair were Bobby and me because we were the youngest. Tony was told that he should understand because he was older, but he'd sit on the side and bite his hand crying. We did have to take turns and Tony would eventually get his turn but by then Bobby and I would have had enough and there was no one to play "Dee Dee" with Tony. When Lulu arrived she'd make one of us play Dee Dee with him.

Grandmother would threaten us with a man named DC Hall to try to control our shenanigans with fear. She said he was coming in a blue truck to take us away. One day we really saw the truck that had DC Hall on it. It stopped in front of the house and a man came slowly walking up the steps. We stood in the hall behind the front door just screaming and hollering and begging, "Please grandmother don't let him take us. Pleeeease grandmother." We were scared to death, just crying our hearts out. She walked out on the porch, closed the door behind her, left us crying in the hall before she sent him away, but she said next time he would take us away if we didn't listen. We were really terrified of DC Hall. As we grew older we figured out that DC Hall was the delivery service that brought the vegetarian food for her to sell. Every time he came we'd wait until grandmother said, "He's gone and I told him you were good today." She always had a slight grin on her face when she told us.

Her other threat was the rat closet. It was just a regular closet next to the bathroom, but it didn't have a light or maybe she'd unscrew it to make it dark. She'd threaten to put us in there with the rats that would come out and eat us up. Even with those kinds of threats hanging over our heads, nothing stopped us when we were determined to do something.

One day we decided to go skating in the bathroom. We put water and soap on the floor and started sliding around. We were really having fun skating and making bubbles. Grandmother came in to see what was taking so long for a bath. When she opened the door, water and suds were everywhere! Bobby and I blamed it on Tony. We always blamed Tony. She put Tony in the rat closet. Poor Tony was screaming and howling, "Please Brandmother (that's what he called her), please let me out." Bobby and I couldn't hold it any longer. The more Tony screamed, the more we laughed. Finally, grandmother put all of us in the closet. Once we calmed down and realized that the rats had not eaten us, we made up a new game in the closet, "Scare Tony." Those were the good old days. We could have fun with anything.

The fun at school stopped abruptly when mother decided that the time had come for me to go to Catholic School. My mother is Catholic. My father was Methodist. Therefore I was baptized Catholic. Therefore I should be in Catholic school. Therefore, I was transferred from Berean and Tony and Bobby to go St. Francis Xavier. Mother was pregnant again, and Daddy did not put up a fight. When she came home with another baby boy, I threw a shoe at him and told her to take him back! Our family now had me and three boys, Dupuy Jr., Ralph and Robert, and I had to go to Catholic School.

Mother was extremely sick after Robert was born and Daddy had to take her back to Flint Goodrich Hospital in New Orleans. He tied a white handkerchief to the antenna of the car driving at least a hundred miles an hour knowing that if Mama could have used a hospital in Baton Rouge, she might be in the hospital by now instead of being on the highway fighting for her life.

Baton Rouge still did not allow Black physicians to practice in the hospitals. So, Mama and Daddy decided to go to New Orleans and be under the care of a Black doctor at a Black hospital. Robert was born at Flint Goodrich because it was a Black Hospital where Black doctors could practice.

While Mama was in the hospital, Mamou came to take care of us. She cooked and made sure we were ready for school. Mama recuperated slowly. When Mamou went home I was left with this new family. My mother was beautiful with blonde hair, blue-grey eyes and very white skin. My brothers looked very much like her. Dupuy, Jr., the oldest boy, and Ralph, the middle boy both had blonde hair and were very fair-skinned. They looked white. Robert, the new baby boy had black hair but blue eyes and also very fair skin. He looked white with blue eyes even. The three boys and Mama could pass for white without question. My father was caramel with wavy black hair and a thin black mustache. He was awfully good looking also, but he couldn't pass. I was brown with thick tight curly black hair and I definitely didn't look like the others.

I quickly learned from people who saw us that my brothers and mother were cuter and prettier because they looked white. Even though my Daddy tried to act like color made no difference in our family, color in the South was hard to deny. Daddy tried to darken Dupuy, Jr. by making Mama put him in the sun to tan but he just got red and burned. Daddy said, "People think I'm his sitter and not his father."

Poor Mama. She received intimidating looks and bad mouth from Blacks and whites and suffered the guilt of the boys looking white and not Black. Even Daddy succumbed to the pressure. I did not realize all she went through until much later in life because I was only feeling my pain as white people stopped her commenting on how cute the boys were and totally ignoring me as if I didn't exist.

While I fought the mental battles of color in my family, Daddy was fighting real battles in the community. Attending school board meetings, he was frequently called a nigger by board members trying to dissuade him from coming and questioning their decisions. He protested Black schools being built on top of waste dumps or on a dead end street that flooded, and inferior books and curriculum. Referring to Daddy, a board member said, "We don't need any nigger janitors turning on any lights for us when we have a meeting… Nigger, where are you from?" Daddy replied, "I'm from Baton Rouge and I'm going to be here every meeting until we get this shit straightened out." He worked with Dr. Gardner Taylor and Raymond Scott. Yet the board used the same old divide and conquer technique by finding a group of Blacks to agree with them on decisions affecting the Black community even to the detriment of their own Black people.

As busy as my dad was at the office and his meetings, I always had a special place with him. His meetings were Civil Rights. I didn't know what was going on but I remember riding with Daddy as he went around picking up people standing on corners and taking them to work. I would always tell Mama who he picked up. I later learned that he was one of the organizers of the first bus boycott of the segregated bus system in Baton Rouge in June 1953 before Martin Luther King, Jr. Blacks boycotted the buses in Baton Rouge. The leaders organized volunteers to take people to and from work in their personal cars. I rode with Daddy as he picked up people standing on corners. He'd stop and ask, "Where are you going today? Can I give you a ride?" They'd get in the car and Daddy would take them where they needed to go. It was fun to hear all the chatter about how they were beating the system. I just remember that they were going to make those "crackers" suffer. The usual talk in the summer was about the heat from the sun, but this year it changed to turning up the heat on the white folks. Daddy would fill up the car with gas and start all over.

Once, as Daddy walked to the corner to ask more people if they needed a ride, a policeman walked up to the car. He asked me if I were alone and I told him that I wasn't as I pointed to Daddy on the corner. He then gave me a slip of paper to give to Daddy. When Daddy got back to the car I showed him the paper and told him that the policeman left him some mail. Daddy said it was not mail but a ticket. Many of the drivers were intimidated but most continued in spite of the threats. Many workers were also threatened with the loss of their jobs. Several people were threatened with a loss of their jobs if they went to that, "Nigger doctor," who's always starting trouble. Daddy had to fight on all fronts.

The boycott only lasted a week with Blacks attaining the right to sit anywhere there was a vacant seat except the first two seats which were reserved for whites. Many of the leaders found this unacceptable and wanted to press on for full desegregation, but one major player sold out for materialistic gains. Daddy was disappointed but understood why it happened. Unlike him most of the Blacks depended on whites for their income and survival. Even though Daddy, Raymond, Johnnie and Murphy Bell were independent businessmen, their businesses were still affected by the boycott and their involvement in Civil Rights. Whites threatened Blacks with their jobs and some with their lives if they were seen patronizing the businesses of "those Black rabble rousers." Many Blacks stopped coming to Daddy. Some were afraid to be seen in the office and came through the back door.

Daddy's involvement in the movement hurt his practice, but he would not stop fighting. He made enough money so that we could live with all the necessities and a little more but never extravagantly. He was always willing to have fewer material things if it meant his freedom, and he never forgot those less fortunate. This was one of those real life experiences to learn as Daddy often explained to me that, "You're never free unless you have the money to control your life. As long as you have to depend on someone else to eat, you're a slave. Remember, you can be anything that you want to be if you get a good education." He believed that education was the key to the future and independence from control of others. He also never forgot to remind me to "Never forget from whence you came and always give back. Reach down and help someone else achieve their dreams and never sell out your beliefs." I loved my Daddy even though we fought constantly because we were cut from the same mold, but one thing about him was that he was never wrong and that's what he told us.

That is why Daddy worked so hard with the school board because he felt that Blacks could and would do better if given an equal opportunity in education and no one could tell him differently. Whites knew this too and that is why they kept throwing obstacles in the way for that to happen. When Civics was taken out of the curriculum in Black schools, Daddy and others started teaching a class of civics to adults to get them to pass the examination to register to vote and hopefully instill in their children the importance of civics and education. Blacks needed to vote to change their status, but they had to get registered first, which meant passing the qualifying exam. Baton Rouge needed new school board members to replace the ones that were not accountable to Blacks, and voting was the way to change the board. The sitting board built a new McKinley High School on a dead end street that flooded. The school had no water, gas or electricity in any of the science labs. Another Black school was built on a dump in spite of protests.

While Daddy fought the school board, led boycotts and struggled to keep his dental practice going, Mama tried to hold down the home front. She was changing diapers, breaking up skirmishes between the boys, and supervising my homework. This was my family.

Mama and me

Bobby, me, Tony

Easter

Dupuy, Jr., Ralph kissing Robert

Baby Freya, Tony, Bobby & Brothers

Baby Freya

Christian Street First Birthday Party
Tony, Lulu, Bobby, Camille, Freya, Maryella, Charles

Christian Street

Miss Frisbie's

Berean Seventh-Day Adventist School, K-12

My brothers and me

First Schools

The Andersons

Six Years Old

I had been in somebody's school it seems since birth. I really didn't need first grade. St. Francis Xavier skipped me to second. St. Francis was the only Black Catholic School in Baton Rouge (remember it's where all the Creoles went), which meant the class sizes were extremely large because Baton Rouge is predominately Catholic with a large Creole population. There were over 100 children in pre-primary with Ms. Hebert (pronounced A-Bear), 90+ in first and 80+ kids in my class, second grade with a nun named Sister Meanie who was at least 80+ years old. She was short, round, wrinkled, wrinkled, wriiiinkled and mean, mean, mean. I had gone from a nice friendly school of teachers and relatives and friends and a whole school of less than 80 children to a mean old witch with more than 80 children in one class. I was scared to death.

I was also younger than everyone else in my class. I didn't know anyone in the whole school but Joella who was in high school and I didn't like her. I think Joella disliked me as much as I disliked her. One evening Mama and Daddy had gone out and Jo was babysitting. Jo told me to go to bed. I told her that I was going to wait for my Daddy to tuck me in. She insisted and pulled my arm. I kicked her right on the bone in her leg with my blue and white oxford corrective shoes with steel arches. I knew it hurt.

I could see she was just going to kill me. I kept looking her straight in the eyes and backing up slowly. She didn't say a word but you could see her eyes turn red. Her hair stood up on her head and smoke started coming from her nostrils. I kept looking in her eyes backing up. I walked backwards through the kitchen talking with every step, "You better not touch me. 'I'm going to tell my Daddy." I walked backward down the hall telling her, "You better not touch me. I'm going to tell my Daddy." I continued to threaten her as I walked backward all the way into the bathroom. I ran out of space. With three brothers, naturally the toilet seat was up, and she pushed me into the toilet. I was so relieved that I was alive but I couldn't let her know. So, all wet and dripping from the toilet I pronounced, "Now you'll just have to clean me up and the bathroom too." She really must've been a real nice person because I lived to tell this story. Jo was graduating the year that I began at St. Francis. That year she broke her arm falling down the second floor of the school on concrete steps. I even felt sorry for her, but my overwhelming fear of the school left me little time to think about Jo.

I could not understand why these teachers all in black were so mean and I heard that they didn't have hair under those veils. This was a strange world. I had no problems in reading and spelling except I wanted to read more but could never read enough because we only read one or two lines and then it was someone else's turn since there were 80 of us that had to read. I had to sit there and try to pay attention while all 80 children had their turn and if you were caught not paying attention when it was your turn you were paddled in your hand. I was never caught, but I was one tense, uneasy child.

One day Sister Meanie began teaching borrowing in subtraction. I really didn't understand her explanations. Aurelius sat right next to me. She called on him to go to the board and work a problem. He did not work the problem correctly. She explained it again, but he still did not understand and neither did I. All of a sudden she slapped him on the back of his head sending it reeling forward hitting the board. His head bounced back like a tennis ball and he started to cry. I wanted to cry too, but I was too afraid to cry. I couldn't look at Aurelius when he came back to his seat. I wanted to tell him I understood how he felt because I didn't understand subtraction either, but I was just petrified. I prayed as hard as I could, "Please Lord, don't let her call on me. I promise when I go home, I'll learn how to borrow tonight." I sat there praying over and over until it was time to go home.

That evening I begged Mama and Daddy to teach me how to borrow. I would not let them stop until I understood and could show them many problems without their help. On the way to school the next morning, Daddy was still reassuring me that I knew it. At every stoplight I worked a problem. Who says brutality does not work? I mastered borrowing overnight. The methodology may have been flawed but I don't remember any child in the room that could not read or compute. Sister Meanie would be arrested today for child brutality and endangerment. Somehow I survived that year, but I had to go back.

My father has always believed that an idle mind is the devil's workshop, so he kept me busy all year and during the summer. During the week, I went to school, came home and ate, practiced piano, studied, took a bath and went to bed. On Saturdays there was Mrs. Durbin's School of Dance on the second floor of the Purple Circle Social Club. My second year recital I was a black cat, drum major and several other things I don't remember, but the night of the recital I was sick with measles and I couldn't perform. As soon as I was well Daddy had me dress in each costume and perform my part for the family. It was my private recital for family and friends. Uncle Bobby had pictures of me in every costume. I tried very hard, but I could see that I was not as good as the best in the class and I never settled for less than best. So, I asked to stop dancing.

That summer Thurgood Marshall won the Brown v the Board of Topeka case in the Supreme Court, May 1954. I never saw Daddy so happy. He and Mr. Scott and Attorney Johnnie Jones started planning the next stages of integration for Baton Rouge. "With all deliberate speed," they kept saying thinking that change would come soon. They were in for a rude awakening. A. P. Tureaud filed suit to integrate LSU, and his son, A. P. Tureaud, Jr., was admitted but kicked out after a few weeks. The University later readmitted him but he did not return. That was a sign that change was not going to come easily.

Dance Recital

FREYA SANDRA ANDERSON

A tiny bundle of vigor, vitality and personality—It is a joy just to look at Freya. There are no words to express the joy received in teaching her. She is a "Beautiful Doll" here, and that is exactly what she is. We want to watch and help with pleasure your growth and development.

Judy, me, Nan

2011 Judy, me, Nan

Seven Years Old

Life got better in third grade at St. Francis Xavier. First of all, Joella graduated and left us and Baton Rouge. Second, Daddy got help for Mama to take care of the house and us—and to cook. We got Aunt Phine who was Judy and Nan's great aunt. All I could say was, "Thank you Lawdy!" She could cook! Just as Ralph was Joella's favorite, Robert was Aunt Phine's favorite. She loved that boy. She liked all of us but Robert was her favorite. I liked her being there because she brought her grandchild, Jo Evelyn, Judy and Nan's cousin, who became my best female playmate in the neighborhood. All the rest of the children in the neighborhood were boys.

Jo Evelyn played girl games with dolls and tea parties. We made up an invisible friend, Mable, to play with us and our dolls until one day we went too far and scared ourselves. I don't know how it happened, but as Jo and I were sitting at the table in my room having a tea party, serving pretend tea to our dolls, both of us heard a noise and it seemed as if it had come from the closet. We looked at each other and said, "MABLE!" We started whispering (as if Mable could hear us!) and determined that she had come to eat us and take the dolls. Afraid out of our wits, we crawled under the bed not making a sound. We stayed there for a long time until Aunt Phine came looking for us. Thank God! When she opened the door to my room, we ran screaming to her telling her all about Mable. Aunt Phine had to look in the closet and prove to us that there was no one in there and our imaginations had truly gotten the best of us.

My third grade teacher was Mother Catholicism. There were only about 70 kids in the class now, but I still had to share my reading time. I had friends now and felt a bit more at ease. That year was my first time taking an IQ test. It may have been a standardized test, but I did horribly. I remember Sister discussing the results with Mama that afternoon and suggesting that maybe I shouldn't have been skipped because I was probably too immature. Shocked, Mama asked Sister if she could see the test. She then asked me to show her the answers. I did. My responses were correct. Stunned, Sister inquired why I had not marked them during the class. I told her that "You kept saying how hard it was so I figured it must be more than I thought and I looked for hard answers." Boy was I stupid.

I sat in the back of the room near the wall next to my best friend Marion Porche. I would stand a large book up hiding behind it to talk to Marion between the 70 children reading and suck my thumb. It was my security blanket and only Marion knew I sucked my thumb, and I didn't want anyone to know. I made a profound decision in third grade that I did not like science.

The third-grade science book read, "Do you wonder what happens when the light doesn't come on? Or where electricity comes from?" I did not care. All I could think of was that when I turned on the switch and the light didn't work, change the bulb or call Daddy to put in a new bulb. If that didn't work, he'd call someone who could repair it. Who cared? That was pretty much my attitude until I became a teacher. That book really turned me off. I think if we had some activities or experiments, it would have been better, but needless to say, with 70 students in a Black school, that was an impossibility.

Third grade did not get by without a trial. Monday mornings Mother Catholicism had every child stand according to their church affiliation and the day they attended church. She first asked the Protestants to stand and name the church they attended. I stood with them because I had gone to Daddy's Methodist church. Then she'd ask for those who went to church on Saturdays to stand. I'd stand with them because I may have gone to church with Grandmother and Lulu to the Seventh Day Adventist Church. Then she'd have the Catholics stand by the time of the mass they attended and I stood with them. After everyone stood she began to talk about the Catholic Church as the one true church and that everyone else was going to hell.

I could not believe that someone who considered themselves a Christian could hurt and humiliate children, not once but every Monday morning. That's why I stood with everyone. If they were going to hell then I was too. I just couldn't believe that God was going to discriminate against good people just because they all didn't go to the same church. If someone did not stand, then s/he was questioned as to why. Were they sick? Did they not belong to a church? I did not see why it was so important since they were going to hell anyway if they weren't Catholic. This was my first revolt against religion.

The summer of 1955 was one of the best summers ever. We went to Los Angeles to visit Mamou and Papou and Disneyland. We were there before the grand opening, before the Casey Jones Train arrived. Daddy sheltered us from racism by providing us with experiences that any child should have. That's why he took us to California. We were lucky that he was a dentist and made enough money, that he was independent, and that he could protect us. When we'd ride past City Park in Baton Rouge and I asked why I couldn't go, Daddy would reply, "That's for whites, but one day you will be able to go. We're going to change the laws, but until then we're going someplace better!" That's how we always ended up in California almost every summer. This summer was really special because of Disneyland.

The trips to California always proved interesting. Generally, we left on a Friday evening when Daddy finished working. I sat up front with Daddy. Mama and the three boys always sat in the back. The boys whined and fought and complained the entire trip and I read the map and road signs to direct

Daddy. He would drive from Baton Rouge to Beaumont Texas the first night, which was only about 4 hours (that was before Interstate 10). We stayed with relatives in Beaumont.

As soon as we arrived, we started visiting aunts and uncles. At each house we had to eat. Mama would warn Daddy to pace himself and not eat a lot at one place because he had to eat at each house. Not eating was considered rude. First there was Uncle Noody's (Mamou's baby brother, Frank) house for gumbo. He owned a gas station. Then we went to Aunt Margie's (Mamou's baby sister) across the street for homemade Texas tamales. She and Uncle David owned a grocery store. We had to stop by Taunte Vic's for some beans, then Aunt Pearl's (Mamou's sister) for dessert. The last stop was Taunte Lou's (Mamou's sister) for fried chicken, dirty rice and German Chocolate Cake. Eating this much was absolutely sinful but required to keep peace in the family and to show love and respect. My kind of family!

About 4 AM Taunte Lou would begin frying chicken again but this time for the trip. We traveled with an ice chest on the floor of the back seat for milk, sodas and water. Taunte Lou packed fruit, raisins, cereal, bread and chicken to put in a bag next to the cooler. Blacks had no place to stop and eat or sleep until El Paso Texas, which was about 18 or more hours away depending on the weather. So, we had to be prepared. That's why Blacks and fried chicken could not be separated and how fried chicken came to be associated with Blacks because we were always seen traveling with chicken. It was the major food that traveled well without spoiling.

There weren't any restrooms either so we had an empty quart jar in the car for urinating if an emergency arose. The segregated restrooms were filthy or sometimes there were none at all for coloreds. We also packed toilet tissue and cleaning stuff for when we had to use the segregated facilities. Mama would wipe toilet seats with Clorox and line them with toilet paper for each of us. Again, I would hold all day. I hated to even smell those places.

Once everything was ready, Taunte Lou would feed us a big breakfast. Then we all used the toilet whether we had to go or not and Daddy would say, "Let's hit the road!" Each trip was riddled with nature's fury. Some of the episodes were terrifying. This particular year we made it through Houston and San Antonio without any major problems.

Outside of San Antonio a Texas storm set in with rain coming down in sheets that you couldn't see through. Traffic slowed to a snail's pace. Flash floods had washed out bridges and traffic made to detour. Daddy had been driving for hours at 20 to 30 miles per hour. The baby Robert was sick with fever and throwing up. Mama was tired and worried. Daddy was trying to find the road and stay on it in the darkness and unending downpour. Dupuy Jr. and Ralph were fighting over whose turn it was to sit at the window when finally Daddy yelled at them to sit down and shut up. Dupuy Jr. cried briefly and went to sleep but Ralph whined softly for seemingly hours.

It was a regular thing with him. Once he started crying, it appeared to never cease. He'd cry, "ahhhhh," on an exhale, then "Uuuh" on the inhale, and "Uummm" for a swallow. Then the cycle began again with no tears for minutes on end. You had to learn to tune him out or go crazy. Mama was a master at tuning out. I locked my jaws and tried to concentrate on the rain and road to help Daddy. A sharp flash of lightning that lit up the night sky followed by a large clap of thunder created a brief silence followed by a scream. I told Ralph that if he didn't shut up, the lightning was going to strike him because noise draws lightning. He finally shut up and went to sleep. After he was asleep Mama said that was not nice for me to scare Ralph like that but I noticed she waited to tell me that after he was asleep. I just looked over and smiled at Daddy and he smiled back. It was so much going on inside and outside that I didn't even turn on the radio.

Usually, in the late evenings we could pick up Randy from Nashville, Tennessee. It was the only Black radio station that had power outside of its immediate city of origin. Daddy and I would listen to Randy "coming to you from Gallatin, Tennessee." Sometimes, Daddy would make the car dance especially in small towns when we had to stop at a red light. He'd press the brake to the beat and dance in his seat. That was a way for him to relieve the pressure on his back, but tonight the weather was too bad for dancing.

We saw an 18-wheeler pulled over on the side of the road. A police car with flashing lights was behind another car. Daddy stopped. The policeman told him that the car in front hit a dip in the road and the driver was ejected, killing him. The white truck driver told Daddy that the weather was getting worse and it wasn't safe, and he offered to take the lead to help. We made it to Fort Stockton following the trucker. He stopped for the night because the weather was too bad to continue. Daddy thanked him for leading us into Fort Stockton safely and offered to give him some money, but he refused. He just wished us a safe journey.

Mama asked Daddy to stop, too. She wanted to bathe Robert in cool water because of his temperature. Daddy kept reminding her there was no place for Blacks to stay, but she insisted. He tried place after place and no one let him in. She even suggested that she go register instead of him. I knew what that meant. They would think she was white. Daddy inquired, "What if they come out to show you to the room?" She said he would be her driver. I guessed that if he were the driver then I would probably be the maid since I couldn't pass for white either.

Daddy refused to stop. As he drove into a service station for gas another truck driver asked Daddy where he was going in all the rain and flooding and did he know how many bridges were washed out. Daddy answered that he did know but he had a sick child and had to continue because there was no place to stay. Again, this white truck driver said he was also going to El Paso and offered to take the lead. We were so very grateful. We never got a chance to thank him for guiding us in safely because we turned off just before El Paso going to Ysleta. Just the "beep beep" of the horn and he went on in the night. How reassuring it was that some white people were nice.

We were so happy to see the Blue Light Motel. I thought that was the name, because I remembered blue fluorescent lights around the edge of the roof, but the real name was La Luz Motel (it means light in Spanish) in Ysleta, Texas. It was considered the "tourist court for colored people." At one in the morning the owner, Mr. Myron Davis, came out, helped us to unpack, got some juice for the baby and offered to feed us. He also told Daddy he'd contact a doctor if we needed one. After Mama bathed Robert and fed him he appeared to feel better. His temperature was low grade at 99 degrees. As soon as we all bathed, we went to sleep immediately. Daddy didn't go to bed right away. He walked around the room for a while holding his back. Later he got down on his knees to pray thanking God for delivering his family safely.

The next morning we were up about 9 AM and Mr. and Mrs. Davis had prepared a big breakfast for us. He said he was shocked that anyone drove through that storm. Daddy said the Lord was with us. Daddy always more than compensated anyone who was nice to us and I remember the owner saying, "Oh Doc, that's not necessary." Then Daddy thanked him again and we hit the road. We arrived in Los Angeles that night rather uneventfully; just a few tumbleweeds here and there, but boy were we happy to see Mamou and Papou!

While we were there we went to the opening of Disneyland. That was the best park I had ever seen. Who cared about City Park in Baton Rouge? I had been to Disneyland. We went to the Grauman Chinese Theater and saw movie stars' footprints and Cinerama, which felt like riding on a roller coaster. We went to the beach and roasted hot dogs. It was wonderful! I wanted to stay there the rest of my life. We visited Aunt Phrozine (Daddy's sister) and Uncle Tiny in San Diego. They took us to a doctor's home way up on a cliff overlooking the city. It was the most beautiful thing I had ever seen. Aunt Phrozine and Uncle Tiny took us to Bali Hai Restaurant for Hawaiian food and entertainment. It was the best ever. I wanted to move to California and live on a mountain so I could go to Disneyland every day, but it was time to go home.

Mamou fried chicken. That meant it was time to leave. Her chicken was never as good as Taunte Lou's but it was good. We hit the road again. No problems on the way back for this trip. On other trips to Los Angeles, we encountered dust and sand storms that pitted the windshield and blasted the paint off the car, fog so heavy Daddy had to open the door to find the white line, and all other acts of nature from snow to unbearable heat. When the weather permitted on some of the trips to California we made special stops at Boulder Dam, the Grand Canyon, the Painted Desert, Petrified Forest, Carlsbad Caverns and the Alamo. Usually on the way home we didn't stop in Beaumont. Daddy would be so tired he just wanted to sleep in his own bed. These trips made summers special.

One time the weather was so bad that we couldn't make it to El Paso and Daddy had to stop in Ft. Stockton, Texas. It was dark and the motel attendant asked him if he was a Nigger. Daddy replied, "Do I look like a Nigger?" The man was shocked and probably thought that Daddy was a foreigner and gave him a room. Daddy always put himself in danger fighting for equality.

That summer right before school started, the Black world was rocked by a heinous cowardly act of racism: the killing of Emmett Till. I never saw Daddy so angry. When he picked up *The Pittsburg Courier* (a Negro national newspaper printed on peach colored paper) and read the article, he threw it on the floor and started cursing. He wouldn't let me read it. I kept hearing all the talk about the beating and that the pictures were going to be in *Jet* (a Negro magazine). Everywhere we went everyone was talking about Till.

The adults tried to keep it from the children but all the whispering and cursing made it hard to not try to find out what was going on. Finally, *Jet* came out and Blacks were even madder. Daddy hid the magazine from us, the children, but I searched until I found it. He had it wrapped in the Pittsburg Courier on the shelf over the hanging rack in his closet. After careful scrutiny, I realized that the picture was of a badly beaten man. It was horrible. That was one time I wished I hadn't been so inquisitive because I can still remember the face or lack thereof. This wasn't the first time for a brutal murder, but it was the first time that there were pictures in newspapers and magazines on a national level with an open coffin for all to see the brutality. I think Till's brutal murder was the catalyst for the Civil Rights Movement.

Eight Years Old

Till's murder ended the summer and I had to get ready for school again. By fourth grade I liked school again because I loved my teacher, Ms. Gladys Joffrion. She had a thick green wooden paddle that she used often and severely. Ms. Gladys had an inmate trustee program where honor roll students, called monitors, took turns writing names of students who broke the rules. If they didn't like you, your name was on the list. If you had done them something five years ago, your name was on the list. If your best friend's friend didn't like you, your name was on the list. Everybody's name eventually made the list, which got their hands spanked. It was just a matter of time. However in spite of her trustee program, Ms. Gladys was nice. She was an excellent teacher. She pushed the slow kids to keep up instead of holding the rest of us behind, but we had to memorize all of those Catholic prayers, which were a waste of my time. If I wanted to say all those prayers, I could always read them, but she insisted that they be memorized. I liked the prayers of the protestants because they just make up stuff as they go along rather than having programmed prayers like Catholics.

By fourth grade all 12 multiplication tables had to be memorized and I had a big part in the school play. I frequently participated in school plays because I had an excellent memory, could speak well and loved to show off. I developed intolerance for people who were not very smart. They always held me back and I'd have to wait for them to catch up. I just thought everybody should be able to learn. There was this good looking boy in fourth grade. He was skinny with wavy black hair, big dark eyes and all the girls like him, but he couldn't remember his multiplication tables. I told him a few years ago as an adult that's all I remembered about him at St. Francis. He'll kill me if he ever reads this because he swore me to secrecy. He's promised me that he's learned them now. I hope so because he is an engineer. He's still fine (good-looking) but married with kids. However I could never find myself interested in him in high school because I always thought of those darned multiplication tables.

I was growing up in fourth grade, tall, lanky, gangly, ugly, no figure and big feet, but I was smart and had a great personality. Most people liked me except Fighty. I found out the day Ms. Gladys left me in charge of the class while she went to the office. Her instructions to me were that no one was to leave the room. As soon as she left, Fighty got up to go to the restroom. I told her she couldn't go. She called me teacher's pet and tried to walk over me. I punched her in the mouth, bloodied her lip, and knocked her glasses off. Ms. Gladys called my parents. Fighty's parents called my parents. The principal called my parents. I was spanked and told to apologize to Fighty the next day. I never did apologize because I had not done anything wrong. I did what I was told to do. Ms. Gladys had turned on me. I never felt quite the same about her after that.

I befriended Pretty who was one of the darkest girls in the class and had short hair. She didn't have many friends because of her color. The Creoles resented Pretty because of her black shiny skin that her mother kept well-greased with Vaseline. She was a beautiful girl, tall and thin and would have made a great model in a later time period. She didn't want to talk to me because she thought I was like the others. She tried to put me down thinking I didn't care but I told her I knew how she felt being dark. I was the darkest at my house. I think I learned discrimination from my family and Creoles before I knew about racism from whites.

Creoles only played with you if you were light-skinned with good hair. Because my hair was wavy I was accepted by the Creoles and the Blacks. I remember trying to bring the two sides together at school sitting on the back steps of the church in the playground with a Creole girl (who later passed for white) and Pretty. The Creole said she didn't have anything against Pretty, but her Mama said Blacks would bring her down and she shouldn't play with them. Creole mothers and grandmothers warned daughters in particular about their boyfriends because "You have to think about your children," and they didn't want black "pickaninny" grandchildren.

My education on people and respect came from my father, not school or the church. The older I got the more I hated the Creole and Black discrimination mentality. It was bad enough fighting whites without having to fight Blacks. My response to any remarks about color was, "The blacker the berry the sweeter the juice." I guess that was part of my strong self-concept and my desire to be darker. I didn't know what "juice" was, but I knew that black grapes were sweet and I associated the juice with black grapes. I always thought, "Black is beautiful."

But beautiful was not how the world saw us. All across the country Blacks were fighting for their lives first and rights second. The Ku Klux Klan was intimidating people and killing them. There were regular hangings and cross burnings. Daddy and Mama were coming back from a Mardi Gras Party in New Orleans one night and they pulled over on the side of the road to change drivers because Daddy was sleepy. He was walking to the other side of the car and Mama was sliding over into the driver's seat. This was before bucket seats. Reaching the back of the car Daddy saw a bright blaze off to his right. When he turned around, he saw a large fire with men dressed in white with hoods over their heads. He turned around and ran back to the driver's side of the car and yelled to Mama, "Move! Get over Inez!" Hurry! We've got to get the hell out of here!"

The Klan was quite active as Blacks across the country began to fight back. Martin Luther King, Jr. came to Baton Rouge that year to find out how we conducted our bus boycott that made it so successful. Even though Blacks in Baton Rouge did not get full integration, they were able to get a big compromise. King asked questions about how the car pools were organized. How money was raised for gas. Who volunteered? Did the leaders file suit in court? He was planning the Montgomery Bus Boycott after Rosa Parks refused to give up her seat and was jailed. Daddy frequently told the story of how Martin Luther King came to Baton Rouge. Daddy proudly acknowledges that the leaders of our boycott met at Mount Zion Baptist Church and gave King the foundation for conducting the Montgomery boycott by suggesting the volunteer cars and drivers and every step that Baton Rouge followed. King used Baton Rouge as a model. One piece of advice that Attorney Johnnie Jones of Baton Rouge gave King was to file suit in the Federal Courts. Johnnie told King that with the '54 Supreme Court Decision, Blacks now had a precedent. King took the advice and made history in Montgomery.

That Christmas when I looked under the tree, there was a doll almost as tall as I was. She was white with blonde hair and if you held her hand, she walked with you. I had seen her at Disneyland that summer and asked Daddy if I could have her. He said, "Not now, maybe later." I remembered thinking, "It's ok. I'm just happy to be here," but to him I said, "OK." I quickly forgot about her as we tackled the next ride, but Daddy didn't forget. He ordered that doll for me while we were there and had it shipped for Christmas. I was elated at seeing it and walked her around the living room all morning.

Later that day, my brothers had her walking across the room and began to fight over her and pulled her head off. I couldn't stand them. They broke all of their toys and mine too. I wanted to strangle them or pull their heads off, but Daddy promised that he'd get the doll repaired. He actually returned it to Disneyland and they sent us a new one with brunette hair that I liked even better, but she was still white. Daddy also reprimanded the boys and threatened to spank them if they touched my doll. I would have liked her more if she could have been brown like me but Black dolls weren't made by Disney.

Nine Years Old

Fifth grade and a great Nun for a teacher, Sister Immaculate, taught me entrepreneurship at recess by rotating students as head of concessions. Academically, the year was fine, but my relationship with my father began to deteriorate. I was no longer his perfect child and he was not the all-loving-me Daddy. Every day he was growling and fussing at me about not eating breakfast or cleaning my room. He always managed to do most of the insulting in front of my friends especially in the morning school car pool. He drove about half the neighborhood to school. I was humiliated and belittled every day in front of neighbors, relatives and friends. If he could find nothing else to fuss about, he could always depend on me not eating my breakfast.

My mother could not cook! That's why we were all so happy when Aunt Phine came, even Daddy, but Aunt Phine was not there for breakfast. The big joke about Mama's cooking was that when she and Daddy got married, she cooked macaroni and cheese without boiling the macaroni. Worse was that he tried to eat it. Well I didn't love her **that** much. Mama "fixed" grits with lumps the size of golf balls. When there is a lump in grits the inside is uncooked so you are chewing this warm mushy stuff when you feel the lump. If you bite into it, the cold flaky inside fluffs all around your mouth, gagging you. If you try to spit it out, the lump breaks with the fluffy inside stuck to your gums, teeth and inside your lips where you need to gargle to remove it. If you try to swallow it whole, the lump chokes you by spreading loose particles in the esophagus. I learned to carefully skim the plate to push the lumps on the side or smash them with my fork before they entered my mouth. However, most of the plate was lumps or uncooked grits from the smashed lumps. So, I was still scolded for not eating. I couldn't win.

Mama's oatmeal was so thick you had to literally carve it off the spoon. We would use a can of cream (evaporated milk), a stick of butter, and the entire sugar dish to try to loosen it but nothing worked. I'd just beg for cold cereal each morning. That's all I needed. Mama's defense was that she wanted us to eat something hot to stick to our ribs for nourishment. That oatmeal not only stuck to our ribs, but it also stuck to our tongue, cheeks teeth and larynx preventing inhaling. I had to gag to try to breathe. She had the nerve to put raisins in it. I guess we really needed the raisins. With all the sticking that oatmeal did, it probably stuck to the intestines and would never come out as poop without the help of the raisins. Sometimes I would feed our German Shepard, Bijou, my breakfast, but even she didn't eat the oatmeal. Only Ralph would eat the oatmeal. We would wait until he finished his bowl and one by one we would give him ours. When Ralph was full we would split the last bowl between the four of us spreading it around our plates.

Maybe that's why Ralph had so many nightmares and walked in his sleep. It had to be because the oatmeal would not digest. Ralph had screaming nightmares of animals under his bed. Daddy had to get up and pretend he was pulling the animal out and throwing it outside to get Ralph to go back to sleep. Sometimes, Ralph would just run up and down the hall and Daddy had to softly talk him back to sleep. One night Mama heard the back door open and she told Daddy to check it out. While Daddy was looking outside, Mama looked in our rooms to make sure that we were all safe. She noticed that Ralph was not in bed and she panicked telling Daddy that Ralph was missing. Daddy searched the house and outside only to find Ralph in the garbage can. He had been sleepwalking and was still asleep. Mama's oatmeal could make you do strange things.

Mama's biscuits were so hard the boys used them as baseballs throwing them across the table, but that was extremely dangerous. If you accidentally got hit by one, you would get a concussion. If it fell on the floor it would put a hole in it. One day Dupuy Jr. got a mitt to catch one. Good thing Daddy was a dentist to repair our teeth when we tried to eat them. I even caught Daddy laughing one Sunday when a biscuit hit the floor and bounced sounding like a Hank Aaron homerun ball hitting the bat.

The one thing we liked, when she didn't burn it, was loss bread. Mama said it was called loss bread because the stale bread was no good to eat and it was considered lost until you threw it in eggs, sugar, cinnamon and milk. One thing about Mama, she always had an explanation for everything even when her lost bread was truly dead after she burned it. Then she'd start scraping the burnt off telling us, "Oh, it's only a little brown. You won't notice it when I finish." Ralph would reply in his long slow whiny Southern drawl, "But it's still burnt." Burned food was another one of Mama's trademarks. She couldn't cook already prepared food. If the food came out of a can or was frozen, you'd think you were safe, but she always managed to burn it. Her excuse was that she was trying to do too many things at the same time. I guess multi-tasking was not a strong point. "Trouble" was definitely trouble in a kitchen.

Just because I complained about Mama's cooking, I was inconsiderate, ungrateful and unappreciative, as Daddy would tell the neighborhood riding to school. He preached that Mama was a good mother who got up every morning and prepared her children a hot breakfast when some kids had no food at all. My response was, "Let me starve! She's trying to kill us with good nutrition."

On a Sunday after a very serious rain, "the bottom" (Black South Baton Rouge where McKinley High School is located) flooded. News commentators were urging the community to stay home because of the danger in the high waters from open sewerage and possibly snakes. Emergency workers asked that people stay away from the area to enable them to get to the people that needed assistance. Daddy didn't listen. He packed all four of us in the car and took us to the flooded area showing us the devastation and how much the people had lost. His next sermon was that the people didn't have food to eat while we were constantly complaining and throwing our food away. The car stalled as water started coming in the car. I was terrified thinking we were going to drown or be bitten by snakes—all because of Mama's cooking. Daddy was risking our lives over hard biscuits. All I could do was pray that the car would start and that God would help Mama learn to cook. This life endangering experience was necessary in Daddy's mind to help us appreciate Mama's food.

The real-life-experience journey in the flood did not help because the bottom line was Mama couldn't cook. Her cooking was the very source of my humiliation every morning. Daddy would emerge from his bedroom in time to take us to school and grab a cup of coffee. He didn't know what breakfast was like or maybe he did and that's why he just drank coffee as he rushed out of the house. I tried talking to Daddy about how he treated me but he was bullheaded and would not listen. I ran away from home. I left after school before he arrived to pick us up. I left a note telling him I was running away and if he tried to find me I would skip the state. I didn't go far. I just wanted to scare him and make him appreciate me again.

I went to Aunt Wilma's, but she wasn't home then I went to Judy and Nan's but they weren't home either. Lastly, I went to Maryella's house, my cousin who was the daughter of George who Daddy ran over in the car. Uncle George called Daddy and they came to get me. Instead of rejoicing over seeing me and having me back safe (like you see in the movies), he got me home, took off his belt, turned me over his knee, and spanked the living daylights out of me for my own good because he loved me. I never ran away again. I was afraid next time he would kill me for my own good. I never understood that kind of love until I became an adult. Some children need to fear something to stay on the straight and narrow path, and I usually feared what Daddy might do if I strayed. If I had cried he would not have spanked me so long, but I knew I was partly right and that he should respect my feelings. So I just clenched my teeth and let him spank me until he got tired. He left defeated and sad. I closed my door gently behind him and swallowed the tears because nobody loved me.

Grandmother came over that evening concerned about where I was and what made me think about running away. She convinced Mama and Daddy that something was wrong and they needed to hear my side. Grandmother could always make Daddy listen. She sat me in her lap and hugged me and told me to tell her what was wrong. After I finished she said, "Dupuy, you have a young lady now and she is growing up. It's time for you to respect her feelings. If you need to reprimand her, do it in private. She does have feelings." She kissed me and we all smiled. Daddy hugged me and I told him I was sorry. He was a little better after that. I had won my first victory. I didn't press that matter again though, for fear of my life. Grandmother may not be around if I needed her again.

Grandmother was the family teacher, chef, mediator and spiritual leader. She could bring calm to any situation. I believed that she could feed a multitude with two fish and a loaf of bread while walking on water. She'd be ashamed to read this because in her view no human could ever be compared to Jesus, but she was close. Every Saturday after church, she'd sit in her rocker and read Bible stories to the grandchildren— the four of us and Tony, Bobby and Lillie—and any other child who may have happened to be at the house at the time. She read from a set of 10 Bible Story books and she'd read from 1 to 3 stories each week. She loved the Bible, and as little kids we loved the stories. She was such a great reader and storyteller. We'd sit there attentively and listen to every word. She was the only adult that could handle all seven of us together without major skirmishes. We all knew to respect grandmother or die. Even though we were bad, we weren't crazy. We knew when and where to draw the line.

All of us remembered the stories, but Tony used to preach the stories to Bobby and me. He'd stand on top of the slide in the back yard and re-preach sermons from church or the books. He was really very good. Neighbors, the white ones behind us, would call Lulu and tell her how good he was. He must have been good because Bobby and I would sit and listen. One day he told the story of Stephen and how he was stoned. Then, Tony slid down the slide and started walking away after his sermon. Without a word between us, Bobby and I looked at each other and started throwing rocks at Tony. Tony ran home crying and as he got to the cut off a dog chased him the rest of the way home. Bobby and I fell on the ground because we were laughing so hard, but we got spanked again for throwing rocks at Tony and laughing because the dog chased him. There was no room in our families for disrespect.

Bobby and I loved Tony. He was just such a "goody two shoe" that we couldn't stand it. We were always getting him into trouble. The neighbors that lived between our two houses were an elderly couple, Mr. and Mrs. Thierry. They were having their driveway paved. After begging and tears and lots of friendly persuasion, they allowed all of us to watch the cement being poured as long as we sat on the porch quietly and didn't get in the way. We all sat side by side on the edge of the porch overlooking the driveway, watching the cement come out of the tube and the men smoothing it over nice and flat.

Tony sat between Bobby and me. We watched and watched until we couldn't stand being still any longer. We had been good long enough. Again, without a word, Bobby and I leaned back, looked at each other, nodded our heads, and pushed Tony into the wet cement. He fell into the soft concrete with his new red leather slippers. Mr. and Mrs. Thierry sent us home and Lulu was fussing at Tony for falling. The new slippers were gone smoothed into the cement. Tony didn't even tell on us. We felt bad about that one...for a little while anyway.

If I'd been Tony, I would not have played with Bobby and me because we never let him win at any sport we played. He never really played. We just used him for us to play, and then we'd get tired and go home. For baseball he was the pitcher. Bobby and I would bat and run all day. When Tony was finally able to put three men out all by himself, we'd change the rules and go inside. One day Uncle Helvius (Tony and Bobby's Daddy) heard Tony crying and came out to investigate. He made Bobby and I let Tony bat and run until he got tired. Tony had such a great time. Poor Tony, he loved us in spite of ourselves. He must be a saint. Only a saint could have had a childhood like that and still retain his faith and belief in God to become a minister as an adult. At least Bobby and I did one good thing. We drove Tony to God.

Another great family story teller was Uncle Helvius. On Friday nights he'd fry fish and all of the children would gather at his house to eat and listen to him tell tall tales. We'd sit around the table with him sucking his fingers as he told the stories about days in Mansura, Louisiana where he grew up. One of my favorites was a wake where the floor board broke, the casket slipped and the woman sat up in the casket causing everyone to run in panic. The way he told it was so funny that we'd request that story more than any other. He also told scary stories about going hunting and seeing this man coming toward them. The man kept growing taller and taller with his pants getting shorter and shorter. By the time Uncle Helvius finished telling the story we were all screaming. Lulu would then appear laughing and saying, "No such thing. Must be silly." With her appearance we knew it was time to go home and say "Good-night."

The summer of my fifth grade year my brothers had ringworm. They had to cut off their hair and wear white hats. Mother insisted that I had to go to Mamou's in California to prevent me from getting it and for Mamou to teach me how to become a homemaker. We went to Beaumont for me to ride the train to Los Angeles with Taunte Vic. She lived in a large house that looked like Norman Bates Motel. She had borders on the second floor and other rental property and business enterprises that I had heard about. Taunte Vic got up every morning and started soaking and cooking some type of beans as her daily routine. She made everyone work whether it was dusting, sweeping, cleaning bathrooms or whatever else needed to be done, and there was always something that needed to be done because she was a collector of everything.

That night we begged to go to Taunte Lou's who had the best chicken and who covered you up with wonderful handmade quilts. All the cousins would gather there to eat, tell stories and giggle at night sleeping together on the floor wound up in a quilt. This time we had to stay with Taunte Vic because the train was leaving early the next morning. None of the children liked to stay with Taunte Vic, not because of the work, but because of the roaches.

Texans bragged about things being bigger in Texas and they were certainly correct about the roaches. Texas roaches were dark reddish brown with a wingspan of about six inches. And they flew. These suckers would land on you and look you in the eye with their big bug eyes daring you to move saying, "This is my place and it's time for you to leave." That's how the roaches were at Taunte Vic's house. Out of the clear blue, a roach flew across the room and landed near the couch. Ralph jumped up running in circles and hollering. Dupuy Jr. and I were holding on to each other. Mother tried to comfort Robert who started crying louder than all the noise. Daddy was laughing so hard at all of us that he could not even try to kill the roach or maybe he was scared of it, too. He caught Ralph and just held him to reassure him that he was all right, but Ralph started whining, "I wanna go hooome…. Uuuuph, Uuuuuum." Eventually Ralph lulled us to sleep with the whining and I slept with the blanket wrapped over my head and tucked under me not allowing any entrance for a roach and barely enough room for me to breathe. I was so happy to see the sun. What woke me up was the smell of fried chicken for the long train trip.

Taunte Vic's chicken was not as good as Taunte Lou's but we had to take it because Blacks were not allowed in the dining car until after we left Texas. Not being able to eat was a real problem for Black folks, but fried chicken was the cure, except that some people's chicken was greasy, but I'm not calling any names. Taunte Vic was a complete pain on the train. Bless her soul. I was excited about leaving home without parents and brothers but that quickly changed. Taunte Vic's adopted son Read was with us. She made Read and I get up at the crack of dawn every morning to use the restrooms before anyone else was up. "There's no telling who might be lurking in those bathrooms," was her daily lesson on the world. She was with me every morning in the bathroom. Seeing her big bloomers every morning was a shock to my system. After cleansing and returning to our seats, we had to say the rosary, which is 50 Hail Mary's, six Our Father's, five Glory Be's, the Creed and more. I never understood why if God is all-knowing why one of each wouldn't suffice. The rosary seemed to be redundant and a waste of time and energy, but we had to do it every morning and in the evening before Taunte Vic made us go to sleep.

After the rosary I had to help Read with his reading. If I were he I would not have liked me very much. Taunte Vic kept telling him how smart I was and that he was stupid. He did get on my nerves but he was nice.

I knew I had to respect my elders but Taunte Vic kept pushing and pushing me to the edge. She didn't know how mean I could be. I had already broken Billy's arm when he bet me he could jump out of the swing higher than I could. He didn't know how to jump. So I called jump when he was back and not forward and he jumped. The swing hit him and he fell down on the ground holding his arm crying. I ran home and left him. I was the neighborhood bully. I could beat all the boys older and younger. I ran Christian Street except for the gang at the end of the street near Bet-R Grocery Store run by Rooney Campbell. Rooney's mom babysat us at night sometimes when Mama and Daddy went out. So, Rooney didn't bother me, but I was a meanie.

I was so fed up with Taunte Vic on the train that given another day, she might have lost her false teeth forever. She wouldn't spend the money Daddy gave her for me, and she would not let me spend what he gave me for me. She said we had plenty of food in our box (fried chicken) and didn't need to spend any money. She was so embarrassing. She was loud, crude, clunky and colored acting. I knew how to act "proper" in front of people, and mother taught me never to be loud and common in public.

Taunte Vic passed that greasy chicken box around to everyone and volunteered my services to teach younger children to read while I helped Read. Even the whites that passed through the colored car were amazed at how well I could read. I guess they thought "All Niggers are dumb." The nerve of them, stopping to praise me like I was a circus event. With every praise, I rolled my eyes and looked away. Daddy taught me early that I was better than everybody, Blacks and whites alike. Daddy said I was the smartest and best person in the world and I could be whatever I wanted to be when I grew up. He promised to take care of me, and he could because he was a millionaire, or so I thought.

Every night Daddy would pull out a wad of money with a rubber band around it. He would lay it in stacks on the bed: ones, fives, tens, twenties and hundreds. It was always amazing. Sometimes he'd count thousands of dollars and sometimes he'd let me count. I saw him give Taunte Vic money for me and told her to get me what I wanted. On the last day I insisted that she take us to the dining car. I told her she could pay for Read and herself with my money if she didn't have any of her own. I was never disrespectful to the elderly but enough was enough. I had stopped eating the chicken because it looked too colored and too many people had been eating out of the box. I only ate the fruit.

I was starving and I told Taunte Vic that if I got sick, it was her fault and I would tell my Daddy she would not feed me. Daddy was my security line. She broke down and took us to the dining car after we dressed up. She enjoyed the meal also. The Black dining waiters were so nice to us. They seemed to be proud to have Black folks to serve. Even though Taunte Vic was cheap, she gave them a nice tip. I realized that she took care of Black people regardless of who they were or what they had to offer. After the meal when we returned to our seats, I had to hear what an insolent, stubborn child I was and she would never take me anywhere again. All I could do was think to myself, "Thank God, because I will never go with you again," but I knew better than to say it out loud. Yet, I knew that she was really a loving, caring and generous woman in spite of all her eccentric behaviors. She took care of anyone that needed help. I just didn't realize that she was trying to turn a spoiled brat, me, into a respectful and humane adult.

If I thought Taunte Vic was bad, Mamou was worse. She did not play. She was a warden over the work camp that summer. I had to iron Papou's undershorts, the sheets, pillowcases, tablecloths, napkins, doilies and clothes. I waxed furniture and "what nots" in every crease and crevice using a butter knife to get the furniture oil in every space. I swept, dusted, dust-mopped, mopped and waxed floors. I vacuumed and beat rugs. I washed and dried dishes. She made me appreciate homemakers and homemaking. I promised that when I grew up and had my house, my furniture would be sleek with no carvings and I'd use paper plates and cups to throw away and nothing would ever be ironed. All the clothes would be wash and wear with just hand smoothing when I took them out of the dryer. People collecting things that just collected dust for someone else to dust never made sense to me.

I finally begged to go to Aunt Gert's house for a while. Aunt Gert wanted me to come too. She said I needed to have some fun. I loved to stay with her family. She let me eat cold cereal in the morning and all her children looked out for me except Bernard. He was a big tease and called me Freya Sandra. No one but Daddy and Judy Faye James called me two names and that was only when he was upset and Judy was mocking him. I felt more at ease at Aunt Gert's house because they were brown-skinned people. Aunt Gert looked white, but her husband, Uncle Earl, was a big giant black man and they had brown children like me.

Everyone at Mamou's looked white except Read, Jules (Aunt Almease's son) and me. Auntie Mease's daughter Patsy and her other son Lee looked white but they were so very nice. Color didn't matter to them. We just had fun, but Mama's younger sister, and her family were passing for white. The children believed they were white. I asked her oldest daughter, "If you are white, then how can I be your first cousin?" She replied, "Your mother married a Negro." I never liked being around them because they didn't like Blacks. That's why I liked being at Aunt Gert's house because Jeannie's children didn't frequently come over there.

Patsy came with me to Aunt Gert's house. We all liked being there. Aunt Gert took us to Knott's Berry Farm, the beach, and in the back of their pickup truck to get a mile high cone. I dropped my cone on the first lick and Bernard laughed at me all the way home. He was a big tease. Bernard was closer to my age than any of Aunt Gert's other children and I guess that's why we had this tit-for-tat going on. In the mornings he'd hide the cereal from me. He laughed at my Southern accent and told me I couldn't talk right. He'd pick a phrase and repeat it everywhere we went to make people laugh at me. He was funny, but not when the joke was on me. His brother Arthur was my friend. He would spend time with me while he was making his conga drum. I could sit and listen to his friends play and he didn't think I was a bother. Thank goodness for Aunt Gert to pull the summer through.

One evening we went to the beach with Arthur and his friends. They were playing their conga drums and dancing on the sand while we roasted hot dogs and marshmallows on the open fire. Wow! Did I like Los Angeles and our family! They made me feel like a grown up being with the older cousins who let me hang out with them.

After I left Aunt Gert's house I visited Aunt Phrozine and Uncle Tiny in San Diego. Aunt Phrozine was the best cook ever. We were going to make tacos until she realized that it was Friday and I couldn't eat meat because I was Catholic. I was so disappointed that I told her it would be ok if I ate meat this once. We just didn't have to tell Mama. She didn't realize that eating meat wouldn't bother me at all, but Aunt Phrozine, being the responsible adult that she was, would not lie, so she made the tacos out of the "not meat." They were very good. I could not tell the difference. She taught me to cook in just a few days by watching her in the kitchen. She had a recipe for almost everything and she followed it to the letter. That was her secret. "If you can read, you can cook," was her belief. I asked her, "Why can't Mama cook?" and Aunt Phrozine laughed, responding that Mama tries to do everything too quickly. They all called Mama, "Ms. Fassy." Knowing my plight, Aunt Phrozine sent me a cookbook for Christmas from which I began cooking for the family. Even Daddy was grateful.

Time had run out and I had to go home on the train with Taunte Vic and Read. I was smart this time pretending to be sick while stretching across both seats. Read had to sit with Taunte Vic. I ate fruit and slept all the way home. I didn't ask for anything or bother anyone. With me being so quiet, they thought I really was ill and they left me alone. When I returned home the boys had gotten over the ringworm and the house had returned to normal or as normal as the Anderson house could be.

Ten Years Old

My sixth grade year was the year of the "Little Rock Nine." Daddy was glued to the television and newspapers. He kept pressing the Baton Rouge School Board more and more for equal facilities and desegregation. The lawsuit to integrate Baton Rouge was filed in 1956 (*Davis v. East Baton Rouge Parish School Board 1956*) with the simple plea that Black children in the then-separate system be allowed to "enroll, enter, attend classes and receive instruction in the public schools on a non-segregated and nondiscriminatory basis," but no action had been taken. Every time I heard Daddy talking about desegregating the schools, I could not wait until it came to Baton Rouge. I knew that if I went to the white schools, I could change the white hatred once they met me and I showed them how smart I was.

Daddy instilled in me that the purpose of life was to right the wrongs of the world, to help the less fortunate and to be the best that you can be. I began this self-crusade at the age of 10. There were 54 students in my sixth grade class. We had a human teacher, not a nun, but she really wasn't a great teacher. The Creoles didn't like her because she was too dark. I didn't like her because she could not teach. The best you could say about her was that she was nice. All year long we, the students, complained to Father Brainwashed the principal, other teachers, and our parents, but who were we to judge. No one listened, not even my own parents, not even my father who fought every cause. Therefore, I knew something had to be done and I had to do it.

I got my chance at midterm. When the teacher passed the end of semester exams back to the class, about half the class had failing grades. I was not in that group but I was sympathetic to their plight and, therefore, came to the rescue. We sat in vertical rows facing the teacher's desk in the front of the room, alphabetically by girls first, then boys. The rules of the class were that you could not speak or move unless recognized and given permission. My last name began with "A" so I was first on the first row. My cousin, Maryella Washington, received an F on a test for the first time in her life. She and many others began crying. I left my seat without permission and went to the fourth row in the back of the room to console her.

The teacher, recognizing that I had broken the sacred rule, demanded, "Ms. Anderson return to your seat." I ignored her. She repeated more sternly and gave me an ultimatum, "Ms. Anderson, return to your seat or go to the office!" I quietly asked some of the surrounding students, "If I walk out how many of you will go with me?" Walking up to me the teacher then commands, "Ms. Anderson, "Go to the office immediately!" I walked out and at least one-third of the class left with me.

I was so proud of our action because I knew someone would have to listen to us since so many had walked out. After all, it was a mass demonstration. Boy was I wrong. This was after the Montgomery bus boycott but it was before the mass demonstrations and sit-ins which meant we were ahead of our time. When my parents were called by the office secretary, they apologized for my actions and came immediately as they were requested to pick me up from school. They were told that I could not return until they had scheduled a meeting and met with Father Brainwashed. When I got home, Daddy spanked me without even hearing my side of the story. Being disrespectful to an elder, not obeying rules and not valuing my education was enough reason for a spanking. Mama and Daddy met with Father Brainwashed who suspended all of us for two weeks, but I was the only one he asked not to return the next year because I was considered the leader and trouble maker. If I went peacefully, there would be no mention of it on my record. Grandmother came to my defense again. She made Daddy and Mama understand that I was only following my role models, "them," to protest when something isn't right. They agreed to listen to my concerns and talk to Father Brainwashed. Father did not budge and that was fine with me. I didn't like Catholic school anyway. Daddy hugged me and gave me a smile to let me know he was proud of me even if he couldn't tell me in front of Mama. Baton Rouge was not prepared for Daddy and me.

I was quickly becoming the defender of the oppressed. My brother, Dupuy Jr. was being bullied by my classmate Danny who hit Dupuy in the stomach during recess. One of Dupuy's classmates told me that Dupuy was crying and hurt. When I asked Dupuy what happened, he told me this boy punched him in the stomach because he accidentally ran into him when he was trying to catch a ball. Dupuy was only a second-grader and Danny was my classmate in sixth grade. I told Danny that he was not right for hitting a second grader and that he should apologize. He responded with, "Who's going to make me?" That was all I needed. I punched him in the face and stomach so quickly. He didn't know what hit him. Classmates pulled us apart before Danny really got a chance to return the punches, but I informed him that he'd better not touch my brother again. It was okay for me to beat Dupuy Jr. but no one else better touch him. The sixth grade finally ended and that marked the end of Catholic school for me. "Thank the white Catholic God!"

That summer was another great experience in the life of the Andersons. The National Dental Association held its annual meeting in Cincinnati, Ohio at one of the newly integrated hotels. This was the first Black convention at the Sheraton Gibson. There were six of us traveling in this loud, hot pink Plymouth station wagon from Baton Rouge to Cincinnati. Daddy stopped buying Oldsmobiles, which he loved, because Plymouth in Baton Rouge hired the first black salesperson, Mr. Fuller. So Daddy bought cars from him. I just wished it could have been a different color but Mama liked it and thought that a station wagon would better suit our needs. Since Mama had never learned to pack conservatively we had trunks of clothes with four large suitcases, one shoe case, one hat case, and one vanity case. The car was so loaded down with luggage there was still no room for all of us in the station wagon. We still had the ice chest on the floor of the backseat and the bags of food, the normal staples for Black travel.

I was in the car with Daddy and Mama, who is this blonde lady with her two white, blonde haired boys and one white boy with black hair and blue eyes—my family. To make matters worse, these three boys were the worst children that have ever existed on the face of the earth. A few of the things they did to get this title were unimaginable. One year they got a toolbox for Christmas. They proceeded to nail nails into newly refinished hardwood floors in the living room and dining room and sawed off the legs of the coffee table. We had the first colored appliances in the world. They painted a chest freezer in the garage along with the floor of the garage, plants and plant stands and the weeping willow tree. All were red. While Daddy and Mama were sleeping one Saturday morning, Dupuy and Ralph, playing with Daddy's lighter at the foot of the bed, set Robert's baby bed on fire with Robert in it. They broke so many windowpanes Mama learned how to replace the glass herself. The broken windows occurred so frequently that the salesman at the hardware store knew the size.

Mama couldn't even take them to church. A "special-needs" man at the church asked her to not bring them back because he couldn't listen to the priest. Mama was the organist and choir director. Those boys threw things from the choir loft and yelled at the statues. They crawled under the pews. They crawled under her feet and mashed the pedals on the organ. I was so embarrassed whenever I had to be with them. It was bad enough having whites think that I was their maid, but it was even worse having Blacks know that I was related. My mother was a further embarrassment. While all this was going on she managed to continue with whatever she was doing as if all were fine with the world. Her typical response was, "If I let them worry me, I'd be insane."

I think she already was because they were driving us all crazy. When we'd visit people they'd look out and see us, then yell, "Put up everything that can be broken! The Andersons are here." Aunt Jerry and Uncle Doc, Judy and Nan's parents, had a dachshund named Jufer. When we walked into the house, Jufer would try to hide behind the stove in the kitchen. Now, I said tried to hide because he was so fat that his stomach dragged on the ground, which meant there was no way he could get behind anything. I said that to say that anytime a dog runs from you, you know you're trouble. That's the reputation my brothers had with everyone we visited. Mama and Daddy's friends must have really loved Daddy and Mama because they'd let us in, but I know they dreaded our visits. When it was time to leave they would count heads to make sure no one was left behind. The worst thing my brothers ever did had to do with playing with fire again.

They inherited this fascination with fire from my father. He followed fire engines. One day he left a patient with a deadened mouth sitting in his dentist's chair alone to follow a fire engine. So the boys did get this minor character flaw honestly. One afternoon Mama and I were lying in her bedroom talking. Robert, the youngest boy, came sneaking inside to get the matches off the stove. As an afterthought Mama said, "Freya, go see what Robert is doing with those matches." I followed him to the backyard and I couldn't believe what I saw. Those three boys had tied the little boy that lived across the street, Greg, to the clothesline pole. They had stacked a pile of wood around him and were getting ready to burn him at the stake playing cowboys and Indians. Greg did not know how lucky he was that they sent Robert in to get the matches. One of the older boys may not have been questioned. I stopped the burning at the stake immediately and went inside to tell Mama. She brought them in for punishment and called Daddy. The boys came in but they continued to play and tear up the house. These were the Anderson boys.

These were the people that I had the pleasure to travel with to Cincinnati. We left early that morning to get through Mississippi in the day light. With all the lynchings and missing Blacks that had occurred there, Daddy did not like driving through Mississippi. He made sure we used the bathroom before we left. We could not have anything to drink. He only wanted to stop for gas and keep moving. The boys were sleepy and didn't fight long over who was going to sit by the window. One got angry with another and threw a shoe out of the window. Mama calmly said, "Dupuy, Robert just threw his shoe out of the window." Daddy started cussing and fussing, but he turned around to look for the shoe. Not finding it, Robert had to wear slippers, which were those moccasin socks. Dupuy Jr. started teasing him because he didn't have shoes and Ralph started whining. The baby, Robert, who started it all, crawled up on Mama's lap with his blanket and went to sleep. If only I could have attached the backseat of the car like a railroad car behind us, I would have left them stranded on the side of the road.

When we arrived in Mississippi we were tired and cranky. The map was almost of no use because the roads were so poorly marked. We drove around in circles for about a half hour. One time we stopped and asked this guy at a "T" crossroad which way to the highway. He assertively replied, "You could go this way or that way." Daddy and I looked at each other. He said "Shit!"

I smiled. Because of the lost shoe and getting lost we had to stop for gas in Mississippi. Before Daddy stopped he warned us that we could not get out of the car for any reason. We had to sit quietly and not make any disturbance. Now, the boys were bad but not totally insane. They knew when Daddy talked like that, he was serious. Disobey him now and you would never breathe again. We pulled into a gas station and Daddy asked to have the car serviced. In those days you got full service. We sat there obediently quiet. Across the street there were men playing a baseball game and the dirt was red, their uniforms were covered with red dust and they looked red and cruddy. I asked mom if that was why whites were called rednecks because they played in red dirt. She said, "Hush!" We saw the people at the station looking at us strangely and Mama became nervous.

The serviceman told Daddy that we needed a new fan belt. He said this one was ready to break, but that he could get a new one within five minutes. Daddy said he could wait until we got to Cinci. The man insisted since we were traveling that far we needed to get the belt or it might break and we would be stuck on the road. Daddy acquiesced. While we were waiting for the belt, a police car parked in the front of our car and another parked behind us. An officer came over and asked for Daddy and Mama's license and car registration. Daddy wanted to know why because we had not violated any law. The officer did not answer but just read the licenses and registration. The other three officers were looking in the car like it was a freak show. I admit with all the luggage and food, we may have looked strange, but we had not committed a crime.

With the arrival of the two police cars the redneck teams stopped playing and walked to the top of the street to see what was going on. Two of the police officers kept the teams across the street but the teams remained at the curb standing and watching. By the time the policeman started asking about Mama's license, the crowd had started to yell, "That Nigger is with a white woman!" We were scared to death. Mama was so angry. I could see her turn past red to purple. I could feel the heat coming from her. She tried to reassure us while telling us to sit still and be calm. "Everything is going to be all right."

The officer asked her, "Do you know that it's illegal for a white and Black to be married in the state of Mississippi?"

"I'm a Negro, she replied."

"Your license has a 'W' for white."

"It must be a mistake. May I see it? Oh, they made a mistake. Every year I have to go down to the clerk's office and have them change it, but I forgot this year."

"You do know that interracial marriages are illegal in Mississippi?"

"Yes, but we are both Negroes!"

"I'm sorry, but I'm going to have to take you to the Magistrate."

The policeman asked Daddy to get out of the car. The officer handcuffed Daddy and put him in the back of the police car. Another policeman got in our car and followed him. I sat as close to the passenger door as possible away from that man. I was afraid. All I could do was blame Mama for not checking her license. She was still "Trouble." She knew that she had to get it checked and changed every year. The clerk's office always wanted to make her white. I think they were more intimidated by labeling a white person Negro so they erred on the part of making a Negro white. This racism endangered Blacks for just being alive, but this was not the time to protest anything. If I said or did anything these crackers might keep my Daddy. I kept quiet.

The officer drove off the highway down a dirt road. By now, I'm petrified. All I can think of are the many Blacks that were hung and never heard from again in Mississippi. Were we going to become a statistic? We could come up missing and the only thing anyone would find would be Robert's shoe that we left somewhere along the highway in Baton Rouge as a clue that we did leave town. The further we drove the more frightened I became and Mama held the boys tightly to her in the back seat. When I saw a sign that read "Magistrate," I felt a little relieved. The policemen did tell us the truth. Now, who is this magistrate and what is he going to do?

The magistrate's office was his home. We waited while he finished eating dinner. Then the policemen told him the story. He questioned Daddy and Mama. We were lucky the magistrate was willing to listen. Daddy asked him to call Judges or elected officials in Baton Rouge and they could verify who he was and that he and Mama were not an interracial couple. The magistrate called a judge that he knew and didn't get an answer. Then Daddy suggested he call Senator Deblieux in Baton Rouge to verify that Mama was Black. Fortunately, the magistrate knew of the Senator and the Senator verified that he knew Daddy well. Deblieux verified that Daddy and Mama were not an interracial couple. The magistrate let us go, but warned Mama that she needed to make sure she got that license changed. All of us reminded her each year after that.

Fortunately, my vision of being tarred and feathered and dumped into the Pearl River did not come true. Daddy drove straight through to Cincinnati only stopping for gas. He usually stopped to give us lessons on the growing crops that we could see from the road, or famous landmarks, but he did not stop. He barely spoke. I could see the tenseness in his jaws and the steam coming from his head. The stillness in the car was permeated with a tension so thick that I could feel the air wrapped around my body like arms squeezing me tightly and choking my breath. I could barely swallow. I could hear my heart beat and feel my pulse throbbing in my arms and legs. The boys even knew better than to act-out. They went to sleep or at least played possum. I read the map when needed and sat close to Daddy to let him know I understood. I couldn't look at Mama because I knew she felt like the incident was her fault. I wanted to tell Trouble that I understood. It wasn't her fault. She could not help the fact she looked white. But the tension kept me from turning and the quiet of the car, kept me from talking.

When we finally arrived at the hotel, it was magnificent. The Sheraton Gibson Hotel was our first major big white hotel vacation. This was the first time a white hotel opened its doors to a major Black Convention, the National Dental Association. However, my embarrassment began immediately. First, just unpacking all of the luggage was a spectacle in itself. The Bellmen took four racks to empty the car. You would have thought the entire Louisiana delegation had us carry their luggage. Not only had we arrived needing four Bellmen and racks but three of the racks had little white boys hanging and climbing from them like "monkeys in the jungle." They fit the stereotype for Blacks – monkeys, no culture, no refinement.

As they played on the rolling racks with Mama oblivious to it all, Daddy was registering at the front desk. I walked away from them but staying in sight not to lose Daddy. Fortunately I was old enough to do most of the activities with the children's program without my mother or brothers. This saved me from further humiliation of having to spend all day every day with those three boys. However one morning Mama cornered me and insisted we all eat breakfast together in the coffee shop. There were five of us seated at a round counter height table, which sat in the middle of the coffee shop. Not only were we the largest party in the restaurant, we were the only Black party there. The faces at the other tables and booths were white. The waitresses were white. The tables had white tops with chrome trim. The stools at the tables had white seats with chrome trim. I was engulfed by white including my mother and brothers.

Naturally, without Daddy, the boys were being themselves, abominable. They began the morning with swordfights using the silverware on the table. The swordfight was followed by turning over the salt and pepper shakers and the sugar bowl mixing them together. In the scramble to mix them, they turned over a glass of milk, which the waitress attempted to clean up as they turned over the table on top of her. They turned over the TABLE! Astounded, I immediately jumped up, looked at my mother, threw my napkin and said, "I'm never going to work for you people again!" I walked out then ran to my room and cried. I'd always tried to maintain dignity and respect to prove to whites that Blacks were not the bad nasty people that people believed. I thought that if whites could see and meet Blacks like me, the rumors and lies would be dispelled, but those heathen brothers of mine fit all the colored stereotypes that I believed were the reasons for discrimination.

When friends and relatives did not want to let us into their house, I fully understood. If I owned a house, I would not have let them in either. It would definitely have taken an act of Congress to get me to let them in. That day I got even. I didn't mind being the maid because it showed I had better manners and etiquette than the whites for whom I said I was working. People thought I was the maid all my life and today I gratefully fulfilled the role to not be associated with my brothers.

Everyone at the convention heard how those Anderson boys demolished the coffee shop. Daddy was also ashamed. He offered to pay for damages but the management was nice and explained that things like that happen all the time. I bet no one turned over an entire table before. It's a wonder the waitress didn't sue. All I could see were national headlines, "Sheraton Gibson hosts NDA and Blacks demolish the coffee shop. Integration is over forever!"

I would not be seen with my brothers anywhere after that. The last night of the convention was the President's dinner and reception. Mother asked me if I would like to go with her and Daddy. I gladly accepted and was proud to be with the adults and no brothers. We dressed up for my first adult affair. The boys were staying in with a hotel babysitter. Mama always dressed as if she stepped out of fashion magazine and she maintained a magnificent figure. I couldn't blame Daddy for marrying her because she was a showstopper. As the three of us walked in, all heads turned but they were all looking at her. She was beautiful. We had a lovely evening. I danced with Daddy for the first time and I had a smidgen (a swallow) of champagne with dinner. I just knew I was grown.

What a breath of fresh air to not be disturbed by the boys. The sitter at the hotel was supposed to be checking the room periodically. Mother left them asleep. When we got back to the room, Mama didn't turn on the light. She just got dressed for bed and got into bed trying to not wake the boys. Just as I was about to drift off to sleep I heard this shrill from Mama. Daddy turned on the light. In the bed, dripping from the ceiling, smeared on top of the dresser was shaving cream.

That was the last straw. Daddy grabbed all three out of them out of the bed, wrapped his belt around his hand and proceeded to spank the living daylights out of them. Naturally mother intervened, "Dupuy, you'll hurt them. Ok, you can stop. They understand. They won't do it again." She always came to their rescue thinking they belonged exclusively to her. Daddy would not injure them. In fact, I felt he should bind and gag them and only force-feed them when absolutely necessary.

We left Cincinnati the next morning. Daddy took the family down to eat in the dining room for breakfast but I refused to eat with them. So I left hungry. I sat in the lobby until they were all packed, and I joined them before Daddy pulled off. We then went to Chicago to visit Daddy's brothers, Bobby and Cliff. Once there we went swimming in Lake Michigan; it was the coldest water I had ever been in, and I didn't consider that fun. I was freezing. Water that cold was not made for swimming. Yet, we did have fun pulling Daddy in the water with us. Later we had a barbecue at Mr. and Mrs. Dawson's home. They were friends of Uncle Cliff who owned the 411 Club and Cliff worked there part time, but the family was more friend than boss. Mrs. Dawson invited her friends and family to meet Cliff's family for a relaxing afternoon of Bar-b-que and cards. As we were preparing to leave Mrs. Dawson discovered that the boys had pulled up every flower she had in planted in the yard. The flowers lay wilted on the grass while the boys covered with dirt from head to toe played in the freshly cultivated beds.

With everyone exhausted after trying to replant the flowers, we quickly headed for home. Daddy said he was not going through Mississippi so we went through Arkansas instead. He was driving non-stop to Baton Rouge but that night he was so tired he asked Mama to drive about an hour so he could rest a little. Mama began driving and did fairly well in the beginning. Then she began to drive slower and slower. I talked to her and we sang songs. I was trying to keep her awake. I gave her a Coke. She started slowing more and I looked to see what was wrong. She said the trees were walking. I looked again and I didn't see anything. She stopped and said the forest had blocked the road. I woke Daddy up and told him to take the wheel or I would drive and I didn't have a license. "Dear Lord, why can't I have a normal vacation? Why do I belong to them? Please don't let me be crazy when I grow up."

St. Francis Xavier, Girl Scout, Jo Evelyn

Freya & Jo Evelyn

Aunt Wilma & Uncle Bernie

Tony's slide pulpit & the Bar-b-que pit

Mama, Aunt Wilma, Aunt Bobbie, Nancy

Uncle Bernie, Dr. Pierson, Dr. Fleet, Uncle Vic

Joella Malveaux

Aunt Wilma & Mama

Family Friends

First Communion

Infamous Tool Box

Robert-trying to take the wheel off the car

My
Brothers

Eleven and Twelve Years Old

In seventh grade I began a secular education. Is it wrong to thank God for not being in a Christian school? St. Francis did not want me anymore and I was quite pleased with that decision. I started Southern University Laboratory School. My seventh and eighth grade years were traumatic ones. I was really lucky that I had such an excellent teacher, Mrs. Wooten. She was a very perceptive person who had a class full of young, above average, borderline geniuses—which meant borderline psychotic pre-teens. Were we ever a severe emotional trip! When we finally graduated it was the greatest bunch of people I've ever been associated with in or out of school. Each person was unique and special in his/her own way.

This was my first realization that I was not exceptional but just ordinary. My entire class was smart. I had been the youngest in my classes before, but now I was the fourth youngest so I was unimportant again. The girls were talking about periods and boyfriends and were wearing bras. I was totally left out. I liked football, didn't want a period and boys were part of a sports team, not lovers. Since I couldn't be the big cheese I withdrew from my peers. I did my work, participated in class, but went home daily and called no one and went nowhere on weekends except with Judy, Nan and Jo, my childhood friends.

I was tall, gangly, awkward, ugly, wore Brown Oxford Girl Scout corrective shoes, carried a big ugly brown schoolbag, and had un-styled hair that only got pulled back in a ponytail with curls. My first year without a uniform and mother still dressed me like I was five, and I didn't like it at five. Mama still wanted a girly little girl. She wanted bows, ruffles, curls and frills, kisses, hugs, affection and warmth. What she got was jeans, cowboy boots, dogs, fights, football and independence without touching. She tried to make me over but I was like, "Polly put the kettle on, Suki takes it off again." Mama would put a bow in my hair and I pulled it out every time. I hated bows. Little Black girls with little hair had the biggest bows stuck to their heads with bobby pins. I couldn't stand it and Mama wanted me to wear bows. She felt curls and bows went together, but I didn't want the curls and definitely not the bows. So, hair became a major issue.

I was so thin and tall I could never find clothes to fit. Most of the time Mama and Grandmother sewed for me. The clothes they made were gorgeous but I only liked a few. My favorite dress that they made was a black velveteen princess jumper with rhinestones. Mama also trimmed the store bought blouse and socks with lace and rhinestones. I still like beads and stones today. Another favorite was a red corduroy jumper that had a flare bottom in a princess style, but no frills. The black velveteen was the only frill outfit that I liked.

A gorgeous dress that Mama made was for my First Communion. I despised that dress. It was a three-tiered imported embroidered organza. Lulu crocheted the hat with pompoms on each side. Utterly priceless! But the dress was just too much for me with all those ruffles, and the pompoms had to go. I pulled a tier off the dress and never wore it again and hid the hat. I would die today for that dress. Mama made another expensive embroidered organza Easter dress with a fitted bodice, a satin ribbon belt and a gathered dirndl skirt. I intentionally tore it on a nail and never wore it again. It just had too much stuff. I'd give my right arm for either of those dresses today. If only I had the fashion sense then that I have now, I would have definitely been more appreciative. All I can say is that I'm so sorry for being such an ungrateful brat.

Mama made me wear corrective shoes because I had flat feet. The shoes were awful, Girl Scout brown oxfords. I had to wear them every day except Sundays at church or special dress up occasions. Since I hated them I would rub my shoes on the bricks of the house to wear them out. I'd have to hold in my giggle when Daddy often remarked, "I can't understand how the tops of the shoes get worn out before the bottom."

With my terrible looks and figure, my awful clothes and shoes, I felt left out and unloved again. I was now too old to be Daddy's girl. He spent more time with the boys. I had no one. I went to school, came home, went to my room, ate dinner, did my homework, went to sleep and started all over again. I felt so alone. I thought of suicide often but I was chicken. With my luck I would live the rest of my life as a vegetable knowing I did this to myself, and I knew better than to try to run away if I valued life at all.

This was my plight in seventh and eighth grades, and this was the young woman that Mrs. Wooten was compelled to change. She saw something worth her time and effort. Mrs. Wooten spotted the little girl in trouble. At Southern High we had student teachers every semester, and every semester Mrs. Wooten assigned one of them to me for their case study project. I wrote so many autobiographies that they were truly sensational by the end of eighth grade, more fiction than truth. I began to prepare them ahead of time. I was quite creative. Each student teacher got a different version from happy to sophisticated to withdrawn and suicidal, a classic case of schizophrenia.

Another student on the list was my enemy, Marion Greenup who was also one of the youngest in the class. We met our seventh grade year and quickly became enemies because we were so much alike. We competed at everything, called each other names and talked about each other constantly to the other classmates. I called her "Nose" and she called me "Yellow." Student teachers and Mrs. Wooten tried to get us to work together and to find out why we couldn't get along but they all failed. When peer relationships fail usually another peer is better at bridging the impasse. That student was Cynthia Davis. I don't remember how or what she did, but she was able to bring Marion and me together as friends and we have been inseparable to this day. Cynthia was a wonderful class leader and friend.

Mrs. Wooten individualized her instruction to meet the needs of each child. Her classes were not lectures and regurgitation of memorized facts. She turned classes over to the students to create, initiate and implement. I've never enjoyed learning as much as I did in those years. Every subject was a project. Mama protested to me, "Doesn't she ever teach? All you do are projects and plays. You're not learning a thing!" Thank goodness Mrs. Wooten didn't cave in to parents. Our classes were so exciting. We learned the Battle of New Orleans by staging it in class. We made the snakes, birds and other animals indigenous to Louisiana out of clay and paper mache for Louisiana History and Natural Resources class. We created plays and quiz shows. We made floor pillows and had class while sitting on pillows.

My group in Louisiana history wrote a play about the New Orleans school system and its benefactor John McDonogh. We acted the entire play on our knees, hiding our legs under our skirts to look like little children. We cut raw onions at his deathbed scene to simulate tears. The whole class cried, but I remember his name today because it was a meaningful experience. The saying, "the Lord takes care of babes and fools," must be true for someone looked after me those two years and allowed me to grow educationally and socially.

If I had to sit through two years of Catholic school in my mental state at that time of my life, I probably would've committed suicide. The gap of being skipped had reared its ugly head and I did not know what was happening. Most of the girls in my class were more mature physically, socially and emotionally and I was none of the above, but I was very creative. Mrs. Wooten began each morning with the devotion. We sang the Lord's Prayer and a few other children's songs, reported headline news, and then someone read the school bulletin and the lunch menu. Some of the songs we sang were "Hands on myself," "Down by the old mill stream," "Teapot," "Little rabbit Fu Fu," and many more.

> Down by the old not the new but the old,
> mill stream, not a river but a stream,
> where I first not second but the first,
> met you, not me, but you,
> it was there not here but there,
> I knew not old but new,

that I loved not hate but loved,
you true, not false but true.

Mackie Jenkins led devotion the best. She remembered more songs to sing than anyone else. She was probably the most popular girl in the class and the class would request her lead. I never wanted to lead, but Mrs. Wooten would try to give everyone a chance, which meant that there were times when I had to lead. When that occurred I tried to mimic Mackie.

The class decided that we wanted our desks positioned in a large circle. Mrs. Wooten did put three disorderly boys in the middle to keep them out of trouble, but they were constantly trying to look under girls' dresses. We arranged and re-arranged the room often but always the students were in charge under the directed supervision of Mrs. Wooten. As much as we loved her, we disliked the student teachers with equal affection. No one could come close to Mrs. Wooten.

Our job was to make the student teachers cry. If they could make it through the semester without crying, they were destined to become great teachers, but if they faltered with a stutter or tremble, their career was over. We knew we had broken them. As long as they were assisting Mrs. Wooten, it was fine, but when they had to take her place and teach on their own, the demons in us came out. Through some miracle most of the student teachers survived.

That summer Judy, Nan, Jo Evelyn and I spent a lot of time together. Judy and I had this bond between us. We were always willing to take risks and do the dangerous, exciting things our parents told us not to do. Nan and Jo always wanted to be with us but were too afraid to do anything, so they'd tell on Judy and me and get us in trouble. We got along well when we played with dolls or went to the movies or when we were at Webb Golf Course where our fathers played golf because those places had few, if any, ways to deviate from being good.

But after a few hours of being good, Judy and I would have to do something to break the monotony. Every time Judy and Nan visited me, Judy and I would go riding our bikes. We had explicit instructions not to leave Christian Street, which was only one block long. Christian Street was a mixed neighborhood with whites on one end at Morning Glory, Creoles splattered between, and Blacks at the other end near Perkins Road. No one bothered anyone else but those who knew each other were friendly and looked out for one another.

Our parents did not want us to leave Christian Street because we were two blocks away from City Park and University Lakes, an upper crust area for whites in the city. The lakes were for whites. It was one of the exclusive areas for whites in the city. On the other side of City Park Lake was City Park where Blacks were also not allowed. So, Mama and Daddy forbade us to leave our street for fear that young Black girls might be preyed upon.

I still believed that no one would harm me because I was such a nice, smart, young girl. I didn't believe I was in danger. Judy and I weren't doing anything but riding our bikes and maybe throwing a few rocks in the water. Not once but every time Judy came, we went riding around the lakes. There was one area with a gazebo in the water that we particularly liked. We never went in the gazebo, but we often wondered how nice it would be. I loved the lakes. Even alone, especially when I was depressed or wanted to get away from my brothers, I would go riding to the lakes and read or sit and watch the ducks. Sometimes I'd ride even in the rain. The summer weather was always so hot causing a daily evening shower or thunderstorm. If it wasn't lightning I would ride in the rain feeling the cool water against my heat soaked body.

One particular day Judy and I sent Jo and Nan inside to get something for the tea party and the dolls. Judy and I sneaked off with our bikes and headed around the lakes. Nan and Jo told Mama that we were gone. When we returned, Mama called Judy and Nan's mother and told her that we had disobeyed. Both parents agreed that playtime was over, and Judy and Nan and Jo had to go home. I was punished, banished to my room. Another time Nan and Jo asked if they could come with us. They convinced Judy and me that they would not tell. We took them around the lake and to our favorite spot, the gazebo, and left them. When we came back, they were still there scared to death and crying. We reminded them of their promise not to tattle or we would leave them there forever. They promised. We took them on Ellisade Street, the street behind and parallel to Christian, and ate honeysuckles that grew wild. As soon as we got home, Nan and Jo told Mama. I was sent to my room. Mama took Judy, Nan and Jo home.

I was sulking when Ralph came to my door teasing me. I slammed the door on him, but when Mama returned, he told her I choked him. I was guilty of a lot of things, but I had not choked him. If he wanted to be choked, I accommodated him. I choked him and then smashed him between the door to the room and the closet door. I left him whining, "aaaaah, ooop, uum." Since I was going to be punished, it might as well have been for the truth. I bet he never lied on me again. I still didn't like those boys, my brothers. They weren't quite as bad by this time, but I just didn't have time for them.

That summer Judy, Nan, Jo Evelyn and I took swimming lessons at Brooks Park, the Black public pool. Judy and I excelled as usual and Nan and Jo were scaredy cats, but we all had a crush on Tampoo. He was about 16 or older with a body like Mr. America. He was a lifeguard at the pool and trained diver. He was probably the first real diver any of us had seen. With his perfectly cut, buffed body, such poise and grace walking the length of the board, he'd dive one of his many show stopping dives, slicing the water barely splashing a speck of water. He looked like a black god with sparkles glistening from the sun hitting the droplets of water on his muscle-ripped deep brown torso. Even though he was cocky and all the older girls flocked around him, he still had time to smile for the giggling preteens. He had to be our first love that summer.

When the class ended Judy and I learned to swim which meant we had to dive from the boards in the deep end of the pool. I successfully completed my dive from the low board and I was challenged by the other life guard, Charles Pickens, to jump from the high board. That was the event that caused me to stop taking dares. Not realizing that heights terrified me until I got to the end of the board, I looked down, got dizzy and started to turn around to go back down. Pickens was behind me and talked me into trying to overcome my fear. After his encouragement, I again walked to the end of the board and stood there looking down. Before I knew it, Pickens gave me a gentle nudge causing me to fall. Somehow I managed to do a 360, turning completely around and grabbing the end of the board. It was only seconds before my hand slipped and I fell in, but I felt like it was an eternity just hanging there at the end of the board. I was too upset and embarrassed. I never wanted to come up out of the water. I just wanted to stay down there and drown. Can you imagine how a pre-teen felt being humiliated in front of the entire Black community of Baton Rouge? My air finally ran out and I had to surface. Good thing I didn't need help because all the lifeguards were doubled over laughing at me. Pickens said he'd never seen anyone do that except a clown at the circus.

At the beginning of eighth grade Mrs. Wooten and the student teachers were still there analyzing me, but I was changing. Physically my body began to slowly develop and there were signs of breasts. After Tampoo, I began to slightly notice other males, but usually they were much older. The ones my age were too silly.

We got a new instructor at the school. He was young, fine, cute, good looking, single and had the most precious smile. Yes, all that! He was the band director, Mr. Ludwig Freeman. Every girl in school joined the band, including me. I selected the clarinet. My father immediately went out and bought a clarinet. After about two weeks most of the girls left the band. They realized this man was serious and not flirting. I wanted to quit too, but Daddy had bought my horn, not rented it. He would not let me quit.

I had taken piano lessons all my life, and I could read music well. Thus, the clarinet was easy to learn. I made progress quickly. Naturally, Mr. Freeman found me a challenge as did everyone else. Here was this intelligent, talented young lady who could play well, knew the music, but never volunteered to answer questions and rarely smiled. To make matters worse he teased me. I stopped going to class. Daddy wouldn't let me quit but I did. I told Mrs. Wooten that I quit, and she stopped calling me to go to band. After two weeks Mr. Freeman called Daddy and Mama and asked to come by to speak to them. He begged them to let me continue to play in the band because I was so talented. Yes, Daddy and Mama were astounded! To their knowledge I **was** in the band. I had a lot of explaining to do. When I wheezled out of the confrontation by playing pitiful for being teased, Mr. Freeman promised he would not tease me, even though he did later, but by that time we were friends. He began teaching me private lessons on Saturdays. He discovered that I had an interest in jazz and he shared his albums. I really liked him but I would never let him know.

Another moment of interest in eighth grade was the movie *Imitation of Life*. Everyone and their Mama went to see this movie at the Lincoln Theater. That was the only Black theater in the City. It was very nice and clean—and all we knew since the other theaters were white. We talked at school about that little Black girl in the movie trying to pass for white, denying her mother. At the end of the movie when she came back for her mother's funeral and cried on the coffin, there wasn't a dry eye in the movie. When Mahalia Jackson started singing, the entire theater was boo-hooing, sniffing, blowing noses and groaning so loudly that you couldn't hear the song. White folks cry cute in public with a sniff, a gentle pat of the eyes and nose, and never a tear falling, but *Imitation of Life* deserved Black tears for all the discrimination and trials and tribulations the entire race had ever endured. This was pure colored crying. It was terrible. Ultimate Hysteria! All I could think of was that I denied my Mama too, not because she was Black, but because she looked white. It was reverse discrimination. Why couldn't I ever be normal?

There were two sections of eighth grade. For our graduation activities our section wanted a prom and the other section wanted to go to Avery Island, the land of Tabasco Hot Sauce. Dr. McKelpin, the principal, denied both requests. He told us that we'd have to decide on one thing for both classes. Our class was an exceptional class. Mrs. Wooten taught us critical thinking and self-assertiveness. She taught us to fight for what we wanted with the research to back it up. We were very independent learners and creative leaders. First, we tried to plan for both events but when we calculated the costs for both events we decided that we could not raise enough money or afford for both classes to do both things. Therefore, the classes voted and the decision was once again that the other class wanted to go to Avery Island and our class wanted a prom. Dr. McKelpin informed us that either we cooperate or there would not be any end of the year experience for either class.

Our class found that unacceptable and decided to fight his decision. We presented a signed petition to Dr. McKelpin stating the reasons why we should have a prom, how we planned to pay for it, the theme and designs, and the food and entertainment. When the other class heard about our petition, they also petitioned him. He again said that both classes had to decide on one thing and do it as one class. We again went back to him explaining that we were two separate and very different classes and wanted our individual activities. He was shocked that we had gone through so much planning and details and that we were so relentless. Eventually he allowed both classes to do their separate activities. We had our prom and the other class went to Avery Island.

Our prom was "Swinging in Spring The Special 8's" with the name engraved on the napkins. We had wonderful food, a talent show at intermission where Lorita Robinson pantomimed "Cry me a River," and a real live band. After the prom Dr. McKelpin complimented us on a job well done acknowledging that we surpassed most senior proms he had seen. It was quite special, but more importantly, we won. We fought the system and succeeded.

The climax of the eighth grade year was graduation. For graduation the girls were supposed to wear white dresses. I knew exactly what I wanted. It was the dress Sandra Dee wore in *Imitation of Life*. I could not find anything close to that dress in any of the stores. So Mama finally consented to make it. One day we were in TG&Y on Highland and State Street looking through the pattern books. The white saleslady was helping me when mother came over and asked, "Oh, did you find something?" The saleslady looked at her and asked, "Does she work for you?" Mother looked at her with glaring eyes and said, "No, I've worked for *her* all my life!" Yes, that was my Mama! I was so proud of her. She dropped the few things she planned to buy and we left immediately. I knew then that she really loved me. She didn't deny me, and I would never deny her again. We forgot about the dress. She didn't make it, but we eventually found one that I liked just as well. She always tried to make me happy.

Eighth grade summer was almost the same as the seventh with swimming, but I was a lot better. Pickens gave me private instruction since I was advanced and I learned the side, back, and breast strokes. He said if I came back the next year I could be trained as a junior lifeguard, but I stayed away from the high diving board. The summer was almost normal. We didn't even take an Anderson adventure trip, but I should have known something would happen. When things are going too smoothly, take a deep breath to prepare for the next adventure or crisis.

Revolutionary II

Daddy decided to run for mayor of Baton Rouge. This was the first time since Reconstruction that a Black in Baton Rouge, and probably all of Louisiana, had run for an elected office. Daddy was more than qualified. He was a doctor and civic leader and definitely interested in the progress of the city and all its citizens, but that was not the issue. He was Black. *That* was the issue.

Daddy listed his qualifications as a citizen of Baton Rouge, his degrees, his dentistry practice, his church affiliation and his military service. He belonged to the Council of Greater Baton Rouge, the Minority Group Advisory Council of a special committee of the Louisiana Department of Labor, the Committee for the Community Services Council, the Quota and Admissions Committee of the United Givers Fund, the National Foundation, the Istrouma Area Boy Scouts Council, and the Board of the Baranco-Clark YMCA.

In a speech made to announce his candidacy Daddy stated,

> As you can see, Baton Rouge is really home for me and I have been an active participant. The city can become progressive with farsighted planning and dynamic leadership under me. My platform issues are: Hard surfacing all streets and maintaining them; conducting a study for sidewalks and prioritizing them based on safety needs; putting signals at railroad crossing and relocating some tracks; including all segments of the population on City Parish Boards and councils; providing equal access for employment for all citizens; enlarging the port to increase business and employment; increasing job opportunities and wages for all; having adequate sanitation facilities for garbage pickup; providing clean thoroughfares; building low-rent housing facilities to decrease sub-standard living conditions; studying delinquency and suggesting solutions; developing a civic center with an art museum to make BR a cultural center for the state; establishing an interracial Commission to better race relations to make the city a model of progressive, democratic administration for the state since BR is the capital.
>
> Finally, I urge all the voters of EBRP to examine my proposal carefully. A discussion of personalities will not get streets paved, better housing or attract more industry, but careful analysis of issues and farsighted planning under dynamic leadership will. This, I assure I can and will provide.

A local TV station provided candidates with a forum to address the community. Daddy's speech to the citizens of Baton Rouge was quite remarkable:

The office of Mayor-President, which I am seeking, is really the nerve center of the administrative process in our government. It requires a sense of direction and purposive action. Proper coordination producing efficiency and economy is a basic goal, which should be constantly sought. In short, this office, as I conceive it must direct the day-to-day routine involved in the governmental process. Furthermore, the occupant of this office should show initiative and creative leadership in policy forma-tion. You see, councilmen are elected by wards and are basically responsible to the constituencies. The policies that they propose are generally locally oriented and their perspective is not neces-sarily broad, no matter how desirable a broad perspective in policy-making might be. The Mayor-President, however, is the one officer whose perspective should be parish wide. He should spend considerable time reflecting on matters of broad public policy and should take the leadership in proposing legislation to the Council and seeking council enactment. Furthermore, the Mayor-President should be able to interpret public opinion and translate that opinion into sound recommendations in keeping with the general interest. I feel that I can do these things and bring dynamic and courageous leadership into the critical and sensitive organ of our city-parish government. In the world over, there is a remarkable trend to young, vigorous and dynamic leaders. People who have a sense of the inevitability of progress and who are equipped to meet the challenge of the future are those being sought. The electorate is no longer willing to be mis-led, but rather has a sense of increasing selectiveness—judging people on ability, sincerity and dedication to the public service. They want imaginative leadership capable of accurate interpre-tation of the issues demanded of governing officials in a highly industrialized and ever-changing socio-economic order. EBRP needs this kind of leadership and I pledge to bring such to the top administrative office if I am elected.

He then described the points of his platform and showed pictures of the areas that needed improvement. One picture was Capitol High School, newly built on a gravel road with open sewerage and no sidewalks. He showed pictures of poor housing conditions and unsafe sidewalks in school areas. He talked about the port and bringing jobs to the area and a civic center. He ended with,

We are living in a period of comprehensive social re-adjustment, most of which involves relations among races. Indeed the need

for consuming so much time, energy and money involving issues based on racial differences, as Adlai Stevenson put it, 'seems quite absurd after almost 2000 years of devotion to the principles of Christianity.' It furthermore, seems a bit incredible to people the world over that the greatest protagonist of democracy cannot and will not make it work at home. I have attempted to analyze the issues as I see them, keeping in mind that we are moving towards a new and prosperous era and that Baton Rouge and EBRParish should be geared to meet the challenges of the future. I respectfully seek your vote on that basis. I feel that I am well qualified to handle the tasks required of the parish's chief executive. I urge you to be selective and vote with an open mind. Let us in EBRP start utilizing the tremendous talent of untapped sources which I represent. It has been a pleasure to be with you. Thank you for your attention.

He was the only one of the mayoral candidates to offer a platform. No one else addressed issues. All of the other candidates played the race card or the "Good ole boy." Johnnie Jones ran for District Attorney, 19th Judicial District, on the same issues with Daddy. They knew they could not win but running put pressure on the white candidates to begin to address Black issues. Running also gave Blacks access to inside information on the election process.

The Black bloc vote was created and became a strong force in the community for elections. Registration drives began. Many Blacks were intimidated and threatened with loss of jobs and even their lives. Daddy, Johnnie Jones, Raymond Scott, Acie Belton and others set up the United Campaign Committee and the "Santa Claus Express." This was the delivery of a sample ballot on Election Day, August 27, 1960 delivered by neighbors between the hours of 4:30 and 7:00 A.M. "In order that we as citizens can make our wishes known to all, *we must answer all Public Officials who disregard our welfare* and give us their *least considerations.*"

One evening Mama, Daddy and I were sitting in the dining room talking and planning campaign strategies. The dining room and living room are on the front of the house with a large picture window in each room. The table in the dining room is directly in front of the window. With lights on and the curtains open, the people in the room are visible from the street. We walked out of the dining room through the swinging door to the kitchen. As the door was swinging closed, a loud noise suddenly erupted that sounded like a firecracker but we also had heard glass breakage. Daddy yelled, "Get down, get down!" A shot had been fired into the house. A second earlier and one of us could have been hit. Hearing the noise, the boys came running down the hall as Daddy ran to catch them. He pulled them to the floor holding and hugging them. Mama and I crawled to the hallway to be with Daddy and the boys. Daddy called the police and reported the incident. The officer was going to send a unit over right away.

We huddled in the hall for over an hour and no one came. Daddy kept looking at his watch because he had a television spot that night, and he had to go. Mama was furious. She said she didn't want to die for any cause and especially when it was putting her children in danger, but Daddy gave her Uncle Jim's gun and told her to stay there in the hall until the police came. He didn't want to leave, but if he got scared and backed down, the cause was lost. How many more people would the whites intimidate? Too many people were looking up to him for support. Almost another hour passed after Daddy left before the police arrived banging on the door. We didn't know if someone was trying to break in or if it was really the police. After we heard them identify themselves, Mama opened the door but told us to remain in the hallway.

Mama took the gun to the door with her. She was as afraid of them as she was the shooter. They stood in the middle of the front door with the door wide open asking questions. She told them to come in and close the door for fear of more stray bullets. They asked a few questions and if anyone was hurt. Luckily we weren't. If we had been, we would have been dead waiting on them to arrive. They left informing us that there was nothing they could do, but they would patrol the street that night. They left and we never saw a patrol.

There was nothing the police would do, but "Trouble" had her gun. She swore that if anyone tried to get in or burn a cross on her lawn, she was going to shoot to kill. We were quiet as could be. I don't know who was worse with a gun, the shooters or Mama. The boys went to sleep together in Mama and Daddy's bed. I stayed up with Mama listening and watching. The dog next door started barking. Mama and I looked at each other. We heard something in the back of the house.

Neither of us said a word. Mama began to walk down the hall, and I was behind her holding onto her waist as she walked. We walked very slowly and quietly. All of a sudden Robert woke up, not seeing Mama, and yelled. Mama turned around startled. When she turned she was facing me and pointing the gun at me! I threw my hands up in the air and yelled, "Mama! Mama! It's me!" She started shaking with the gun now pointed to the floor. She then held onto me and started crying. She was so scared. I guess with all the noise we made we scared the person away. Daddy and Uncle Helvius found footprints by my bedroom window in the back of the house the next morning.

During the election the klan repeatedly burned crosses in the vacant lawn across the street from our house and the police did nothing. The klan is a bunch of sneaking, yellow-bellied, sons-of-bitches cowards. They come in quietly, wreak havoc, burn, kill, and run. I kept wishing I could catch them.

I sure wanted to set those damn white sheets on fire. Sometimes I'd sit up at night watching and wishing that they would come. I had it all planned that while they were in their circle erecting that damn cross, I'd sneak as near as I could get without them noticing. Then I'd pour gasoline on the grass as I crawled away leaving a single line trail for me to leave. Once I was safely out of the way, I'd light a match on the trail and watch it burn all the way to those sheets. I guess someone looked after me because I had carefully designed this plan to work. The gasoline can was ready in the garage and I knew where it was without turning on any lights. I wanted to do this alone. I wanted revenge.

Daddy was always under attack. As he was leaving a meeting at one of the local churches, someone threw acid at him but the acid fell onto the front of his car as he was getting in. It barely missed him. The acid landed on the hood of Daddy's car and burned off the paint. Again he was lucky. It could have hit him in the face, blinded him and scarred him for life. The city for us became a war zone. Where ever we were we had to always be alert. There was little down time, but Mama insisted that we have quality family time when and where possible.

For relaxation Daddy and the men of the bridge club played golf on Sundays when possible. The Black golf course was Clark's Park in Scotlandville. The Black doctors played on Sundays and on their day off, Thursday afternoons. If Black folks needed a doctor on Thursday, all they had to do was to go to the golf course. On Sundays the families of the doctors followed with the children playing in the park and the wives cooking out, playing bridge and watching the kids. We came in two cars one Sunday because Daddy was going to be a little late. When we left, Daddy was driving in the lead with Mama following. I had just remarked to Daddy how slowly he was driving and that he must be sick since he usually speeds. We were going under 35 miles per hour when a police car started flashing its lights and pulled Daddy over. Both of our cars stopped, Daddy's and Mama's. The police went through the normal routine asking for license and registration while Daddy inquired why he was stopped. The officer told him that he'd find out on the ticket and not to give him any lip. Knowing the power of the police and that we could be locked up for resisting arrest or a weapon that the police might pull out from anywhere or anything else that they decided to wrongfully do to us, Daddy did remain silent and waited for the ticket. He was ticketed for speeding which we weren't and Mama too when they found out who she was even though they had not pulled her over.

We went to court and I had to testify on the stand. Johnnie Jones was the attorney. He said that it was harassment. I had to repeat my statement of Daddy driving so slowly and that both cars got a ticket when only one car was initially pulled over. The judge dropped charges for speeding. We didn't have to pay a fine but the officers were not even reprimanded. All summer there was one episode of discrimination, threats and acts of intimidation after another. I was usually with Daddy when he thought it was safe, but we never knew when a fool might try to do us harm.

I enjoyed going to the meetings with Daddy and watching him on television and listening to his speeches. We all sat on pins and needles when he was on television because Daddy was a great extemporaneous speaker. Verbatim script reading was not his strong suit. He preferred his tangents. He also cursed profusely when upset. So, we were afraid he'd say, "Shit! Damn! Bastard! Son of a Bitch!" and in summation maybe "Cracker" or "Honkie." That's why we sat on pins and needles until he concluded his speeches. Afterward Mama and I would look at each other and smile and shake hands. We were so proud of him and what he was doing even if our lives were in danger.

The entire Black community knew Daddy was running, and most people recognized us. I felt safe in our community of Black people. With jobs and lives threatened, Blacks were willing to try to help even my friends. One day Aunt Phine took Judy, Nan, Jo, Donald Ray (Jo's brother), my brothers and I to see the *Angry Red Planet* at the Lincoln Theater. We were watching the movie until it got scary. As we slouched down and put our hands over our faces, Henry Howard, Judy's neighbor and our friend yelled out, "Stop the movie! The Mayor's daughter is scared!" I was just too embarrassed. I truly held my head in my lap for the rest of the movie. The whole theater was laughing. I needed that relief of laughter. It reminded me that humor, teasing, and fun could be good.

I had become somewhat of a celebrity among my friends as the "mayor's daughter." A Black running for mayor was a novel idea. Even though most Blacks knew we could not win, they were going to vote. Daddy came in third place the night of the election and fourth place after the absentee votes were counted. It was an excellent showing but more than that, the election brought Blacks to the bargaining table with whites who were running, and even better it brought Blacks to the table of those whites in the run-off election. Blacks were now a power force that had to be dealt with and could no longer be ignored. The bloc vote was important and critical in determining the winner. In the eight predominantly Black precincts, the bloc vote was 4114 for Daddy as Mayor with the six white candidates only garnering 1008 between all of them, less than 200 each. Attorney Jones had 4118 votes with 1011 spread between the five white candidates. An ad was run by whites in the newspaper publicizing the bloc vote to intimidate Blacks.

The registrar listed Daddy and Johnnie Jones' names on the ballot as

Negro. Later Daddy filed suit and took it to the Supreme Court to eliminate race from the ballot. The case was the U.S. Supreme Court, ANDERSON **v. MARTIN, 375 U.S. 399 (1964), 375 U.S. 399,** ANDERSON ET AL. v. MARTIN. APPEAL FROM THE UNITED STATES DISTRICT COURT FOR THE EASTERN DISTRICT OF LOUISIANA. No. 51. (Argued November 20-21, 1963. Decided January 13, 1964.) The Supreme Court reversed the appeal court's decision and race had to be removed from ballots. Mr. Justice Clark delivered the opinion of the Court ending with, "Race is the factor upon which the statute operates and its involvement promotes the ultimate discrimination which is sufficient to make it invalid. Goss v. Board of Education, supra, at 688. The judgment is therefore, Reversed."

He filed another federal lawsuit attacking the constitutionality of a new Louisiana law banning electioneering within 600 feet of a polling place on election day. He asked the Federal Court to issue a restraining order against enforcement of the new law by the Sheriff and Police Chief.

Daddy also ran for School Board Ward I in 1962 along with Acie J. Belton for School Board in Ward II and Johnnie Jones for District Judge. He never gave up his fight for equality in education, which was his ultimate goal. He called American schools "racist by design." In 1956 when the suit was filed against EBRP Daddy worked with the school board and all types of city and interracial committees for the desegregation of the schools. He was determined that this was going to happen in my lifetime. He attended almost every school board meeting and was pushing the board and the courts for a decision. By this time I was in high school and almost hoping that nothing would happen right away because I really didn't want to leave my school.

Daddy worked with and served on the Board of the National Foundation of Infantile Paralysis. He was also on the Committee to Desegregate the Istrouma Council of Boy Scouts of America. During his association with the Council, he served as Treasurer for 25 years. The 75th year Eagle Scouts' Celebration, March 29, 1985 was named in his honor and he subsequently received the Silver Beaver Award from the Boy Scouts. The program read,

> *Over the years, he has been involved in the cause of Scouting, both black and white. He has worked to improve race relations wherever there has been a need. He was involved in the nego-tiations to obtain and open Camp Carver (a camp for Blacks). Until this time there had been no organized council effort for blacks to attend Summer Camp. He was also involved, years later, in the closing of Camp Carver and integrating Camp Avondale. There was criticism on both sides, but the committee was bound to do what was right. He was also involved with the Capital Fund committee when the former Scout Service*

Center at 1000 Scenic Highway was purchased. Dr. Anderson has served on the Executive Board of the Istrouma Area Council for many years. In his positions with the Black community, he has been able to give leadership too many projects and activities that have improved race relations during troubled times. He was instrumental in the formation of the Lewis Sewell Memorial District as a viable geographical district, rather than a service area for Black membership only. In addition to scouting, his other civic activities include service with the United Way, organizer and Board member of the Baranco-Clark YMCA, Board of Southern University Foundation, Board of Directors of the National Foundation for Infantile Paralysis and Board for State Labor Committee for Minorities. He is also a member of the Capital City Dental Association, Pelican State Dental Association, National Dental Association, American Academy of General Dentistry, American Endodontic Society, the American Analgesic Society, Alpha Phi Alpha Fraternity, National Association for the Advancement of Colored People, and the Human Relations Council. For his many efforts on behalf of Scouting, the Istrouma Area Council recognized Dr. Dupuy Anderson in 1978 with the Silver Beaver Award. As he looks over his 50+ years in Scouting, he is proud of the improvements in race relations. "When I (Dr. Anderson) joined Scouting, things were very different because of my color. Now I am serving as the Council Treasurer. My progress represents all Blacks. Scouting can instill in everyone development of character to improve our community and our world."

He also received the 1996 Trailblazer Award from the Cultural Development and Support Guild of the New St. John Baptist Church. Eventually there were numerous rewards and plaques—and some are still on the family room wall—but the Boy Scouts was his first revolutionary project, and it was dear to his heart.

He initiated several law suits for Blacks to become registered voters. During the 1950's Daddy was instrumental in obtaining equal participation in the use of radio and television by serving on the Federal Communications Council. He also served on committees to integrate the hospitals and give the Black doctors equal opportunities in the hospitals. Black doctors were still not allowed to practice in the hospitals and had to turn their patients over to white doctors once admitted. As late as the 60's Black doctors were not considered qualified to work in the hospitals. Charles Drew had created blood plasma. Dr. Daniel Hale Williams had performed open heart surgery and Black physicians across the country were performing remarkable feats, but Baton Rouge did not think Blacks were qualified. Daddy, Johnnie Jones and Raymond Scott continued to fight that battle. Finally, they were able to get Dr. Louis James admitted as the first Black doctor in the hospitals. Soon afterward other Black doctors were admitted. Dr. James, or Uncle Doc as all the children called him, also became the first Black coroner in the city.

Daddy served on the Human Relations Council, the Mayor's Bi-Racial Committee, the School District Desegregation Committee, and the Baton Rouge Area Inter-Racial Council. The Inter-Racial Council believed "the advance of the whole must include the advance of all its parts. The progress of the majority racial group is necessarily affected by the condition of any minority group, and one of the factors influencing the realization of a greater Baton Rouge is the quality of the relations between racial groups living in the area" (from the Bylaws of the Council).

They basically adopted Daddy's platform with its direct purpose as "education, health and medical care, sanitation and safety, housing, recreation, streets and transportation, employment, child welfare and general living conditions." Daddy's candidacy for mayor opened many discussions city-wide that began a movement in Baton Rouge for constructive changes from infrastructure to housing to environment to equal treatment.

He helped get Black salespeople hired at white stores by threatening that he and other Blacks would close their charge accounts. The Sternbergs owned Goudchaux's Department Store, which was one of the largest stores in Baton Rouge. Daddy had a confrontation with them when Dupuy Jr. was only five years old. Mama was shopping, and the boys were with her. She was stopped in the store and asked if she'd allow Dupuy Jr. to model in one of their mailers. Mama agreed. When Daddy showed up for the shoot, they suddenly changed their minds. Well, Daddy and Mama had not changed their minds, and they proceeded to tell the Sternbergs that they would cancel their charge accounts and get every Black in the city to do the same. Needless to say Dupuy Jr.'s photo in the mailer appeared and was mailed all over the city. Not that his picture proved anything to anyone but Mama and Daddy and our family because Dupuy Jr. looked as white or whiter than the whites in the book. No one knew that there was a Black child in the mailer, but the Sternbergs knew not to argue with Daddy. So, when he came back to them in the 60's requesting that they hire Blacks for salespeople and they refused, the store was immediately hit with a boycott. The Sternbergs put up a little fight because they did not believe that Black folks would stop shopping or be able to pay out their charge cards and cancel them, but after only a few days, they realized that picket signs did keep people out and the people with the largest balances began cancelling their charges. Goudchaux's began hiring

Blacks. In fact in 1973 they even hired me as the first Black buyer in a major white department store.

Daddy helped desegregate Baton Rouge in many different areas. He worked with over 15 different organizations from the NAACP and the United Way to the American Academy of General Dentistry. He was president of the Black Chamber of Commerce in 1947 where he greeted and welcomed visiting organizations to the city of Baton Rouge. In an expression of welcome to the Louisiana State Beauticians Association, he urged them "to be alert and to participate in activities that will be for the uplift and betterment of our racial group. Remember, too, that women everywhere are coming to the front and joining hands with other organizations in the promotion of all activities pertaining to happier living for all."

Daddy was truly an amazing man. He was ahead of his time, not only fighting for Civil Rights for Black people but also for women's rights. He believed in equality and justice for all people. He was a humanitarian that practiced what he preached, and he did preach! He may not have had a pulpit but that didn't stop him from giving sermons on the Constitution and human rights. He believed in respect and dignity for all people. In spite of all that he had done up to this point, his major fight was just beginning.

VOTE FOR AND ELECT

NO. 22

DUPUY H. ANDERSON
MAYOR-PRESIDENT
Parish of East Baton Rouge

Mayoral Push Card

Anderson-Jones Campaign Dinner

Theme: "The Dawn of The New Day"

DR. DUPUY H. ANDERSON
Candidate For
Mayor-President

ATTY. JOHNNIE A. JONES
Candidate For
District Attorney

CAPITOL SENIOR HIGH SCHOOL DINING ROOM

SATURDAY, JULY 9, 1960

Eight o'clock p.m.

Campaign for Mayor

United Campaign Committee

BENEFIT DINNER

Theme: "Crusade For Responsibility In Local Government"

Dupuy H. Anderson
Candidate For
School Board
Ward I

Acie J. Belton
Candidate For
School Board
Ward II

Johnnie A. Jones
Candidate For
District Judge

SCOTLANDVILLE SENIOR HIGH SCHOOL DINING ROOM

SATURDAY, JULY 14, 1962

Eight o'clock p.m.

Campaign for School Board

Daddy

Top: Daddy, Mama, me and Dupuy, Jr. Ralph in the belly. Bottom: Dupuy, Jr., Mama, Daddy, Me, Ralph, Robert

Daddy & Raymond Scott

Family and Honors

Trouble Again

Amid all the chaos, fear, struggle and everything else going on in our lives, Mama decided we needed more. She had been a stay-at-home wife, housewife and mother, but she wanted to fulfill her dream. She told Daddy that she wanted to go back to school and get her degree from Southern. He kept telling her that this was not the time. He had asked her to wait until all the children were in school because he did not want to leave Robert at home without a mother. So, she waited until Robert began school.

When Robert started school she told Daddy again that she wanted to get her degree. He found another excuse not to let her go. He did not understand why she needed a degree since she didn't need a job. His rationale was that he was making enough money to support his family; his wife did not need to go to work, therefore, she did not have to go to school. Mama protested that she had a mind, too. She needed intellectual stimulation and some independence. She also promised her mother, Mamou, that she would get her degree. No matter how hard she tried to persuade Daddy he remained adamant that she needed to be home with the children. All of her arguments were in vain.

One Saturday morning Daddy received an emergency phone call from the police that his car, the pink Plymouth station wagon, had been in a wreck at Swan Street and Scenic Highway. He was in shock. There was no way the car should be in Scotlandville. Mama had left with the car to go shopping, so the car must have been stolen! But where was Mama?! The police verified that it was Daddy's car and that it was Mama who had been driving the car; they then told Daddy that she was being taken to the hospital but the injuries were not life threatening.

I had heard the entire conversation because Daddy was loud and afraid. He did not know what to do. Ms. Campbell, the lady that took care of us on Saturdays who lived at the end of our street, said that she would stay until he returned. Daddy left immediately for the hospital. Mama's leg was twisted, and she was in a cast. Her face was bruised, but her stubbornness had won.

She had been attending Saturday morning classes at Southern when she was supposed to be shopping. She had slowly been taking money out of Daddy's wallet to pay for the courses and making excuses why she needed more money for different items in the house. Since she was a stay-at-home mom, Mama didn't have a checkbook and rarely had cash, but she did have charge cards. The only place she needed cash was the grocery store.

Every morning Daddy's pants would travel up and down off the corner of the door where he hung them when he came in from work at night. Mama would pass out money to us as we were leaving for school. A Catholic school nickels and dimes you to death! Every day there was a need for money for something: a bazaar, a saint's day, a special novena, just think of something and the school was begging.

Also, every morning we had to have lunch money. We loved eating at school. It was far better than Mama's cooking. In fact, St. Francis had gourmet meals. The ladies in the cafeteria prepared all of our meals from scratch. There were hot homemade biscuits and rolls that would melt in your mouth with butter dripping from them. The chili dogs were my favorite and every holiday we had turkey and cornbread dressing. Usually, I was not one to eat a lot of food and most of the time had to be forced but not at school. I always cleaned my plate and the desserts were literally the icing on the cake. We had cake, pudding, bread pudding, ginger cookies, and pies. Maybe, if Mama could have cooked, I would have liked food better, but I guess I'm glad that she couldn't cook because I stayed thin.

So, Daddy's pants went up and down, on and off the door with the morning parade of trying to get all of us out to school. Daddy often remarked that his pants walked more than he did when he was wearing them. Morning after morning Mama would take a little extra from the pants or extra from the groceries to pay for her tuition. She was determined to get her degree and was not going to let anything or anyone stop her.

After the accident, Daddy stopped protesting. He gave in and paid tuition and helped in any way that he could. Mama wanted to pursue a degree in elementary education. She studied and went to classes and became a regular college student. Amazingly, she was able to maintain all her other commitments. Aunt Phine cooked and cleaned and was at the house during the week, and Ms. Campbell kept us on Saturday mornings. Mama never had night classes, so she was always home by the time we arrived from school.

I remember Mama had difficulty with biology. She told Daddy that she never had science classes in high school because the school required all girls to take home economics and would not let girls enroll in science and math past the very basic courses. She told me that she hated home economics and I believed her because she never liked anything to do with keeping a home. She didn't cook. She didn't clean. She didn't iron. The only thing she did all the time, even though she didn't like it, was wash clothes, and they were bound to come out any color. When Mama took home economics she told me she'd bring her sewing projects home and Mamou would sew them for her.

I couldn't believe that Mama would actually cheat in a class—but I also understood that even though she was smart as a whip, she only did what she wanted to do—but that is how she passed home economics. She couldn't do the same for biology, so Daddy sat down with her in the evenings and showed her how to study. He had her draw diagrams and label them to help her remember. He worked with her and quizzed her until she understood. What a team! He didn't want her to go to school, but once he realized that she was determined to do so, he was right there to help. He was so proud when she received her degree. We all went to graduation and took pictures to celebrate, and since there was no place for us to go out and celebrate, we had a party at our house.

I think Daddy knew that once she had the degree, his troubles were only starting. The next argument? Mama wanted to go to work. After student teaching she had the bug, and she wanted full time work. Daddy tried and tried to convince her that she did not have to work, but what he did not realize was that money was not the issue. Mama hated being in the house and without any of us home to take care of she was not going to sit and watch TV or clean or cook and we didn't want her to do any of those things either. We fought for Mama to work and for Aunt Phine to be with us every day especially to cook.

Thinking about coming home every day with Mama bored and having to cook and clean would not be a pretty picture, and I think Daddy finally realized it. So, he gave in again. Mama went to work. Aunt Phine remained and we ate well. Mama began teaching at Arlington Elementary in South Baton Rouge and loved every minute. Initially, most of the teachers at Arlington thought she was white but a few knew her from the community and stood up for her. Arlington was in one of the poorest communities of Baton Rouge. Mama had many challenges but she persisted and excelled as did her students. Her annual school operettas with costumes and scenery garnered standing room only crowds. Black teachers were still not paid the same as whites and the supervision of Black teachers was different from that of whites, but Mama persevered.

A few years later Mama went back to school for a Master's Degree in Educational Counseling and became a counselor. She was also one of the first cross-over teachers to go in the white schools. We laughed at her because no one but our family and friends would know that she was Black. She always replied, "Oh, they know who I am because I make sure to let them know that I'm Black and they better not say anything racist around me." Occasionally, someone would forget that she was Black and tell a racist joke in front of her, but they definitely had to feel her wrath. She'd come home and tell Daddy, "Oops, I might be fired because I had to tell them off again." Daddy would just smile and let her know that he had her back. She was as feisty as they come. I wonder where I get it from?

Trouble settled down after she got her way. She had manipulated Daddy and all of us to earn her degrees and go to work. She no longer had to stay home and be a housewife, which she despised. Wife and mother were fine, but cooking and cleaning were not her thing. She demonstrated that she could multi-task and keep the home front secure and operating like a finely tuned engine while she attained her personal goals. Daddy wasn't the only fighter in the family. Mama, too, stood up, struggled, and fought for Black and women's rights. What a household!

Mama
Southern Graduation
Education

Masters in
Educational
Counseling

Inez Anderson's Graduations

Dupuy and Inez
25th Wedding Anniversary

Dupuy Anderson 65th Birthday Celebration

...oh, Robert, Mama, Grandmother, me, Dupuy, Jr. & Daddy seated

Celebrations

Ninth Grade

I think the nightmares began after the shot in the window. I'd wake up screaming and shaking. Mama and Daddy would both come running down the hall to comfort me. Then Daddy would walk me to their room and I'd sleep with them until I could calm down. Most nights Daddy would walk me back to my room after he convinced me that it was just a dream, but sometimes everyone was too tired and I'd just sleep on Mama's side of the bed next to Mama or curl up at the foot of the bed wrapped in a blanket. The nightmares began to happen so frequently that a few times, Daddy tried to just call me and tell me to come to their room, but I couldn't move. I was paralyzed with fright hiding under my sheet and blanket. Eventually, when Daddy didn't hear me coming, he'd come and get me.

There are a few of those nightmares I remember because they were recurring. One was about the model city Tony, Bobby and I built with houses, shops, train station, airline terminal and even a rocket launch center. It was on a large rug and the plastic pieces were arranged around roads, lakes and parks. Tony, Bobby and I would work on it and imagine the other places our city needed. It had cars and buses and emergency vehicles. When we finished playing we'd pull it under my bed for safe keeping from my brothers who destroyed everything. I started having a dream that the family was at Clark's golf course during the 4th of July celebration and everyone there was shooting fireworks. Somehow the children got a large rocket to shoot. Just as they lit it, Daddy noticed us playing with the fireworks. He came over to prevent us from getting hurt but the rocket blasted off and shot him through his stomach. I saw the rocket exit through his back and as he fell forward. His innards fell forward in a cylinder shape. This nightmare would not go away.

What made nightmares worse in my family is that Mamou and Mama had ESP (extra sensory perception or mental telepathy). I prefer to call it transcending time with brain waves. At any time, Mama or Mamou could have a dream and tell us about it; then it would come true. Of course, not every dream they had would come true and they wouldn't tell us every dream, but they seemed to know which ones to recount. That was scary to know and most times I didn't want to know ahead of time. When Mama was sick after delivering Robert, Daddy didn't call Mamou because he didn't want Mamou to worry, but Mamou called him and told him that Mama was sick. He told Mamou that Mama was all right, but Mamou didn't believe him and took the next train from California to Baton Rouge. That's how she ended up at the house to take care of us.

Mama told me about a dream in which a family was killed in an automobile accident describing a woman decapitated and a child thrown through the front window. She didn't know exactly who it was but she saw the accident in her dream. Mama and Daddy were at a dental convention when I got the news and had to call them and tell her that it was her friend, Fern and her family that she'd dreamed about. Most of the dreams were minor incidents, but occasionally the dreams were extraordinary.

That's why my nightmares were so frightening. I imagined that I was seeing the future as Mamou and Mama did. After that dream with the fireworks I refused to be near or around them and would not go to Clark's Park for the 4th of July. I made Daddy change the plans and have a backyard bar-b-que like we used to have when we were younger. Every 4th Mama's bridge club would get together in our back yard for the annual bar-b-que. All the children and adults would have one, big, happy, extended family gathering. The women played bridge and the men cooked the meat on the grill, but each year there was drama. One year Daddy couldn't get the fire started, so with the help and encouragement of Dr. Pierson, Uncle Doc and Uncle Bernie, he doused the coals with gasoline. Needless to say the brick pit exploded sending bricks flying and men, women and children running. We were grateful no one was injured. Another time Daddy was swabbing the meat with sauce when Dr. Pierson started looking closely at the towel tied around the fork that was being dipped into the sauce and onto the meat. He took off the supposed towel and opened it up. To his surprise it was a pair of Daddy's briefs. He exclaimed, "I'll be got damned! Inez may love you that much but damned if I do." Mama replied, "Oh, Dr. P. they're clean. Last year we used the baby's diaper. The fire will kill any leftover germs." Everyone laughed because Mama was quite sincere thinking clean undies were ok to use to swab meat. That's why I didn't eat the bar-b-que. I knew the bottom line and didn't want it flavoring my meat. This was just another day in the life.

Another nightmare that was recurring and caused me grief was the closet in my room. I was neat to the degree of being fanatical. There was a place for everything in my room, and I knew if a pen or pencil had been moved. My brothers kept trying to invade my privacy, but I would always catch them because they never learned to put anything back where it belonged. I'd report them to Mama because they were not supposed to be in my room without permission. I had built-in wall-to-wall shelves with a desk in the middle. On the shelves were my books, my rock collection, my TV, my record player, and a few dolls that just stood up and looked pretty. Under my bed was the model city, but after the nightmares, I gave it to Tony and Bobby to keep at their house. My clothes were neatly hung in the closet or folded in drawers on the wall shelf unit, but the corner in the left of the closet had everything that I had no place for or did not want to get rid of or just stuffed there because I ran out of time while planning the neatness of the rest of my room. Daddy used to tease me using a scary voice pretending to be a monster that was growing in the closet that was coming to get me. Well, every time the closet became overwhelming, I'd have the nightmare that this monster was coming, and I'd get up in the middle of the night and clean it after I finished screaming and Daddy and Mama calmed me down. This happened about three times before I finally stopped letting the junk pile up. I couldn't fight the monster any longer.

A good recurring dream that I had was that I could fly. Tony, Bobby and I would begin the dream by sitting on the roof of the house just talking to each other and enjoying the view. I'd open my arms wide and lift off and fly. They would follow me and we'd pick up other children in the neighborhood and fly over the city. It was so much fun doing whatever you wanted. I felt free looking down at the people. I'd try to make myself dream of flying when I went to sleep because I enjoyed it so much, but those dreams happened rarely even though they were recurring. I had more nightmares than fun in my dreams. Most of the time I was glad to wake up and go to school.

Ninth grade was wild! I came of age. No longer shy, withdrawn, feeling different and left out of the mainstream, I now created the mainstream. Everything that could possibly happen to the kid happened. My homeroom was in the chemistry lab because my homeroom teacher was the chemistry teacher, Mr. Jenkins, who had a stiff leg that caused him to walk with a limp. We called him "Hoppy" and "Hopalong." Our homeroom was boring. A few of the class leaders were in our room: Marion, Wanda, Wesley and me. We would sit on the stools and kind of hang out the windows to get a look at Mr. Freeman as he walked to the band room. He'd wave at us and the girls would have a major meltdown each morning. He was so cute with his little ditty bop walk. Hanging out the window was more fun than whatever was going on in the class.

Hoppy was the only homeroom teacher that made homeroom a class. He had to organize everything. We were required to report on current events and weather and have discussions on the current news topics. After all of that we then had time for silent study. Other homerooms had free time and discussions and/or study hall. Hoppy was a pain in the butt. We were constantly disrupting his plans, but he persevered in a militaristic style unlike many of the other instructors who just gave up and took the homeroom time as their own prep time.

One of my classes that year was English literature with BB. She was a little plump but quite voluptuous and young. We called her BB for Bridget Bardot who was a French actress that frequently disrobed in her films, which became the first nude productions allowed on the screen in the U.S. Her films were extraordinary for that time period, not particularly good, but X-rated. BB tried to be sexy with a walk that could keep a hula hoop in perpetual motion. She wore skirts that rose above her knees when she sat on the front of her desk and crossed her legs. The boys started dropping pencils as soon as they walked in class so that they could look under her skirt. She was not a great English teacher. She was merely a babysitter who kept us in line by requiring lots of homework, but I learned my lesson well in sixth grade about trying to tell on adults. So, instead of complaining, I found as many ways as I could to keep the class interesting.

The classroom was on the first floor of the high school wing with doors on both sides of the room that opened to the hall and vertical transom windows the length of the doors on one side of each door. One day BB did her usual walk out of the room to go down the hall to practice the hula hoop hips. I got up from my chair, walked to the door then walked back to her desk imitating her walk. I sat on the front of her desk and crossed my legs mimicking her every move. The class was hysterical. Not only were they laughing with me for what I had done, but at me because BB was standing at the transom window watching me. She had seen my entire performance.

She suspended me from class for a week. That was fine with me. Since I wasn't suspended from school, only from her class, my time was spent in the library with Ms. Fisher, the librarian who I deeply admired. When I returned to class BB had assigned me *Vanity Fair* as the book report due for the nine weeks grading period. I could not get through that book no matter how hard I tried. I tried and tried time after time to read it but to no avail. It was just too boring and about white people that I could care less about. It was not relevant to anything in my life. It was not an interesting time period or of historic consequence to me. I asked BB to please assign me another book, and she denied me. I asked her for permission to read two or more books to replace *Vanity Fair* and she again denied me. I tried to read *Vanity Fair* again but could not do so.

However I began to read other books on the list without her permission. I read *Exodus* and *Gone with the Wind.* I loved to read, but *Vanity Fair* was a problem. In fact, Mama would have to make me go to bed when I became engrossed in a novel. One night with only a few chapters left in *Gone With the Wind*, Mama told me to cut off the lights and go to sleep. I couldn't put the book down, but I did turn off the lights so Mama could not see them. I put my lamp under my sheet and read in the tent I built but the sheet began to burn. I smelled it and realized that the lamp was too hot so I went to the bathroom and got some water to cool the burnt spot and stop the smoldering. After that I went in my closet to finish.

I also read James Baldwin's *Fire Next Time* and *Go Tell It on the Mountain.*

I turned in all those book reports along with *Manchild in the Promised Land* and *Mandingo* for a total of six reports, but none of that made any difference to BB. The one great thing that BB did for me was spark an interest in reading Black literature, but I could not get through *Vanity Fair*. I continued to beg and plead for another book, but she did not change her mind and did not accept the other reports as a substitute even though I read more than any other student in the class. She gave me an F for the year—not the nine weeks, not the semester, but the year. Well! This time she had gone too far. Daddy and Mama raised hell. They talked to Dr. McKelpin and Dr. Felton G. Clark, President of the University. If she wanted to flunk me for a nine week period because of a one week suspension and not doing that one report on *Vanity Fair*, she technically could, but she could not flunk me for the semester and definitely not for the year. I had A's and B's that balanced even an F for the nine weeks to a minimum of a "B" for the year. She was required to change my grade. I ended up with a "B" overall for the year and BB did not return to the lab school the next year.

In Algebra our instructor was Mr. Reynolds. He was an excellent teacher and made math interesting and challenging. We really had to know what we were doing as he forced us to give detailed explanations of every problem. His favorite word was, "Why" and his favorite phrase was "Are you sure?" He could turn simple definitions into major explanations. An example might be to define a line. Most would think that it could be explained easily, but when he finished asking questions to deepen your insight, that line became a total half hour or more lesson. He'd tease students who made mistakes and the class would follow up with more insults and jokes. We worked hard in his class because we enjoyed it but also because we did not want the teasing. I loved his class and truly enjoyed math. It was my favorite subject.

Mrs. Holmes taught science but she always seemed pregnant. Her belly kept a pregnant pooch. We never knew when she was or wasn't pregnant. She was a permanent fixture on a counter stool at the end of the science counter, reading, with a lisp. Mrs. Holmes rarely moved from the stool, and I don't remember what we learned in her class.

Ms. Jordan was the Physical Education teacher, but she was such a terrible gossip. She started and passed on so much mess that she could have run her own scandal sheet. She not only discussed teachers and students but parents, lovers, future lovers, pregnancies and predicted disagreements. She tried to be everyone's friend. Along with the gossip, she taught sports and health. We learned the rules of the games and played the sports in class and had teams for intramural sports. We played volleyball and basketball, ran track, and learned the basics of gymnastics or all that we could without equipment (except for dirty, smelly, tumbling mats). I loved PE.

French was yuck with Ms. Patterson spitting all over students saying, "Ques que c'est?" No one wanted to sit on the front row and everyone would move when she got near. The main interest in class was who she would get today with the flying spit. You sat and watched very carefully every misguided flying ball of spit trying hard to make sure it didn't land on you. Whoever it hit was the laugh out loud of the day. There was never much space to move in the room because it was so small. I remember it being almost the size of a closet. Listening to French conversations on earphones and trying to repeat the sentences were our daily drills. I did not learn much French. Today, I remember "ferme la bouche," which means close your mouth and "ouvrez la fenetre," which means open the window. Why these two phrases stick in my memory, I can't imagine, other than I always wanted her to stop talking and the room was so small that a window needed to be opened. I doubt if these phrases will ever be of major use to me, but I can't seem to forget them.

Every class had a memorable experience because the Class of '64 left a big impression on everything we did. Each grade at the Lab had to present an assembly program once a year for the entire student body, and parents were invited to attend. The lab was Kindergarten through twelfth grades so we had all the grades in the gymnasium for our program along with a few parents during the monthly assembly. Our class sponsors allowed us to create our own assembly program. They should have known better. Even though we were creative and wrote each scene in the show, the sponsors should have monitored the production. We decided to write our script because first, we could, and second, we did not want to pay royalties for someone else's work that wasn't as good as ours. That's how vain we were. I guess the class sponsors tried to supervise us, but basically their complaints fell on deaf ears and we wrote our own scripts, produced, directed, and presented the program much to the chagrin of the sponsors, parents and Dr. McKelpin.

Hoppy could have cared less about an assembly. As long as he could teach chemistry, he was fine. Just let him teach. The extraneous activities were of no interest and he left the details to Mrs. Patterson and BB. Mrs. Patterson tried to supervise but realized she just didn't have the support from the other sponsors, so she gave up and left the final say to BB. Now BB was in charge. She was hot lips herself, a wanna-be actress, an adult in charge of a teen program that needed to be critiqued and supervised, but that just was not part of her demeanor. She reminded me of a frustrated actress/hooker waiting to be discovered by Hollywood. So, the idea of a TV special for our program was right up her alley.

Our class assembly was "An Afternoon of TV." It recreated scenes from some of the most notable shows on TV at that time. Two of the most infamous scenes in our assembly were takeoffs from Art Linkletter's "Kids

Say the Darndest Things." Our show host asked questions of the kids we were pretending to be and got answers like, "I saw Mama kissing the milkman." That may not have been so bad but my part was, "My sister was circumcised." Then, I began shaking and squirming in the chair and raising my hand through the whole scene. The host ignored me, and I finally ran across the stage saying, "I have to go pee!" The students in the audience were laughing out loud and having fun. We thought we were doing great.

The closing scene was a takeoff of a soap opera with adultery and risqué jokes and ended with a major bend your back kiss on stage. The curtain closed and reopened for a curtain call and they were still kissing. They weren't really kissing. We didn't think that would be appropriate. It was just a dip with Jewel's head turned backwards and her hair falling over Tony's face to hide the fact that they were not kissing, but it looked like a kiss from the audience. Again, the students in the audience were howling. We had a hit on our hands, or so we thought.

Understand that this was 1960. There weren't ratings for movies because everything at that time compared to today would have been rated G or at the maximum PG. Nothing in the theaters back then would have an "R" or an "X" rating. On TV, husbands and wives did not sleep in the same beds. They had twin beds in the same room. Sex could only be imagined after a cut away from a kiss or embrace. Kisses were not open-mouthed, and all clothes stayed on. My parents banned me from seeing *Madame X* and *Backstreet,* because of implied sex with adultery, and *I Want to Die* with Susan Hayward because of her violent death in the gas chamber. Our program was performed in that climate of Puritan ideals, mores and values, and in front of a school assembly of Kindergarten through twelfth grades with parents also in the audience.

That's why the adults were shocked—even Hoppy. He had no idea what we had planned and were presenting. He left the supervision to the other class sponsors. I thought he was going to have a heart attack. I felt sorry for him because he was taken aback and did not know what to do when Dr. McKelpin called all of our sponsors together for a meeting to threaten their jobs if anything ever happened like that again. Hoppy could not believe that he was a part of that program. He was ruined. He apologized to Dr. McKelpin for not overseeing what we were doing and accepted the blame for not being there for supervision. Mrs. Patterson and BB feigned ignorance for the debacle but apologized for our behavior. Then Dr. McKelpin had a meeting with the entire class. He not only reprimanded us for our program, but he also informed us that if we did not learn to act appropriately, befitting high school students and not streetwalkers, that we would find ourselves on the streets because we would be expelled from Southern University Laboratory School. We didn't really understand what was so bad or wrong with what we had done because it was all in fun. We told him that they weren't kissing, but we missed the point. Ultimately, we understood that Dr. McKelpin was very serious and that we were in great trouble. We knew we had to make amends for our actions, and we did try. We managed to heed his advice and remain in school in spite of ourselves.

We were an interesting bunch. We took nothing seriously except the desegregation of the public schools in New Orleans and the Southern University Student Demonstration. Federal Judge J. Skelly Wright ordered the Orleans Parish School Board to integrate its schools in July 1959 and after a series of aptitude tests, Gail Etienne, Leona Tate, Ruby Bridges, and Tessie Prevost were selected to fulfill the court's mandate. We watched the evening news on November 14, 1960 as a little Black girl, Ruby Bridges, walked to William Frantz School at 3811 North Galvez Street amid crowds of people yelling insults and racial epithets. I was so very angry. How could human beings act like that? She was just a baby. What made anyone that cruel? As I continued to watch, my jaws tightened around my clinched teeth and I swallowed tears of pain for Ruby and tears of hatred for the ones causing her that pain.

In March 1961, 5000, or so it seemed, Southern University students plus the senior class of Southern High walked out of classes from Southern University to downtown Baton Rouge. The students were dressed up, young women in heels and Sunday dresses and young men in suits and ties. They were carrying picket signs to end desegregation in Baton Rouge. Most of us at the Lab school wanted to go too, but we were too young. I contemplated walking with the college students and our seniors but my behind was getting a little sore from not listening. So, I just stood in the front of the high school with the other high school students watching the marchers go by. No one went to class until the last student passed.

I remember that day clearly. I walked from the cafeteria with Marion and Bert. I was wearing Bert's coat. It was a big gray wool three-quarter-length jacket with sleeves that hung past my fingernails. Bert had taken it off because it was really too warm for it, but I liked wearing his jacket. Bert, Marion, and I were best friends. Marion and I were walking to the front of school singing,

> Nobody loves me, everybody hates me,
> I'm going to eat some worms.
> Long skinny slimy worms
> Short fat fuzzy worms
> I'm gonna eat some worms.
> I'm going to chop off their heads
> I'm going to suck up the guts
> I'm gonna throw the fuzzy wuzzy away

Nobody loves me, everybody hates me

I'm gonna eat some worms.

That was a real depressing day. Harold Robinson joined us upon hearing this mournful song as we were sitting on the ledge in front of the school. He said that he had never heard such ridiculousness, and Marion and I taught it to him and Bert. Naturally, we drew a small crowd. Ernest Sterling was among the group. He was standing on the ledge when someone opened the window from inside pushing it outward. Ernest was standing directly in front of the window which caused him to lose his balance when the window opened. He fell off the ledge and onto the spotlight in front of the ledge breaking the glass in the light and cutting his knee through to the bone. All I saw was blood and bone and I must have blacked out for a minute. I remember the salty brine taste in my mouth then everything went around, then black as I held onto the ledge. I came to on my own, but it was one of the few times I felt faint. I couldn't even help Ernest. Others tried to help but I remember coming to and yelling not to move him and send someone to the office to call an ambulance. The timing of his fall could not have been more inappropriate because the demonstration was just beginning. Students had started trickling down the street. Trying to get an ambulance to the school was a nightmare, but somehow it was done.

After the crisis with Ernest was over, we moved from the ledge for safety reasons to the front of the school to watch as the students began streaming by, going downtown, filling the street. I stood there feeling so alone even though I was surrounded by hundreds of students from the high school. I was proud as I watched the Southern University students. I was transported to my own little world, seeing myself with them, walking for freedom. I thought they'd never finish as more and more kept walking by. I just wanted to be with them.

Daddy was downtown with the students when the police turned the dogs loose on the students and shot teargas at them. He came home smelling of teargas so strong that it made our eyes water. He was angrier than I had seen him in a long time. It was amazing that he withstood the violence himself, but he broke down and cried as he told us of students running away from dogs and teargas trying to find a way out of the crowd to breathe and find safety. Daddy spent the evening bailing students out of jail while negotiating with other black leaders in the community to raise more money. They were able to raise thousands.

The Black community was unified in its resolve to stay behind the students. Daddy stopped work at his office and devoted all of his time to this new effort. He met and talked with community leaders, both white and Black. A group met with President Felton G. Clark. They argued, begged, and pleaded with him to support the students and stand behind them. That time was the peak of the Civil Rights movement in Baton Rouge. The Black community had become a unified force with many white supporters. This was the time to move. The demonstration was viewed as the catalyst for change. Even Black ministers stood firm, all except one. He and President Clark "Uncle Tom'd" to the white politicians and expelled the leaders of the demonstration, Donald Moss and Melvin Tolson. The community was devastated.

The Southern University faculty and staff fell apart. That was the beginning of the downfall of Southern University. About one third of the PhD's on campus begin leaving. Over the next few years the faculty at the high school was recruited for the University. Worse than that, there was a split in the Black community that never healed. Dr. McKelpin was forced to give a one-week suspension to the high school seniors that participated in the demonstration, and he threatened their participation in the graduation ceremony. My faith in Black unity was truly diminished.

Although my protest and revolutionary personality was bruised, I really "came out" that year, as the old folks would say. I was wearing a 32 AA bra and a straight skirt. I had been to California for Christmas vacation with the family because Mama was still trying to get Daddy to move out there, and this Christmas he was seriously trying (or so he told Mama). He was taking a special course for the California dental boards during Christmas school break. Meanwhile, in California I was getting pretty. All of my cousins had a new perm. It was called a reverse perm. I had tried straightening my hair with the hot comb and curlers, but even with grease, the humidity in Baton Rouge never kept my hair straight. My hair curled in waves through all the burns on my ears and neck and hot curlers searing my scalp. My cousin Agnes put this reverse perm in during the Christmas holidays. The perm was Lilt, which is a white hair curling perm, but instead of rolling my hair on little rollers, she combed the perm through it. Then after combing the hair straight, she set it on very large rollers and dried it under the hair drier. My hair came out bouncy and straight and fluffy. I couldn't believe it was me. I stayed in the mirror just looking from side to side, turning my head and bouncing my hair. If only Daddy would let me wear a little make up, all would be well, but he didn't.

Do you really think that stopped me? When I got back to school, the new me emerged from the bus after the holidays. I had new hair. So, I had to put on lipstick and eye eyeliner for the completed look. On the bus to school I changed the old Girl Scout shoes to my gym sneakers and put on lipstick and eyeliner. I just had to make sure that it was all gone before I got home. The lipstick usually was because I didn't get home until after 6 PM after band practice. I was hot! The new me. I looked good, and I felt good. Self-esteem is a monster. When you believe you can do, you can do, and you do do, and I did.

Pretty new hair and makeup, sexy 32 AA bra, and smart aleck if nothing else, I was armed to fight the world. I loved my school and class at Southern high. If Dr. McKelpin thought he would drive us apart with his threats, he did just the opposite. We developed camaraderie in our class that no other class ever had or will have again. We pulled together in all that we did, good or bad. We became family. We could talk about us, but no one else could.

We were vicious with our mouths, teasing others, and I didn't realize how cruel we were until our 13th year class reunion. Just a few of us had gathered the night before the reunion and jokingly reflected on nicknames and fads of our class and the 60's. One female was named "Speckled Trout" because she had chickenpox that left her with pox marks all over her body. One male was called "Tits" because he had protruding breasts, and these were a few of the mild nicknames. Others were called "Goat," "Dent," "Pinhead," "Monster." The list goes on. I was called "Yellow," "Red," and "Freckles" on good days. If girls had a run in their stockings, someone would stick a finger in the run and tear it off. Nylon knit shirts were the fad called Ban Lon, but don't have a loose end because it would be pulled until your whole shirt was unraveled as you walked down the hall— compliments of Mackie or Wesley. You were better off not wearing a watch than wearing a Timex since it was considered cheap and your name would be loud-mouthed through the hallway for wearing one. No one or nothing was sacred. Your father, mother, brothers, sisters, religion, car or home were all likely subjects for the daily laughs. It was a wonder any one of us came out sane. If you survived Southern High, you could make it anywhere. You had no feelings of shame, and your self-esteem became impenetrable. The worst you could do was to let the ribbing affect you. Then it only grew worse. If you laughed and kidded with the kidder, no matter how badly it hurt, you could survive. Today, we would be expelled for bullying, but then it was called, "The Dozens."

On the other hand if you were in trouble and needed help, we all pulled together for support and assistance even when you thought no one cared. One student, who was always on the receiving end of jokes, was hospitalized for a ruptured appendix. It was feared he would die. The class pulled together, visited him, brought gifts and flowers and even stayed close when he went home from the hospital. Upon his return to school, the ribbing started all over again just as if he never left, but this time he knew we all loved him in spite of what we did or said.

To culminate my freshman year, I was the featured soloist in the concert band. I played "Concertino." I had never enjoyed performing in front of an audience, regardless of size. Even though I had played piano for years and had several concerts, I never played well in public. My legs would shake so badly on the pedals that I couldn't hold them down. I'd forget the music or totally make mush on whatever I was playing even though I had played it perfectly for a month or more at home alone. My father always said, "Practice makes perfect," but it never seemed to matter how much or how long I practiced, the jitters of performing never allowed a perfect recital. I screwed it up every time in some way or fashion. The mistakes were really miniscule, but I was a perfectionist and therefore never satisfied.

So, I was petrified with this clarinet solo that Mr. Freeman insisted I perform. He was still giving me private lessons, and I had developed into a pretty good clarinet player. Daddy bought me the top of the line clarinet, a real wood Selmer horn, a professional instrument. This instrument added to my tone with a beautiful and a full resonant bass sound that took a second seat to none. Mr. Freeman gave me the confidence I needed and encouraged me to relax and give the solo my all.

I played the solo about three times in different venues before the main concert at school. Each time Mr. Freeman would patiently wait until I was ready. He'd take a deep breath, look at me, smile, and nod to see if I were okay. Once I nodded back he'd then raise the baton. I'd completely lose myself and become absorbed in the music. My best performance was at Cheneyville High School. I even cried when I played the Lento part of the solo. It was magnificently slow moving with that full bass sound filling the auditorium exposing all my emotions for public view. At the end I received my first standing ovation. Mr. Freeman was so proud. I could see the twinkle in his eyes. I was embarrassed. I had tears in public. They were almost unnoticeable to the public, but I knew. My wall had fallen and so had the tears. I could not swallow them. I was not invincible after all. Mr. Freeman made me human.

Ninth grade was a totally new me. More growth— physically emotionally and intellectually—occurred in one year than all the other years put together. I really shouldn't have talked about BB so badly because in spite of everything else, I really began my love of reading in her class. True, *Vanity Fair* was not for me, but James Baldwin's novels were and *Mandingo* and *Uncle Tom's Cabin*. Those were the beginnings for me in Black readings in history. Ralph Ellison's *Invisible Man* was a soul wrenching experience because for the first time someone Black had been able to express feelings and emotions that were realistic. In spite of our families, our jobs, our communities, we lived in a society where we just didn't exist in the eyes of whites, except when something negative occurred, then Blacks were made the scapegoats in the news and our presence was acknowledged. Ellison captured that reality.

My emotional, racial turmoil and thirst for knowledge of Black people that began in ninth grade has never subsided. The history of the rape of Africa, of its peoples and resources, the inhumaneness of slavery and its degradation and brutality, the Jim Crow segregation and institutionalized racism, and worst of all the omission from history of our contributions to humanity were all facts that had to be researched and validated. The stereotyping of Blacks was blatant in all forms of media with white superiority and Black inferiority flaunted like medals of honor.

Like many Blacks I have gone through phases of what and how to do for us as a people to survive and thrive in this country. In the 60's we fought for Civil Rights in the courts. Many people marched, sat-in, boycotted, went to jail, suffered abuse, died, or endured whatever was necessary to be recognized and accepted as equals. White folks eventually let us in, hired us, took our money, and then sent us home to be good boys and girls. If you played the whites' games and obeyed their rules, they gave you the crumbs, and you were acknowledged as a good Black, but if you did not play their game, you were criminalized by both Black and white society. The norm in Black culture was to try to act and look white by mimicking white culture and not disrupting the status quo, but change was coming.

The Supreme Court in its 1954 decision hit the nail on the head by noting the psychological inferiority that segregation creates, meaning that separate but equal could never be equal because people would always assume that Black was inferior if there were a segregated venue. Part of this was due to what Carter G. Woodson observed about Blacks and noted in *The Miseducation of the Negro* (1932): Throughout history, Black people have been brainwashed of their inferiority to the degree that it has become inherent. Woodson made a powerful statement. It took me a while to realize that he was saying if white folks took all the barriers down, we Black folks would still believe we were inferior because we had been trained to think of ourselves in that manner. With all my readings, travels, and experiences, I began to try to understand this concept and deal with it, but the superiority/inferiority is so deeply imbedded that we truly don't realize the extent to which we are affected. Not knowing exactly what was wrong or how to conquer this debilitating fact/ disease, I began my personal fight to break the chains oppressing my own mind and body.

My first attack was the Catholic Church. Since I was not in a Catholic school the church mandated catechism classes once a week for public school students. I knew all the Catholic dogma because I had attended Catholic school from second through sixth grade and had been confirmed the year before daring the Bishop to slap me too hard or I would slap him back. Someone was looking out for both of us. Can't you see why I could never truly embrace Catholicism? There were too many hypocrisies and contradictions. I wondered as a child, if all men were created in the image of God, why was God always portrayed as a white male with blonde hair. I am a Black female. This did not compute. That God only belonged to white males with blonde hair. My God should look like me. If God were all-knowing, all-loving, and all-forgiving, why did he not like Protestants? I have not believed since third grade that God would send everybody else in the world to hell because they were not Catholic. What kind of God creates people, is all knowing, loving and forgiving and condemns his creation to hell for not being Catholic?

However, the good Catholic that my mother was insisted that I attend catechism classes once a week on Saturday mornings. The instructor was none other than Father Brainwashed. The first week of catechism class, I questioned the Trinity and the reality of it. Three people in one? Now, be for real. How can that be? If I walked around telling people that I was three people in one, I would have been committed to an insane asylum. Yet, Father said you must have blind faith, and you don't question the church. Ok, so who's crazy?

The next week of class I asked why Catholics had to go to confession. I told Father that I did not need an intermediary. If God was all-knowing and all-forgiving, he could hear me, and I should have a direct line. Father replied that Jesus had given the priests the power to forgive. I told him I preferred to go to the Boss himself.

The next week Father and I had a true battle. He read a passage about a man who had to make a decision whether to save his wife or the life of his newborn in a difficult birth. The Catholic answer was to save the infant and let the wife die. Catholics always have a preset answer. No exceptions! No alternatives! Everything is always right or always wrong. My questions were, "What if there were other children at home, who would take care of them? What if he had no other family to help and he had to work? What if the wife could have more children later?" I thought people should have options depending on their circumstances. God should understand that each of his creations is unique.

In that same class I continued the birth conversation with the Catholic Church's stance on birth control that I felt was totally ridiculous. It's more of a crime to bring a child into the world that you cannot feed or provide for or that will be abused out of resentment than not conceiving that child at all. I wasn't talking abortion, just preventing its conception. After all, I do value life. With that statement, Father asked me not to return to the classes because I was a disruption and clearly not interested in learning. No, I was not willing to be brainwashed. I wanted to think for myself.

Boy was I glad! He really did me a favor by putting me out of catechism. Of course, my mother had a few choice words with me, but I could not sit idly by and not speak my mind. I only wished Father could have forced my parents to stop making me go to church on Sunday. I believed in a Supreme Being, but She was Black like me with pretty, nappy hair, and She was sassy too, who truly loved all people, and She did not make you sit in the back of white churches.

Yes, BB started a revolution. I have never really thanked her for it, but she forced me to read more and get into the books that made a difference in my life. No, it wasn't that damned *Vanity Fair,* but all the other books that I read opened up a whole new world.

At the same time I was going through this conflict with church and racism and identity, my family went through a crisis that drew them closer to the church. One morning about 3 AM my mother was awakened by a strange noise. I heard her get up because I was a light sleeper and was accustomed to everyone going to the bathroom, which was between my room and my brothers' room at the end of the hall. Instead of going to the bathroom, she went into the boys' room and started screaming for Daddy. I held the covers tight around my head afraid to move as I waited what seemed like an hour. Daddy came running down the hall frightened to death, not knowing what to expect. He found mother holding Robert in her arms crying and screaming at the same time, "My baby's dead! He's dead! Oh God, why? My baby's dead!" Daddy had to literally pull her away so he could check Robert. He was not dead but in a sound sleep, in almost a coma. Daddy reassured Mama that Robert was not dead as he called Dr. Yates who lived next door.

Dr. Yates came over quickly and listened to Mama's description of what happened. He said it sounded like a convulsion. Dr. Yates checked Robert and said to watch him carefully and that he would probably sleep for a while but when Robert woke to call him. Upon awakening, Robert said that he couldn't feel his left side. Dr. Yates examined him again and they decided to take him to the hospital. Mama and Daddy took him to New Orleans to Flint Goodrich where he had been born. The white hospitals in Baton Rouge were known to let Blacks die waiting in the emergency rooms while they took all the whites first or they kept Blacks waiting in the hall until there was a bed on the Black ward. How could Blacks trust their sick children to people that discriminate in the practice of medicine? You can only figure that they just want to get rid of more of us. Dupuy Jr. was born at Baton Rouge General Hospital, and they broke his collarbone during his delivery, so we have always tried to go to Black hospitals when possible.

Imagine having to drive 98 miles to a hospital when you don't know your condition and you're in pain, but we knew the doctors at Flint Goodrich. They knew us, and they cared about us. Flint may not have had all the latest technological advancements as the white hospitals, but it made up for it in its care. Uncle Bernie had now specialized in internal medicine and he and Aunt Wilma had moved to New Orleans to work at Flint. He was the one that took care of Robert. After two months of tests, the final diagnosis was epilepsy. Most of the time Robert was without seizures on his medication, but then he'd have petit mal seizures and sometimes grand mal seizures and his medicine would have to be regulated as he grew. Many times he stayed with Aunt Wilma and Uncle Bernie at their home as Flint tried to regulate his medicine. Usually, Mama or Daddy stayed with Wilma and Bernie also, but when they couldn't be there, he was home with family, Uncle Bernie and Aunt Wilma.

I really missed Aunt Wilma and Uncle Bernie when they left Baton Rouge because their home was my escape from the boys. Daddy did not believe in sleep overs and would not allow me to stay overnight with anyone except Aunt Wilma and Uncle Bernie. She'd pick me up on Friday evenings to spend the weekend. We'd always do something special together, but we'd never fail to get Muffelato's hot tamales on Friday. We knew Mama would kill us both, or worse stop me from sleeping over, if she ever found out that Aunt Wilma and I ate meat on Friday. So we'd go get the hot tamales about 11:30 PM. Then we'd sit up watching TV until one second after midnight and we'd eat those hot tamales. Aunt Wilma was very special to me. She had a boxer named Mugs who would sit in the chair to watch TV with us and cross his legs. Whenever we smelled something, we knew he farted because he would immediately leave the room.

Aunt Wilma's house was always wild. She didn't have children but I was her child. She was a one-woman party. Trying to keep up with her was like trying to hold onto a tornado. She had one of the first Thunderbirds. It was green and convertible and wonderful. We'd take the top off and go riding downtown to shop and everyone would turn and look at that Black woman and me in this new green convertible Thunderbird. One day while she was parking the car a white man remarked, "I wonder how niggers can afford a car like that." No one was immune from racism, and Aunt Wilma never let anything stop her. She was traveling to the Bahamas and abroad before that kind of travel was even popular for white folks. She owned Dior originals and had traveled to Paris to buy them. She was one-of-a-kind, and I loved her. She taught me to enjoy life in spite everything else that was happening. Thank goodness for her during Robert's illness; Mama and Daddy would have lost their minds.

Robert was in and out of the hospital for almost two years before his epileptic seizures became controlled by medication. During those two years I saw Daddy at his weakest while Mama's strengths surfaced. Daddy had never been able to see us in pain. He needed solutions, immediate solutions. Mother held him and our family together. She kept the family moving as normally as possible. She had definitely matured over the years. I usually thought of her as a dumb blonde personification but she had asserted herself and gone back to school over Daddy's protests. She received her BS in education and Master's in counseling and was beginning her profession in education. She had become the rock of the family. When one partner was weak, another took over. That's the way a family should be, equal in all respects.

In need of some down time after Robert was stable that summer, we went to California. This time we made it to El Paso with no problems, but between El Paso and Los Angeles we ran into a sandstorm. Daddy had just bought a new green Plymouth Fury. As we traveled through the shifting sands, the sand blew mountains of sand onto the road and across the windshield. Visibility was zero. Traffic came to a virtual halt. Daddy drove about 15 mph through the storm. We were frightened to death, but at least the boys were older, and we didn't have the fighting and crying. When we finally got out of the storm, the car was not new anymore. The windshield was pitted and the front of the car was literally sandblasted. It had to be re-painted while we were in Los Angeles. We were lucky to have survived with just car damage, but Daddy had always been an excellent highway driver.

I specified highway because in the city, he was dangerous. He stopped at green lights, went through the red ones, never yielded and never, never looked where he was going. He could drive down the street and tell you what the lady two blocks over was wearing when she served barbecue ribs, potato salad and mustard greens for dinner with cherry pie and ice cream for dessert. He saw all that while he went through the red light and stopped at the green.

On the highway he was a different animal. He still noticed all of his surroundings but there was less traffic and you felt a bit safer. I really don't know why I felt safer because he was usually traveling at 95 mph as he read the billboard five blocks away. Suffice to say, he loved to travel. He was always showing us interesting sights as he drove. He wanted us to appreciate nature and travel and the beauty and wonders of the country.

All we ever wanted to do was get to Disneyland. Onward Ho!

L.A, Disneyland, Knott's Berry Farm, the beach, and, this time, Universal City! As boulders came crashing down onto collapsing train tracks while we rode across them, Universal City became our new adventure. The major point of interest was when I found out how the Red Sea parted in *The 10 Commandments* by just reversing the pouring of water. How un-melodramatic! My favorite second part of the trip was Lawry's Restaurant. The head chef was Lee Davis, my uncle, Patsy's daddy. He was married to my mother's sister, Auntie Mease, but they were divorced. However, that never made any difference with our family. Lee attended all the family gatherings and checked on Mamou just as we all did. Mamou stayed in touch with all family, the in-laws and out-laws. So, when we went to Lawry's we were treated like movie stars since we were related to the chef. The salad was prepared at the table with the waitress spinning this huge bowl tossing salad in the air. I realized then that I loved being waited on and pampered. I had never been a great lover of food, maybe it was because Mama couldn't cook, and I just ate to live. However that was the best food I had eaten, down to the creamed spinach, which I never would have tried at home. The crowning glory of the meal was a chocolate pie—even the crust melted in your mouth—full of pecans and meringue. To this day it is still my favorite. I became addicted to chocolate and fancy restaurants. What made the evening perfect were no brothers and no tables turned over. That was a great culmination to my ninth grade year.

Tenth Grade

The tenth grade year was not as exciting as the ninth but better in many ways. I had settled down and was more relaxed. Our class continued to get closer and closer as family members, and we never wanted to be apart. We enjoyed school so much that there were a couple of days of school closings due to severe freezing weather, but teachers had to report, and guess who else showed up? We did. Our class came to school just to have fun with each other. The teachers could not get rid of us. We just hung around in the classrooms and halls, played games, ate, and acted like it was a school day. We taught class for ourselves.

I was president of the band that year, and we finally raised enough money for our uniforms. They were the greatest uniforms I had ever seen in Louisiana. We couldn't wait to get on the field and beat the University in a Battle of the Bands, but we had to wait until my junior year because the uniforms didn't come in until March of our sophomore year. I continued to have my battles with Mr. Freeman in our constant love/hate relationship. He still teased and picked on me constantly. He still taught me private lessons on Saturday mornings, and we really got into the jazz that I loved. Usually I could play the average song without practicing, and I remained in first chair, but every now and then he'd have chair competition, and I'd get moved down from first to second and once to third. It was always a fight between Charles Burchell, Comie Barges, Herbert Robert Carter, and me. A chair position was really not that important to me because whatever chair I was in, I'd still play my best. All I had to do was practice every now and then, but I played his game of trying to keep me interested.

Our 10th grade class had to maintain its reputation as the best, or at least the most exciting class at the school, and we did not fail. Our assembly program was a talent show. We left the audience with their mouths hanging open, but this time it was at the shock of our overwhelmingly magnificent talent. From vocals to instrumentals to acting, it was all there, and it was all good. I did a monologue of Edgar Allen Poe's "The Tell-Tale Heart." Dressed in Mama's turquoise silk, black velvet embossed full length lounge robe that had a wide tie attached belt, a black lace scarf, and deep black eye makeup, I walked slowly out onto the dark stage emerging almost as a ghost. Walking to the front of the stage gazing at the audience, I stood there silently, looking out, making eye contact with everyone in the first few rows, slowly lifting that gaze to the back of the auditorium. Holding my breath as if waiting for something to happen, I began to move very slightly but nervously. When the audience was totally quiet, almost eerily quiet, anticipating what I was going to do or had forgotten to do, I began, "True, nervous, very very dreadfully nervous I had been and am, but why will you say that I am mad!" I held the audience in the palms of my hands until I finally tore up the floorboards trying to end the beating of the heart that was driving me mad. The curtains closed to thunderous applause.

Tony played "Autumn Leaves" on the trumpet accompanied by Nancy Walton on the piano. They began in a conservative traditional tempo and ended with upbeat jazz. The audience brought them back for an encore. Dr. McKelpin commended us on our excellent performances. He told us he knew we could excel, and we had proven him correct. However, before the end of the year we would cause him heart ache again.

We planned special dress up days that we called mix-ups. On these dress-up days we wore plaids, stripes, florals, or whatever all mixed together. We looked terrible. We looked like we had dressed from things we picked up on the street. We just didn't stink. Mackie Jenkins pressed black gum against her front teeth scaring all of us because it looked like she didn't have any teeth. She actually walked around all day like that. We had baby dress days where we dressed like young children or babies with pacifiers. We had 50's days with large appliqued hoop skirts, crinoline slips and bobby socks. We also had dress up days when we were dressed to the "nines" with heels, hats, and gloves. We just kept school interesting as we continued to excel academically. Teachers never could predict what we were going to do next and neither could we.

In homeroom, Mr. Jenkins was determined to have scheduled activities just as we persevered in trying not to do them. Wesley Bean was in our homeroom; he was a star athlete. He was the quarterback on the football team, one of the five starters on the basketball team, and the pitcher for baseball. He ran track, threw the discus and was simply outstanding in all sports, but he never did his homework. Marion and I would do it for him in homeroom almost every morning. It wasn't that he couldn't do it; he was just damn lazy and refused to do it. I'll never forget a math test of 100 square root problems where he worked only enough to get a "C" and then he quit and turned in his paper. That's all he wanted: just enough to pass. Being smart didn't fit his macho image, so he never really tried very hard to get "A's" if it required too much work. Yet, he was brilliant.

Fortunately, most of us did not subscribe to Wesley's theories of learning. Mrs. Holmes, the science teacher, was having another baby, and we had Mrs. Nash, a nice little old lady with false teeth who substituted for Mrs. Holmes. Mrs. Nash was always clicking and sucking on her teeth. So naturally, everyone in class was always clicking and sucking when they responded in class. She had no control over us, and we all played dumb, which caused her to explain over and over again. We could talk her into anything.

That year in science class, we taught ourselves sex education. We convinced Mrs. Nash to divide us into panels to make presentations, like we did in Mrs. Wooten's class. Our presentations were excellent, and we learned quite a bit from each other, or more than any adult had ever taken the time to explain, but even if they had, they would never have given us the information that we presented. Again Dr. McKelpin was called by some parents who thought the information in the class was much too explicit for their children. He was astounded that we would have been discussing such things. We reasoned, "After all, it is a biology class, and sex education is part of biology."

Thank goodness for that class or I might have missed quite a bit. Mama gave me a book and asked if I had any questions, but who asks parents about those kinds of things? Remember, this was the early 60's before the flower children and promiscuity. Sex was taboo until we opened it up in the classroom. There was no sex education, and it did not enter the school curriculum again until at least a decade later. We were always ahead of our time.

Dr. McKelpin initiated an advanced honors program for a summer school session. He was also ahead of his time and was an outstanding principal. He truly understood his population and met the needs of each one of us. Most of us would have been suspended, expelled or worse, possibly not graduating, had it not been for his intuitive resourcefulness, constant understanding, creative manipulation, and supportive nurturing. Even though he impaled us with the fear of God, we knew he loved us and wanted us to succeed.

That's why he initiated the honors summer program. There were so many applicants that he had a waiting list. I was accepted in the writing class with Ms. Isabel Herson and Marion was in world history with Ms. Couch. I wished I had had the chance to study with Ms. Couch because she was one-of-a-kind and received nothing but accolades from all who studied under her, but she left after that summer, as did many more of the PhD's who continued to leave Southern University. I blame her for my failure to develop an appreciation of history until much later in life because she left before I had the opportunity to experience her talent and wisdom.

However, that summer, I wrote my first short story, "The Girl in White." Edgar Allen Poe was one of my favorite writers, and his works gave me the inspiration to write mysteries. The story was about a little girl dressed in white who appeared to a family over a brief period of time but upon investigation she had been dead over a year. She appeared suddenly without parents or anyone having any knowledge of her. She described how she was killed and where she lived. She was always dressed in white, with ribbons in her hair, never leaving a trace of where she went. After several visits, the girl was never seen again. However, one of her contacts found her ribbon in the spot that she frequented. That left everyone to wonder if she were real or not. I thought it was pretty good, and so did my class. That summer became the foundation of my writing quest.

The enrichment classes spawned discussions of philosophies and doctrines. We began to question existence, religion, love, the world, war, and the scarcity of Black people in all of what we were studying. As I looked back, I realized how white my education was. Even though we were Black students in a Black school with Black teachers and Black administrators, we were educated white. We could not blame our teachers because they were educated the same way. Blacks did not write the curriculum texts or any of the materials that we used, and therefore Blacks did not exist in them. It is one of the classic signs of racism—omission.

We only found ourselves in history as slaves. We only existed in the news as criminals or welfare mothers. We only existed when we were a problem to white society. Ralph Ellison's *The Invisible Man* caused me to scream more loudly, "I know how you feel!" I found myself drawn back to *Exodus* to try to understand how the Jews survived their Holocaust. First, they were able to maintain their religion and culture. Second, they constantly taught their religion and culture, which was the bond that tied them together worldwide. I wanted a bond like that for Black people on all continents. I wanted us to understand that in our history, enslavement was a totally destructive institution that demolished our religions, our families, our culture, our self-concept, our financial enterprises and even our names. We could not rebuild like the Jewish people because we knew nothing about who we were. I wanted us to understand that society was continuing to dehumanize us, and we had to begin to take control of our lives and teach ourselves about our history, our culture, our religions, and begin to like who we are and STOP trying to imitate whites.

As my education expanded, Black survival and thriving became my life's challenge. I had always been on my father's coattails in Civil Rights. I followed him to meetings and joined a group of black and white youth who came together under Wade Mackie, a Quaker trying to better race relations. We met once a month to discuss the racial problems in our community and our feelings about each other and our families. One white girl's father was a member of the klan. She said she could only come when she was visiting her older sister because her father would kill her if he found out that she was meeting with Blacks and white sympathizers. She was petrified of her family. She talked of the violence at home between her family and with others, and she said she hated Blacks too until she began coming to the group with Wade. I felt sorry for her because she was pitiful, poor white trash, but I didn't want to be bothered with her. I had no sympathy for PWT (po' white trash). I had little patience for people that had all the resources needed to succeed but didn't. I did, however, garner insight by meeting and talking to a few whites. The main thing I learned was that no matter how poor, ugly, trashy, dirty, or ignorant they are, whites still feel like they are better than Blacks and know more than any Black ever will. I know that's why they joined the klan, and that's why I joined the youth NAACP.

13th Birthday Party

Aaron,
Merrill,
me,
Mackie,
&
Jackie

Dental Convention,
Cincinnati Sheraton Gipson

Top: Southern High Band with new uniforms
Bottom left: Mr. Freeman, Band Director
Bottom right: Freya 10th Grade costume for *Tell Tale Heart* by Poe

LABORATORY SCHOOL
Southern University

                    B U L L E T I N   March 5, 1962

STUDENT OF THE WEEK

        A young lady who is recognized as having "exceptional"
musical talent is our student of the week from the Sophomore
class. Not only does she play the piano well but she plays
clarinet in both the marching and Concert Band- which organization she serves as President. Although a serious musician,
she is an ardent jazz fan and as such participates actively
in the Jazz Club.

        If you were to ask, she would probably tell you that
her favorite school subjects are Band, English and Physical
Education. Her out-of-school activities include dancing,
sports-spectator and participant - and travel. By way of the
"grapevine", we learned, too, that one of her hobbies is
acting.

        You should have guessed long before now that the student
we are honoring this week is Freya Sandra Anderson.

_____

        Homeroom teachers will make arrangements
students assemble in Gym Tuesday for 8:15 at
band uniforms will be christened (modeled).
play a number or so prior to their departure
they will participate in a Mardi Gras Parade.

_____

TODAY'S MENU

Roast Pork Loin
    and Barbecue Sauce
        Au Gratin Potatoes
            Creamed Peas & Carrots
                Hot Rolls
Chilled Apple Jelly   Milk

SCHOLARSHIP COM-
MITTEE PROJECT
    The Scholarship Com-
mittee of the Council, chaired
by Constant Essex '64 has
begun an interesting project-
that of saluting persons of
outstanding scholarship and
and citizenship of our school.
The person selected is entitled "Student of the Week",
and a brief biography of that
person appears in the Daily
Bulletin on the First day of
the Week.
    Claude Tellis, '62 whom
you have already met, was
the first such student honored. Freya Anderson, '64 a
sophomore was honored this
week. Last week the honoree
was Rosalind Fletcher, '63.
    Till Next Time,
            Adele, '62

Student of the Week

Dress Up Day
Carmen, Brenda, Elaine, Joann, Veronica, Anna Jean, Freya

Sweat Shirt Day
Brenda, Pat, Mackie, Helen, Joann

Talent Show
Anna Jean
Joann, Pat

Classmates

Junior Year

"Ain't no stopping us now, we're on the move!" That should have been the theme song for our class as we became known city-wide. We had the finest and prettiest girls in the city or at least we thought so. Every Black high school had guys making a play for the girls in our class. The senior girls at our school despised us, and we stayed in a constant rivalry mostly because we were going steady with the most popular senior and junior boys. The senior girls didn't stand a chance! The tension came to a head after an intramural volleyball tournament. The finals were, you guessed it, the junior girls against the senior girls, and the tournament came down to the last two points. Of course, the mighty juniors beat them.

We even won the fight afterwards in the locker room. I was getting dressed in the area behind the first row of lockers when one of the senior girls started threatening to beat my ass. Naturally, I couldn't let that go, so I was responding appropriately—selling wolf tickets—telling her that I was not going to take her shit and would definitely reciprocate beating her ass, all the while backing up into the aisle checking to see if I had any support from my classmates. Looking around the corner of the lockers, I saw Mackie Jenkins and Joann Simon were listening and I could see that they had a plan. So, as quickly as I was out of the area of the row of lockers and in the aisle, Joann motioned for me to move further back into the aisle and she and Mackie turned over the entire first set of lockers on the senior girls who were taunting me. That row falling over started a chain reaction of lockers falling on top of each other. We were damned lucky that the last row hit the wall, which stopped all the lockers from falling to the floor. They were braced against each other, allowing room for everyone to get out. They must have been very good lockers because they didn't buckle. Luckily no one was injured (some of the senior girls may have been, but they were too embarrassed to complain about it). The rest of the senior girls that were in the locker room came to the rescue holding up the lockers and standing them upright to get their friends out from between the lockers as we started dumping trash cans on them. Good thing Dr. McKelpin was gone that year or he would've been in the middle of the girls' locker room breaking up the fight. I don't think Ms. Herson, the new principal, even knew there was a fight. From that time on the senior girls and the junior girls were on the warpath over any and every thing.

Our football team was great that year, and for the first time my parents let me follow the team. They really had no choice because I was in the band, and the band played for the games. We had our new uniforms, and we were unbelievable. Wherever we marched and played, we turned out the stands with new routines that even the universities had not seen! We were just waiting for band day, the big showdown at Southern University where the local high school bands were invited to a SU football game to perform.

On band day, the high school bands would perform for the pre- and post-game shows, and SU performed at half-time. In the stands during time outs, the University was supposed to play, but whenever they didn't pick up their horns, we picked up ours. The Mighty Kittens had the stadium rocking and turned out the pre-game with our dance routine. None of the other high school or college bands were doing dance routines at that time, and our St. Louis Blues always stole the show along with Mr. Freeman's jazz songs arranged especially for our band. He choreographed our routines with steps to the music and marching. He would have had a stroke if we'd lay our instruments down on the ground and shake our booties as the bands do today. We were the best I had ever seen in anybody's band. Our motto was, "Not as good as but better than," just like Daddy's, and we were. We took pride in how we looked. We were cocky, but we deserved it. When one moved, we all did. No time for solo showoffs. Our band was truly an effort in unity.

The uniforms were designed by Mr. Freeman. They were wool, dark green, almost black, with cross ties across our chests pulled together by a square brass buckle. We wore white gloves with half fingers cut out so that we could play, and we had black shoes with black soles to accentuate the white spats. There was a green cape with a gold lining that flashed with every turn, and the hat had a gold feather plume. You couldn't afford to make a mistake because if one flash were out of line it would be seen. When we marched, our knees and thighs had to be parallel to the ground, guiding left for straight lines. We were one precise unit on the field marching eight steps to every five yards. Harold Robinson and Tommy Davis, Jr. led the percussion section and would come up with the most outstanding cadences. Once the drums started, people began to line up to watch us coming. I think if I were to research Drumline, the history began with the Kittens. The University mimicked us, and later when Mr. Freeman went to the University, our cadences went also. Under Mr. Freeman's leadership the percussion section of the University band became known as "The Funk Factory," and they began challenging other bands after the half time show. It all started with the Kittens.

That year the Kittens played Grambling High for the first time in ages, and our band went to Grambling. We had eaten tuna in the Grambling cafeteria earlier that day before the performance and many of us were sick, but the most amazing thing was that we still performed for the halftime show. The minute we began walking off the field from performing, band members began literally falling out and throwing up on the sidelines. The drive to complete halftime and finish our routine was undeniably a mind-over-body act of will. That was devotion—and probably a little vanity and insanity.

The band played and fought together, but the girls probably did more fighting than the boys. That year, we played T. A. Levy High School for their homecoming game. It was a big rivalry of ours, so we knew there was going to be trouble. We headed straight for the bus as soon as the game was over. I was sitting on the third seat from the front of the bus with Jerome, whose nickname was Coon. He played saxophone. All of a sudden we heard fighting in the back of the bus. The rival band had opened the emergency door and was fighting the people at the back of the bus. Kids were screaming and fighting. Students were running across the tops of the seats and hiding under the seats. Coon said, "Here Freya, hold my horn." I took it thinking he was probably going to help our friends in the back of the bus, but he proceeded to crawl under the seat in front of us. All I could do was laugh. When I came to my senses, I told him how low-down he was for leaving me holding his horn while he was hiding. He replied, "Every man for himself." I never let him live that down.

The football team won every game and made it all the way to the semi-finals for state championship with our junior class leading the way. Wesley was the leading quarterback, Henry Howard was a running back, Stuart Freeman was an end, and Joseph McGhee was just all over the field. Matthew McKines played offensive guard and linebacker on defense. We were such a small high school that several guys played both offense and defense, but they played relentlessly. How excited we were to have made it that far. The game played out to the last second with us down in the red zone but missing the last pass. What a heartbreaker! It was the first time in a long time that the Kittens had made it that far.

Then we started basketball season. McKinley High School, Daddy's Alma Mater, was the number one team of the year, and their star player Leslie Scott was being recruited nationally. Little did anyone expect the Southern University Laboratory Kittens to be a threat. The other schools were always teasing us and putting us down because our mascot was a Kitten compared to McKinley's Panthers, Capitol's Lions, and Scotlandville's Hornets, but we weren't just kittens, we were the Mighty Kittens, and we were invincible.

The All-City Basketball Tournament was held at McKinley, and all bets were on McKinley to win. We had no chance, if we had listened to the newspapers and other coaches, yet we made it to the finals. Game after game of the tournament, we held our breath. We had six players who were called by the *Newsleader*, the Black newspaper, the weary six. We had no bench. The weary six were Henry Howard, Stuart Freeman and Maurice Haynes all seniors and Wesley Bean, Ernest Sterling and Milton Wicks, our juniors.

Wesley guarded McKinley's Leslie. There were no three-point shots in the 60's, but balls were flying from all over the court. Leslie would hit two and then Wesley would hit two. The entire game was shot for shot. Talk about exciting down to the last second. Then, Wesley put up a long shot and it went in! We won! There wasn't even a fight after the game. It was such a great final. Everyone was exhausted, but we went to the Black YMCA and partied afterwards. I don't remember whose party it was, but it had to have been someone Mama and Daddy knew or I would not have been allowed to go.

The girls' basketball team was just as good. There were just so few teams at that time for girls. This was before Title VI. Our team was led by a skinny junior nicknamed Goat (Joann Simon, the one who turned over the lockers with Mackie). Don't ask why we call her Goat because it's another story, and Marion and I will take it to the grave with us. Goat was a super hero on the court! Girls only played half-court in those years, which meant that there were guards on one side and forwards on the other side and neither could cross to the other side, but this year the new concept of a roving forward began. The roving forward could play both ends of the court, unlike the other players who were restricted to one end. Goat was the rover. She crossed the line guarding on one end and shooting on the other. She was tough, for all of her 80 pounds. Watching her made me want to join the team, but mother insisted I stay in the band. Dag! Mr. Freeman stopped a lot of my extracurricular activities.

I don't remember baseball because I'm not a baseball fan or track fan, for that matter, but in intramural track, our junior girls did it again. The junior class girls had another first at a relay against our boys where the girls beat the boys! The first time was just in fun, a fluke. The next time was serious. The guys' feelings were hurt because we beat them. The boys we beat were not the real jocks of the class, but they were still boys. They challenged us to a "real" race, and we accepted. We were cocky.

The day of the big, "real" race was the day after we had run our hearts out. We went out and didn't warm up. No practice. We felt that we did it before without warm ups and practice, and we could do it again. We were fast, just unadulterated speed. We lined up on the track, got into position, and took off! Then, cramps set in. Thigh and calf muscles began pinching, getting shorter, tightening up, and grabbing the legs saying, "No! I am not moving." Each person in each leg of the relay seemed to get worse. We almost crawled to get the baton around for the 440. Goat started, I was the third leg, and Mackie brought it in beating Marvin Eames for the win. He said she blew him away. He has barely forgiven her to this day as he reminds her how she embarrassed him, but did we suffer! Somehow we did it, just like the band members finishing the Grambling show. There was no one to help us as we lay on the field in pain from the cramps. Not even the boys' coach, Coach

Owens, offered assistance. He insisted no one help us off under the pretense that we should continue to stretch the muscles or they would get worse. We tried to make it across the street to the school, but I couldn't even make it out of the stadium. Eventually, Wesley and Endas Vincent carried me, one on each side of me, laughing the entire time and talking smack. When we got back to the gym Coach Owens had Ms. Jordan rub us with some hot liniment that burned so badly, I thought my skin was going to fall off.

However, everything was not fun and games that year. The Cuban Missile Crisis had started getting attention. At 6:50 AM every morning, I would step on Wilbert Johnese's bus for the more-than-hour-long ride to Southern High with not only high school students but also college students. We never had any problems with the older students on the bus. They usually looked out for us and developed a big brother/sister relationship advising and helping us in any way that they could. If we felt we had something to contribute to their conversations, they'd even allow us to participate without intimidating us. On the morning of October 23, 1962, everyone on the bus was nervous. Some were listening to transistor radios. Some were quiet and praying. Mama and Daddy had discussed whether we should go to school that day or stay home. Daddy called us together and we all prayed. He decided that God would not let the world end this way and sent us off to school, but just in case he wasn't reading God's mind right, Daddy made an emergency plan. If anything were to materialize Daddy would get me and the boys, and we would meet back at the house as soon as possible. This was the emergency plan for our family, but once at home, what was the plan?

There was a small group of mostly college students on the back of the bus discussing what they were going to do if it happened. I knew what they were talking about because President Kennedy had given Russia an ultimatum to either get the missiles out of Cuba or prepare for a third world war, and this time, it would definitely be a nuclear one. Our family had all sat around the television the night before listening to the gravity of the situation as President Kennedy made his speech to the nation. Baton Rouge was one of the top five cities that would be bombed because it was home to the Standard Oil Refining Company. We were all told that if a nuclear bomb hit Standard Oil, there would be little chance of survival not only because of the nuclear fallout but also because we were next to the Mississippi River, which would surely wipe out the entire city if a large bomb hit it directly.

So, with all this news on October 23rd, I boarded the bus acutely aware of the conversations and emotions. We all knew that if Premier Nikita Khrushchev of Russia did not back down and turn his ships around, there would be war, and we were all going to die. I had always known that, as a Black—especially one involved in Civil Rights—death was a possibility, and

I was still willing to take that risk, but this was "in your face death" now. In a few hours, the world as we knew it might not exist, and I was on my way to school, sitting on Wilbert Johnese's bus with the possibility of not returning on the 5 PM bus looming over my head.

As I walked to the back of the bus I listened to the college students talking about the world coming to an end. Freddie Pitcher asked me, "What would you miss if you died today?" All I could think of was that I was going to die a virgin and never know what all that "feel good stuff" was like. The way everyone was always talking about sex, it had to be what life was all about, and I had never experienced it. Seemed like a shame to die before it happened. I said that if war started, I was going to find someone and "do it." I refused to die not having had that experience. That brought a little levity to the situation. Everyone laughed until they cried. Freddie asked me to just hold on a little longer, at least until we knew for sure that the war had started, and then he was sure someone would oblige me. Fortunately, Russia backed down, the world continued as normal at the Lab, and I didn't have to do anything foolish. Freddie later became the first Black elected to a judgeship in Baton Rouge in 1983. He was always wise.

The unstoppable Mighty Juniors continued setting new heights. We began another legacy that year: our parties. Segregation limited the movement and activities of Blacks. Neither young nor old had any real entertainment outlets except the movies, at the Lincoln and Ann Theaters, and house parties. Adults had a few clubs and their social and civic clubs. All other activities in the city were open to whites only, so that left us with creating our own activities. Since we worked so hard all day at school and after-school events, not getting home until 6 PM, the only time left was the weekend, which usually involved house cleaning chores and church, but at least once a month we'd have a house party for the class.

The real house cleaning took place on Sunday mornings after church with Daddy supervising. We had hardwood floors throughout the house; the living and dining room floors had to be cleaned at least once a month. We'd wax on our knees, then skate across the floor to buff using the electric buffer as the final touch. We had to dust and wax every piece of furniture and artifact. Fortunately, there were not a lot of artifacts because the boys managed to break them shortly after their arrival. When we finished, we called Daddy in to inspect. Most of the work was done by Dupuy Jr. and me with Ralph sitting on the couch holding the can of wax and Robert running into our legs while we were trying to buff. Regardless of how hard we cleaned, Daddy always found something that we missed, and we'd have to clean again. One Sunday I dusted everything: the mantle, the end tables—even underneath!—the coffee table, the dining room chairs and table, the china cabinet, the music cabinet, and the speakers. We called Daddy after I inspected and I was sure that he would not find anything to complain about. Daddy walked in and looked at the floor and said we did a good job. Dupuy Jr. and I looked at each other and smiled. Then Daddy started wiping his hands over the furniture and could not come up with any dust. Dupuy Jr. and I looked at each other and smiled again. I said, "Wow, this is the first time that you couldn't find anything. I guess we did a great job." He went over to the speaker in the corner and wiped his hand across the metal strips in front and found some dust. He looked up and smiled. I wanted to cry. Couldn't he just once congratulate us on a job well done? Daddy wanted perfection and settled for nothing less. Dupuy Jr. and I were devastated. I think Daddy saw the disappointment on our faces and said, "But you did a good job. Next time it will be perfect." That didn't make us feel any better. We had tried and failed again. Sundays would remain the day of cleaning and never quite being perfect.

House parties were our way to escape reality and forget our troubles. Wanda Cage gave the best ones. You just had to get there early enough to get your spot on the wall. No one moved because you could lose your place. That Christmas Charles Brown's *Please Come Home for Christmas* played over and over and over again. Folks was sweating and hair was going back (if you're not black or if you're too young, "hair going back" means that your hair was getting nappy from perspiration or heat or humidity after being straightened). The guys would have to walk away a little stiff legged every now and then or they would have lost control, which would have been embarrassing, having wet pants and all.

This was the 60's. We weren't dating. We weren't screwing. At all of our parties, there were parents supervising and usually more would join the kitchen gossip of adults as they brought their children to the party. Sometimes the parents had not met each other, and this gave them a chance to share notes. At any time parents could wander in the party and turn on all the lights, so we had to listen carefully and prepare for bright lights. During the interim, though, we would hold on to each other real tight and move to the music, hugging and kissing, trying not to get caught. Our junior class parties had guys that represented all the schools in the city, and we never had any fights even though other schools or even other classes had parties that had cigarettes put out on furniture, broken furniture and police called. Our homes were off limits to fights. It was just understood.

Whenever any of us gave a party, it was an event. I'd have about two parties a year at my house because my parents always felt it was better to have us at home than in the streets. As long as we didn't mess up the house, they did not mind. No drinking allowed, no smoking, no fights, and lights on. Those were the rules. A few guys drank and smoked outside, way outside away from the house. The lights were off until Daddy came through and turned them on. He'd walk through the living room door, and the whispers started, "Doc, Doc!" He'd turn on every light that he passed continuing through the dining room exiting through the swinging door to the kitchen with the usual, "Alright, keep those lights on." I was embarrassed at first but no one else got upset. Everyone's parents did the same thing, just not quite as often.

I was glad that I stayed in the band for that year because we had a spectacular season. We entered the state band festival for the first time. Now we had our new uniforms. We had already shown up the University band at band day, and we were going to the state championship. We worked our butts off every night. Mr. Freeman had us marching until dark with our parents' cars' headlights aimed at the makeshift field (the cow pasture) for us to practice trying to find the five-yard lines, marching the eight steps to every five yards of white stripes that Mr. Freeman had to mark himself. I was marching in my sleep most nights because I was so tired.

Mr. Freeman was so uptight. He didn't know which end was up. He was also a spoiled brat and a perfectionist. Why were all these neurotics in my life? The week before the festival Mr. Freeman had a tantrum, throwing his baton and hat down and walking off the field saying we didn't listen to him. He went on a tirade complaining that we had no spirit, and we were not going anywhere representing him if we weren't perfect. If I could've grabbed that little man and spanked him, I would have, but as president of the band and his private lesson student I knew him even better than he knew himself. The band members left practice feeling dejected and hurt. We had looked forward to the state championship since last year, but I knew I could make Mr. Freeman change his mind. I started a petition from all of us in the band asking him to please let us participate in the state rally and assuring him that we would not disappoint him. All of us signed the petition, and I presented it to him after school in a special band meeting that I'd called.

We also surprised him with a cake and gave him a new baton with his name engraved on a gold band. He had tears in his eyes. I knew how to get him. He couldn't resist us and he resumed practices. We were the best looking band on the field with our new uniforms. No one could touch us with our white spats, cross bars, gloves and plumes, our gold capes flashing when we turned and the brass buckles on the cross bars that shined in the sunlight. The deep green suits were the backdrop for the flash of the gold and whites. Every move was precise with legs and arms snapping at the same time, straight lines guiding left, hitting our marks simultaneously and a sound that filled the stadium. Our dance routine of St. Louis Blues was amazing and it brought the stadium to their feet in a thunderous standing ovation. They had never seen anything like it.

Our state championship concert selection, the Overture of 1812, was equally as impressive, with our timpani vibrating the souls of the judges. Mr. Freeman smiled because he knew we had clinched first place, but we almost flubbed the sight reading. I don't remember what the selection was but there was a long rest for most of the instruments in the band except percussion. Everyone lost count as to when to come back in, but I managed to weakly come back in on time after that long rest with Mr. Freeman giving me a nod, and eventually the rest of the band caught up to finish with a big bang. Mr. Freeman was sweating on that one. Yet, we won first place in concert and first place in sight reading. We found out that no one else even finished the selection. We won first in marching in points earned, but we had to settle for second place in marching because of a time default that was not specified in the rules that were sent to us and five points were deducted. We were so disappointed. But we were state champions, and I received a superior award for my individual clarinet solo. Our famous dance routine to St. Louis Blues has never been duplicated anywhere. No one has ever topped any of Mr. Freeman's shows. He was the best, and I loved him and that band.

The academic classes were coming along, but who really cared? The camaraderie and friendships took precedence over all. I had made the National Honor Society, and I always did enough to make the honor roll each grading period. I did not hurt myself to do much more, but I always did more than Wesley because I was never too old for my Daddy to spank. My one problem was chemistry. Yep, Mr. Jenkins, Hopalong, Hoppy, himself taught chemistry, a new program piloted at the school called "CHEM Study." It was an experimental approach utilizing inquiry, prediction, and finding solutions on your own by doing experiments without the teacher providing answers. It was not my forte at all.

I started pipette fights over Bunsen burners melting the glass and pulling them apart during sword fights with other students. I put mixtures together that would stink up the class, and I screeched the stool during one of Mr. Jenkins' lectures. On top of not liking science, I simply did not get along with Mr. Jenkins. Couldn't you tell? I knew I was heading for a showdown sooner or later, but it did not happen over chemistry. I was two minutes late for class because I was coming from gym, and Ms. Jordan let us out late. Still, I took a shower since I was hot and sweaty, and that made me late for class. I had a reputation to uphold and refused to go to class smelling. When I arrived in class Jenkins told me to stand against the back wall for the entire class period. Naturally, I refused. He was calling me out in front of the entire class, and it really wasn't my fault. I tried to explain, but he cut me off and would not listen. He gave me an ultimatum and said, "Either stand on the wall or go to the office." I took the second alternative and went to the office. He suspended me for two weeks and gave me a "D" for that marking period. I deserved it. I was wrong. I was insubordinate and insolent, showed disrespect for authority, and I did not do my work. I finally learned just enough to get a final grade of "C" the only one that I ever received in high school. I had a mental block against sciences. In spite of chemistry I managed to stay on the honor roll.

That wasn't enough for my father. When he found out that I was suspended from Chemistry, he talked to me about my behavior. He began rather rationally, but I could see his anger mounting as he continued his speech. Finally, he took off his belt and had me turn around as he whipped my behind. I didn't cry. I swallowed the tears of anger and disappointment. All I could think was that he had lost his mind if he thought a whipping was going to make me change. As a child the belt may have made a difference, but now if words could not convince me, a belt surely couldn't.

Mr. Jenkins had to have a meeting with my parents in order for me to return to class. He was quite nice and spoke highly of me and my potential, but he told me something to remember. He said that you never back a panther into a corner because the only way out is to attack whoever or whatever is in front. Always leave an opening for a retreat. I really didn't know whether he was talking about me or him. Did he realize that he didn't give me a way out or is it that I didn't give him one? Either way, I remember that lesson to this day and always give my students a way out, except when they directly attack me causing physical injury. Mr. Jenkins and I were able to resolve our differences, and he was gracious enough to tutor me to help me pass. Thank God. Mr. Jenkins was an excellent teacher but very regimented in his views. I guess that personality goes with being a Geek in science.

One day Mr. Jenkins was absent and Ms. Nash was the substitute. We decided to do some science experiments on our own and give her a hand by cleaning the storage room. A few of us went into the storage room in the back of the class with good intentions of cleaning up, but others of us were just playing around with the chemicals. We created a small explosion that shook the building and had a little fire in the closet, but nothing major. We put the fire out with the extinguisher. There was a loud noise and small tremor with a few broken beakers. By the time someone in authority had reached the class, we were all in our seats looking like we had no idea what had happened. We never told who the leader was or who created the explosion. We all took the blame. Fortunately, we were not expelled.

I loved my school and my friends. Every few weeks I'd cut homeroom and hang out in "Lovers Lane." That's what we called the top of the stairs on the second floor, east side in front of the math room, next to the restrooms for an easy getaway. There were a few regulars that hung out there in the mornings, not making love or even petting, just not going to homeroom. We'd talk and play around, harass people who walked by and create devilment. It was one of those times that I tried smoking a Kool cigarette in the bathroom with Mackie, but I got sick as a dog. I threw up. The room was spinning, and the girls in the bathroom were laughing at me. I left cigarettes alone. Being KOOL was not for me.

Hanging out in the morning missing part of homeroom got you marked tardy. The trick was to go in just near the end of the period so you could be marked tardy in the office before it was an absence and the secretary called home. No way could I explain even a tardy because my parents knew that I caught the bus and should have been at school on time, but homeroom was boring, and I could not stand listening to Mr. Jenkins every day. Usually, Steve Sterling (Dent) was hanging out there too. He was called that because he had a dent in the middle of his head. We just harassed folks and clowned around joking and laughing until one night I had this nightmare. I dreamt we were hanging out as usual and Dent was sitting on the railing when I accidentally pushed him in the chest, playing, and he fell off the railing and down the stairs. I woke up terrified. That cured me of cutting homeroom. I took it as a warning, but only for cutting homeroom. I'd usually end up there at least once a week for getting put out of math class.

Mr. Reynolds, our great math teacher, had left and he was now at the University. SU was raiding our school to try to fill the gap of the PhD's that left over the student Civil Rights Walk-Out. So, we had a new math teacher, Ms. Chaos, who really didn't know how to control us. She had been our student teacher under Mr. Reynolds, and she knew Algebra II, but she just had no discipline. She introduced a topic on Monday, reviewed Tuesday, Wednesday and Thursday and had a test on Friday. The smarter students who understood the work by Monday after class or at least by Tuesday would just start jokes or something to disrupt the class, and Ms. Chaos would put them out in the hall. So, we hung out in Lovers Lane.

On an average middle of the week for math, five or more of us ended up in the hall telling jokes and clowning around. On one of these occasions the girls started talking about who was the best kisser. Joseph McGee ended up being the number one choice. I had never kissed him. In fact, there was only one person that I had kissed, but this day I really had the devil in me. His ears must have been burning with us talking about him because just then Joseph came walking down the hall. I informed him of the verdict, and he just smiled. He had gorgeous eyes, and they were twinkling. Without saying anything, he put his arms around me in a bear hug, slightly bent me backwards over the railing and kissed the fire out of me leaving me breathless. When he finished and I could talk again, all I could say was that he had my vote. He is still number one in my book for kissing. He walked off smiling without saying a word. He enjoyed his work and took it seriously.

Another thing that we'd do when we were put out of class and were just hanging in the hall was to play "Pick a topic." We started this game with Paul Domingue, Carmen Williams, Marion Greenup, and me. Robert Ford wanted to join us and we eventually let him play, but he threw our numbers off from four to five making the teams uneven. When we'd come together, one of us would say, "Pick a Topic," and someone else would throw out one ranging from abortion to war to Civil Rights, to existentialism to right to die and more. Another person would narrow it down. Then the person who suggested the topic chose the affirmative or negative and picked a partner; the two remaining people had to take the opposing side. We'd debate an issue right then and there whether we agreed or not with the position. This game kept us on our toes for what was happening in the world and made us think about all perspectives, and it kept our minds actively engaged in academics. Thinking back this was an extraordinary game for "play."

In the Spring, Muhammad Ali (then called Cassius Clay) and Wilma Rudolph visited our school while they were attending the Pelican State Relays at the University. They had both won gold medals at the Olympics and were there as role models, inspiration, and motivation. Wow! What an event. Classes were cancelled, and we all reported to the gym. I left the gym before the end of Ali's motivational talk to see his new red metallic convertible Cadillac that had been given to him for winning. Someone told me that Dundee had given it to him for signing and going pro. All I know was that the guy who was watching it let me and two other girls (I don't remember who they were) sit in the car. We sat on top of the back seat smiling and laughing too hard. When Ali arrived, he shook our hands. No one knew that he would go on to be "The Greatest" fighter of all time. He moved Joe Louis out of first place.

The finale of the year was the Junior-Senior prom. The 60's proms for Blacks were held in the schools' gymnasiums since the only other venues open for Blacks would have been nightclubs, and that was not an option. Our theme was Tahitian Holiday. The tradition at our school was for the juniors to give seniors a prom. We had to pay for the band, the decorations, and the food. We really didn't want to do anything for the senior girls, but we couldn't break tradition. We did research to make authentic decorations for the gym with real plants foraged from the campus ravine to look tropical. Mackie led the way, and we all followed like a bunch of nuts down in the ravine. There could have been poisonous snakes or spiders or any of Louisiana's deadly indigenous creatures, but we persevered going back and forth until we had everything we needed. I was scared to death but when Mackie summoned, we followed her anywhere, maybe even to death.

We created indigenous Pacific Island homes and trees, but the most remarkable piece was the volcano that encompassed the stage. A professor from the University helped Jewel Richardson and Endas Vincent build the volcano using a frame and paper mache'. It erupted that night every half hour spewing smoke and flames (lights) that made the evening magical. It was as large as the entire stage with lights and greenery making it look real. The gym was totally transformed into a Tahitian island. My father still did not permit me to date. He drove me to the dance, just the two of us, walked me to the door of the gym, spoke to the class sponsors, and picked me up afterwards. In spite of that embarrassment, I still had fun. Mama had purchased this lovely, long, pink gown with spaghetti straps and a dirndl skirt. The bodice had tiny pearls all over the front and back. Naturally, I didn't like it, but everyone complimented me and I enjoyed the night.

I shouldn't have been embarrassed, though, because two thirds of our class girls were still not allowed to date. I was not alone. My parents told me that they were not going to be one of those fathers or mothers lamenting over their elementary, junior high or high school student who they can't control or who may be on drugs or alcohol or pregnant with no one to blame but themselves. They said that they were parents, not my peers which, meant that they called the shots and didn't care about what any other parents did. "When you give a child adult freedoms, they will try to be adults without adult responsibility or adult accountability. That's why adults are supposed to be parents, not friends. It is our responsibility to supervise and take care of you so that one day you can be independent. But until that day, we are in control." My parents kept me so busy in school with homework and extracurricular activities that I didn't have time to do anything else. I was well supervised. No TV raised us and they definitely did not try to be my friend.

Our family came first in all of our activities. My father and mother were the greatest role models any child could aspire to imitate. Now that Daddy was involved intently in the desegregation of the East Baton Rouge Parish School District, I could see that it would be coming soon. I remembered the Little Rock Nine and Ruby Bridges and became fearful that my time was near. New Orleans began their integration in first grade and Little Rock in high school. Ruby, a baby in New Orleans, was taunted, spat upon, jeered at by crowds of racist protestors, and threatened with her life. If those racist pigs could act like that towards a baby, they were truly not human. I tried to imagine what she felt as I began to get nervous about the desegregation in Baton Rouge.

The governing bodies of our city and state always planned everything for failure instead of success. They did not want change, and anything new was doomed before it began, especially as it related to interaction between the races. Deep down inside me there was a gnawing sensation that daily left my gut twisted causing bouts of diarrhea. This is when my IBS (irritable bowel syndrome) began. Somehow I knew my turn to face the ugly reality of desegregation was coming. With the ultimate decision resting with the school board, I knew they would plan the worst possible scenario to deter Black students from attending the white schools.

Just as I feared the summer of my junior year, the summer of 63, the East Baton Rouge Parish School Board announced its plan. Their plan began with the 12th grade of high school, "My senior year!" The seniors would be the only students allowed to transfer to white schools. "Oh, God! Why me?" I knew I had to go. I could not let my father down. He had fought so long and so hard and now the decision was resting here with me, for him and for history. He used to promise me when we passed Baton Rouge High School that one day I'd be there and he kept his promise. As soon as the announcement was made and even before it went public, Daddy told me the decision. He asked me to sit down and he called Mama to sit with us. Then he said, "The board decided to begin desegregating the schools with the 12th grade and each year thereafter add one more grade level descending one grade at a time. You know how important this is for the city and the country and for Black children. You don't have to go. We can shelter you and always give you the best education. I can afford to do so, but there are many Blacks that can't offer their children the same opportunities as you have been given. We've traveled and stayed in nice hotels, and eaten in nice restaurants and been to Disneyland and Knott's Berry Farm and Pacific Ocean Park. You will be able to go to the university of your choice whether you do this or not. I'm not forcing you. You don't have to make this sacrifice. I'm not going to feel any differently about you if you decide not to go. It must be your decision. You will be giving up a lot and it will not be easy. Your mother and I will stand by you and love you whatever you decide. Don't say anything now in haste and emotion. Think about it and weigh the pros and cons. We love you."

My decision. I knew I had to go and that I didn't have a choice. I had been fighting with Daddy since the boycott in 1953 over ten years ago. I had been to court with A. P. Tureaud when he was arguing various Civil Rights cases. I had been to court with Johnnie Jones when he represented Donald Moss and Melvin Tolsen, the expelled leaders of the mass walkout and demonstration at Southern. There was no choice for me.

I knew I didn't want to destroy my senior year by transferring to a white high school. I had too much to look forward to as a senior at "The Lab." I had been with my classmates since seventh grade and we stuck together in good times and bad, but the real reason was the band and Mr. Freeman. Our band had come from nothing but squeaks and wrong notes to State Champions, and I was president. I loved that band. In just a few years from nothing to greatness, I had given my all. Nothing stopped me from going to practice. Never had I worked so hard for anything or been so dedicated. It was my true passion. My life revolved around the band.

All of my great Lab memories ran through my mind. I just couldn't leave now with the senior class trip going to New York and D.C., signing the memory books, class night and graduation. All I wanted to do was walk down the aisle with my friends, receive my diploma from Southern High, and sing the Alma Mater. Giving up all of this was too much to ask of anyone. Remembering Ruby Bridges, I would gladly have done this in elementary school or middle school or even the beginning of high school, but my senior year? "No, I can't give up all of my hopes and dreams. Desegregation would have to be done without me. I was not going to do it."

I really did not want to go, but I did want to break down racial barriers and I wanted to show those crackers who I was and I wanted to make the world right, but that meant I had to leave Southern High and I didn't want to do that. I cried for weeks silently at night alone in my bed. I cried riding my bike around the lake, cried as I sat and watched the ducks and the ripples in the water as the stones skipped across. I cried with my friends as we considered leaving each other. But I swallowed the tears in front of Mama and Daddy. I tried to put up a positive front for them as I was bleeding inside. With all the excuses that I made, nothing was noble enough to overcome the obligation that I owed to my Daddy.

The Civil Rights movement. Integration. Desegregation. Better schools. Better educational opportunities. Nothing! No, nothing was greater than Daddy. He left the decision to me, and he had not said another word, but I knew I could not let him down. After all of his hard fought years and sacrifices and putting his life on the line, I could not let him down. What would the people think if I did not transfer? Doc's daughter isn't going to desegregate! How would that make him look? How would he feel? His disappointment in me would be something that I could not bear. People would tell him how sorry they were that his daughter wouldn't go and pretend to understand or blame him for not sending his daughter when he was asking others to make the sacrifice. With less than a week to make the decision, I felt abandoned and defeated. I literally wanted to die...to not exist.

I drove up to Southern High and talked to Mr. Freeman, who did not want me to go. I talked to friends who did not want me to leave. I talked to friends that were going to transfer who had assumed that I was going to do the same, and I didn't have the courage to tell them that I hadn't made up my mind. What if I told them that I wasn't going? Would they change their minds? We cried together while reminiscing about the good times we had. I also cried alone. Mama almost caught me crying one day, but she didn't see the tears, only red watery eyes. She told me that she did not want me to go, but she would respect my decision whatever it was. I knew she couldn't tell Daddy that she encouraged me not to go, but she was always protecting us.

On the fourth day, I told Daddy to send in the transfer slip. I walked into my room and closed the door, then crawled into my bed and balled myself up into fetal position. Holding my folded legs with my arms and hands, resting my head on my knees, I began to cry. I felt like a fetus being aborted … before life begins … you're dead. My high school was the womb that had provided me with warmth, kindness, affection and love. It nurtured me with food, knowledge, and instructions for life. It had wrapped its arms around me with friendships that protected me from harm, and now something foreign was invading that womb … invading my world … forcing this premature fetus into a cold, cruel, hate filled world that would try to destroy it. I was being taken too early. Could I survive not really being totally developed and alive? Could I function on instinct and reflexes while feelings and emotions are nonexistent? Could I become a non-feeling being? I was afraid that if I allowed my feelings to come forth I would drown in my tears. Fearing death I chose to live without emotion and swallowed the tears.

Weekly Newsleader 1963

HOLD BAND TROPHYS — Holding the first place trophy in concert performance for the Southern University Laboratory School, in left photo, is David. Mayes, III as Samuel McCormick of Morehouse Parish Training Schools, holds the second place award. The Laboratory School Band, AA school, won three first place positions during the annual high school band festival held at Southern University. Displaying a second place trophy in marching is Frey Anderson, in second photo. The Laboratory School, having more points than the winning school, lost the first place position by a one minute overtime default. Herbert Davis, Herrod High, Abbeville, holds the trophy for the first place in marching.

State Band Trophy

State Festival Band Award

Weekly
Newsleader
1963

Marching Band Trophy

Wesley and Joseph

The Weary Six
Ernest, Stuart, Wesley, Milton, Maurice, Henry

UNDEFEATED KITTENS — Southern University Laboratory School's cage Kittens are undefeated in ten straight games this season. The Kittens, coached by Larney E. Owens and assisted by Paul Bailey, are the new champions of the Capitol City Kids Basketball Tournament held during the Holidays. The "fighting six", left to right are, Ernest Harding a junior, senior Stewart Freeman, Westley Bean, a junior and the leading scorer on the team, Milton Wicks a junior, Maurice Haynes a senior and senior Henry

Sports
at the
Lab

Junior Prom Volcano

Janice on top,
Marie, Mrs. Patterson, Paula, Lorita, Betta, Veronica

Endas and Ernest
and
"The Volcano"

PART II

Desegregation

The Beginning

Before I made my decision to desegregate, the year had already made history. January 1, 1963 marked 100 years since the Emancipation Proclamation, which really didn't free the enslaved even though that is what most people believe. In 1865 the 13th amendment to the Constitution abolishing enslavement had to be passed to make enslaving human beings illegal, for a second time. After the ratification, Congress passed the Civil Rights Act of 1866 that was supposed to guarantee previously enslaved African people the same rights as whites but unfortunately for Blacks it did not happen. The Civil Rights Bill was vetoed by the president and Congress did an over-ride, passing the bill, but rights for Blacks were not granted. Another amendment was needed to grant Blacks, who had been defined as 3/5 of a human being in the Constitution, citizenship since the Supreme Court had taken away citizenship in the Dred Scot decision. Blacks had now been freed and granted citizenship; a Civil Rights Bill had been passed that gave Blacks the same rights as whites, but Blacks still were denied the right to vote, which was supposed to be a right in this country. So, in 1870 the 15th amendment was passed giving African American males the right to vote.

After the Civil War, Reconstruction, Emancipation Proclamation, ratification of the 13th, 14th, and 15th Amendments, and the Civil Rights Bill, laws were passed that began to reverse these gains and deny Blacks their rights. Terrorist organizations like the klan and white citizens councils and others formed. They lynched, threatened, jailed or forced Blacks into voluntary servitude. The Supreme Court sanctioned "separate but equal" in Plessy v Fergusson (1896), then struck it down in 1954 with Brown v Topeka Board of Education, but most southern school systems remained segregated. Not only were schools segregated but restaurants, hotels and transportation facilities continued their past practices of segregation. Not only were facilities segregated, but Blacks were also discriminated against in jobs, admissions to colleges and universities, salaries, housing and every facet of life from the toilet to the water fountains. These were the new obstacles and barriers placed by the white oppressor to keep Blacks enslaved or at least working at slave wages. This country could not have become a world leader had it not been for the free and forced labor of Blacks, and whites were not willing to change the system without demand and/or revolution. So, in 1963, 100 years after emancipation we found ourselves still fighting for justice, fighting for equal rights, fighting to vote, fighting to live and survive as Black people in the United States of America, the land of the free.

The Civil Rights fight in Baton Rouge began in 1953 with the bus boycott to Rosa Parks/MLK Montgomery bus boycott, to 1960 with the Southern University demonstration to North Carolina lunch counter sit-ins to the Little Rock Nine and Ruby Bridges in New Orleans. The Freedom Bus Riders in 1961 had been under attack until Bobby Kennedy, the Attorney General of the United States, stepped in to protect them. The rise in Black protests continued to escalate across the country, and East Baton Rouge Parish Schools were right in the middle of the witches' brew. The court case to desegregate the schools was moving forward, and the community was getting more and more aggressive in fighting desegregation of any and all kind, but 1963 marked one of the most violent years.

On April 16th Martin L. King, Jr. was arrested in Birmingham, Alabama. This empowered the racists in Baton Rouge to think that they were in control. On Saturday, April 20 in the *States Times Newspaper* (Baton Rouge's afternoon newspaper) there was an article entitled **"Signers of Protest Petition against Integration Listed."** There were thousands of names in the paper of white people who signed this petition against integrating the schools. The petition was presented to the school board. These individuals were not embarrassed to have their names listed in the paper and at public meetings. In fact they were proud to uphold the great southern tradition of segregation, and they were hoping that when other people saw their names against integration that more citizens of the Baton Rouge community would follow suit. The tensions mounted in the community, but Black citizens pressed on. Violence against desegregation intensified across the south but in particular the states of Alabama, Mississippi and Louisiana.

May 1963 the children of Birmingham, Alabama held a mass protest that suddenly turned violent when Bull Connor, Commissioner of Public Safety, turned fire hoses and police dogs on the children. Connor arrested 959 children ages six to 18 on May 2nd. The event was televised; the nation was infuriated.

On **June** 9, 1963 Fannie Lou Hamer was arrested and savagely beaten almost to the point of death by police officers because of her initiatives to get people registered to vote. On **June** 12 Medgar Evers, a field secretary for the NAACP, was shot and killed outside his home in Jackson, Mississippi in front of his children. He was organizing voter registration drives and boycotts, and he was investigating crimes that had been committed against Blacks. The klan shot him to send a message to Blacks that desegregation and voting were not going to be tolerated. From King to Hamer to Evers, these were messages for Black folks to stay in their place. These acts of violence ignited more violence throughout the country once the oppressors realized that there was no containment, repercussions or consequences for their actions, but the murders, jailings and beatings did not stop Blacks from continuing their protests, picketing, and court suits. Evers' death became a catalyst to continue even stronger. The violence had backfired.

National Black leaders called for a mass March on Washington for civil and economic rights to be held on August 28th. It was summoned by A. Philip Randolph, the president of the Brotherhood of Sleeping Car Porters and vice president of the AFL-CIO, who had planned an earlier march in 1941. Other organizers were James Farmer of CORE (Congress of Racial Equality), John Lewis of SNCC (Student Non-Violent Coordinating Committee), Martin L. King, Jr. of SCLC (Southern Christian Leadership Conference), Roy Wilkins of the NAACP (National Association for the Advancement of Colored People), and Whitney Young of the National Urban League. Baynard Rustin, a Black national organizer, was in charge of making it happen with advertising, arranging transportation, providing security and all the other logistics for the success of the march.

A *Morning Advocate* (Baton Rouge's morning newspaper) editorial against the march was posted on July 22nd ending with, "We do not believe that the intelligent leadership of the Black citizens, the kind of leadership that rejected intemperate counsel here in Baton Rouge, for example, will care to become involved in such a venture." This prompted Daddy and Raymond Scott to respond in an editorial that read,

> *... the implied message of your editorial is that local Negroes are satisfied with our progress in the field of Civil Rights and would not become involved in any regional or national effort to protest the snail's pace of desegregation. We have in the past offered our services to those who were ready and willing to find equitable solutions to our problems. We do the same now and expect to continue to do so in the future. We believe it is possible to solve our own problems and to make this an ideal community. The opportunity is ours and of which we can make a capital asset, providing we, the community, are susceptible to progressive changes. The services of the Negro segment of the community are and will continue to be available so long as there is hope. This is an opportunity which we have now in our hands. There are individuals, public and private, who have worked hard for long hours to help solve our problems. There are organizations working full-time towards the same goals. For all of these efforts we are deeply grateful for they are making tremendous contributions to our community and community relations. After having pointed out the necessity of our community to solve its own problems, we feel we would not be honest if we elected to point to the glaring weaknesses. East Baton Rouge Parish School Board*

recently approved a desegregation plan which was sanctioned by the minimum legal requirements, which we doubt that anyone can question the truthfulness of this evaluation. There can be no equivocation, our community is at a very low ebb, when those entrusted with its administration deemed necessary to grant its citizens, or any segment of them, the bare minimum legal requirements in any given area of human endeavors and relationships. How do you determine whether a government imposition should be accepted by its subjects? Certainly, if it is possible, an appraisal of the facts should first be made. Yes, then attempt to negotiate. This should be enough, and in many cases it is enough for the solution to the problem at the conference table. We know that anticipated plans of protest demonstrations in Washington are in a fluid stage and therefore we have no specific plans of our own for now. We feel reasonably sure that no such protest demonstrations will occur, provided normal democratic procedures are followed in Congress. Finally we recognize the basic American constitutional right to protest as exemplified by the Boston tea party. Our participation or non-participation, support or nonsupport of such protest demonstrations will depend upon the total collected facts in the case, as well as in any other case.

After reading Daddy's editorial I knew I had to let my dream of graduating from Southern High die. I had to desegregate. I tried to reconcile myself to the idea of a new school. I thought of making it a new adventure, a challenge. Pressed with my back against the wall, I decided to take the reins and go out and organize to get students together to make this horror a success. Marion was one of the first that openly said she was going from Southern High. My best friend had decided to go. I told her that I was going too only because I felt guilty. I was tormented by the fact that I couldn't let my Daddy down. I knew it had to be done, and I was all for making a difference and changing history, but my bottom line was Daddy.

Marion and I immediately went from friend to friend recruiting from Southern High trying to persuade them to join us in the desegregation. Our first hope was that, even though we had submitted our names, maybe the superintendent wouldn't accept us, but we knew that would be too good to be true. The school board was only accepting Black students to transfer to white schools if they had high academic grades, stable homes that included both parents in the home, good student discipline records, and social and mental competence. We knew our grades and background were more than sufficient. We were Honor Society students. Dr. McKelpin never put any of our antics in our records, which meant we had a great discipline record. Maybe they would find us mentally unstable. We laughed hard at that one. Both of us were a little crazy, but no one knew it but us and our friends at Southern High. Knowing we were going to be selected, we decided we wanted to go to Baton Rouge High. If enough of us went, we could turn that school out. The white folks would never know what hit them. We thought about our courses, and I decided to stay away from any science. I definitely didn't want white folks to know my weakness. Marion could take anything. She was a genius. We would work together to make sure we succeeded, and we tried to think of everything that we needed to fortify ourselves to maintain our sanity and dignity.

Dignity and humaneness were ethical considerations that we never lost sight of in all our planning. Whatever we thought of as part of our protection, we always considered the ethics behind it. Our mothers had instilled in us from childhood that whatever we did was a reflection on our family, and we were to act appropriately at all times. We were told to never lower ourselves to someone else's level. If ever we were confronted with trash and filth, we should not put ourselves in a position where an outsider may not be able to differentiate the "chaff from the grain." We had to maintain our dignity at all costs. We were told to ignore name calling or insulting words. "Sticks and stones may break my bones but words will never hurt me." HA! We knew that wasn't going to work. How long could you take insults without responding in some way? But we had to find a way that did not make us act like them. Our strategy became whatever names we were called, our response would be, "Your Mama." For some reason after white folks have called you every name under the sun, talking about their poor white trailer trash wanna-be Southern Belle Mama really hurt them. This was the best way to get back. We would not call them all the names I just mentioned or succumb to trite profanity, which is what I would have loved to do. Instead, our simple response was, "Your MAMA," with our heads held high. We tried to think of other nonviolent strategies or ways to respond without dehumanizing ourselves, but it was very difficult not having been put in a specific situation. We knew we would find the appropriate response when needed. Both of us were pretty quick on our feet. We felt like we could handle anything. We would be invincible.

The next week Marion and I were together every day recruiting other students by talking to friends and their parents trying to convince them that the more of us there were, the better we all would be. The students that were applying began to meet at Bethel AME Church on South Boulevard, which was Daddy's church. One of the first students that applied, even before Marion and I, was Doretha Davis, whose mother was threatened with losing her job if Doretha transferred, but Doretha and her mother refused to be intimidated and both came to the meetings. Her mother defied her employer saying, "If that's the way you feel, I guess you'll have to fire me. My daughter wants to go, and I'm going to stand behind her." I remember this because it just made me realize the conviction and the sacrifices people were willing to make to do what needed to be done. I felt as if we were carrying the future of the entire Black race on our shoulders. I knew I would have to succeed, as would we all. As I thought of my petty reasons compared to what Doretha and her mother were risking, I felt even more ashamed for considering myself first, before the greater good of Black people and future generations.

A few days later an article appeared in the *State Times,* **"30 Negroes Asked School Transfers."** Day by day the newspapers continued to count the number of Black applicants who were requesting transfers to attend the white schools. As of August 7th, 47 applications from Negro students had been obtained. The plan adopted by the board allowed 12th grade students to transfer to white schools with only a 10 day enrollment period set by Judge E. Gordon West to begin Monday, July 29th. The judge allowed the review of the applications, which included 16 criteria to disqualify an applicant, by Superintendent Lloyd Lindsey. No other school district or school had such regulations for enrollment. Daddy protested the criteria, but the judge allowed it since this was the first time for desegregation in Baton Rouge. West and Lindsey justified the criteria by saying that they wanted all the transferring students to be successful. Since when did they start caring about us? More criteria included not only the student's academic record but also their parents' financial condition, as if being poor was a prerequisite for failure. When the cut was made, we went from a group of 47 down to 28. Almost half of us were gone. There were only a few guys because if boys transferred they would not be eligible to play sports. They would be red-shirted for a year, which caused most boys not to transfer since that might make them ineligible for athletic scholarships for college. Recruiters would not be able to see them play.

After the final cut, we filled out transfer cards with the school's name that we would be attending. Mine was not accepted. I had requested Baton Rouge High; I did not know that I was not in that district. I was in the district of Robert E. Lee High whose colors were red and gray, the Confederate colors, and whose mascot was the confederate rebel. After all of the recruiting of friends and our plans of being together, I was being sent away all alone to a confederate school. I wanted to secede from the union and go back to Southern High. We were in a meeting at Bethel when I found out. I had to quickly swallow the tears that were trying to escape along with the salty brine taste in my mouth making me feel like I was going to regurgitate. Somehow I managed to keep all my innards contained while maintaining my composure to listen to the rest of the school assignments. There were three guys from McKinley assigned to Lee High with me. I didn't know them. The three Black guys were Louis Morgan, Melvin Patrick, and Murphy Bell. Murphy Bell was the son of Attorney Murphy Bell who assisted in some of the discrimination cases. There were only four of us. I would be the only girl at Lee High. I wanted to scream, "It's not fair! I'm going to be alone!" I wanted to throw a tantrum and beat on somebody and kick the pews but it was too late to change my mind. Daddy was already bragging about his girl going and our names were already known to the Black community.

Soon after the school assignments, shit started. At night, cars would speed down the street and eggs and rotten fruit were thrown at the house. Mother stopped the boys from playing in the driveway and front yard because once, while they were riding their bikes in the driveway during the day, rotten fruit was thrown at them. The klan burned a cross on the empty lot directly in front of the house again. Dead animals, like rats, possum, and even cats were found hanging from our front porch. The audacity that people had to come up to the house to threaten us. Mama and Daddy even stopped all of us from answering the phone because of the threats and defamatory language. Our phone was tapped to spy on us and find out what was going on in our home. You could actually hear the click and the open line when someone else picked up. Mama and Daddy knew not to say anything sensitive on our line. Sometimes Mama would just start talking terribly about white folks and when she finished she'd say, "I hope you got an earful." Where were the police? They were never around when you needed them. Their excuse was that they had more to do than just patrol Christian Street. I always thought the police and the FBI were behind most of the harassment. Later in the 1990's, the public found out about COINTELPRO, which was an FBI operation to keep track of Black "terrorists" by phone tapping, surveillance, and infiltration of Black organizations. The operation was under the guidance of J. Edgar Hoover, director of the FBI. What few people knew was that the Japanese camps of World War II were being prepared for the Blacks of the 60's. And we thought we lived in a democracy.

With the start of the violence, Daddy, Wade Mackie (a white Quaker who worked with us), and Raymond Scott met. They were the committee that took care of all our needs. They realized more protection would be needed. Some of the parents became apprehensive even though most of the attacks were happening to my family. The names of the transfer students had not been made public, but the Black transfer parents feared what might happen once school began and the public knew who the students were. Parents were afraid for their children, which was perfectly natural considering the climate in Baton Rouge. Their questions were, "How are the children going to get to school? Who is going to protect them on the school campuses? Would they be able to participate in school activities?"

Daddy, Wade, Raymond and the others began with the transportation issue. The school board said that they would provide school buses but that they could not guarantee our safety. Daddy knew that we would not be safe on a school bus, which made that possibility null and void. He would not allow us to drive our own cars arriving at differing times, going to and from a car by oneself or someone vandalizing the car, but more importantly no one ever wanted one of us alone on the white school campus. There were no parents that could commit to drive every day. So, the committee had to come up with a transportation solution. TAXIS! The NAACP and the community, along with Daddy, Wade, and Raymond, paid for taxis to bring us to school for the entire year. There was one taxi for Lee High, two for Glen Oaks, one for Istrouma, and three for Baton Rouge High. There were Black taxis in the city but none could afford to donate their service for a morning and afternoon pick up the entire school year, so that became a major issue.

Meeting with ministers and community leaders, the committee raised funds and hired taxis to take all of the students to and from school on a daily basis. Black businessmen Horatio Thompson and Earl Marcelle, owners of gas stations, volunteered to provide gas to those taxis at a reduced rate. The churches, Black businesses, Black social and civic organizations and individuals paid for those taxis. Many times during the year the money ran out and there were special drives, and many times Daddy and others just paid out of their pockets, but somehow the community managed to support us for the entire year, and I want to say thank you to the Black community. We would not have been able to survive without the protection afforded by those private taxis.

Wade Mackie suggested that we might need tutors and a place to meet to debrief and share stories for encouragement during the year. The committee then solicited volunteers from the community for tutors and the YWCA became our meeting place. Committee women Ms. Simmons, Ms. Shade, Ms. Roberta Tyson, Ms. T. Lois Tacneau, Ms. W. W. Williams and others took over the task of finding the volunteer tutors, providing refreshments on Saturdays when we met, and overall just being there to counsel and let us vent. I remember two of my tutors: Dr. W. W. Williams for math was Carmen Williams' father. She was one of the students at Glen Oaks and a former "Pick a Topic" partner. Her father, Dr. Williams, taught math at Southern. My other tutor was Dr. Harry Faggett who taught English at Southern and helped me with my research paper. They were both wonderful. Any time of the day or night did not matter to them. If there were a problem, they were there to help, and I truly appreciated them for all that they did. With the major plans in place, we were just waiting for the final selections.

Guest speakers were brought in to talk to us about nonviolence and how to handle difficult situations if needed. We had a mock lunch counter drill where people stood over us and called us names and threw stuff on us. We were supposed to sit and take the insults without responding. That was the hardest activity I experienced. I wanted to throw the stuff back and literally fight back. When it was over, I told them that I could not and would not tolerate that kind of abuse. I was not non-violent. They laughed at me but I was serious. The speakers tried to think of everything to help us get through the year while maintaining some sort of normal fun teen social life in the process.

Another guest speaker who talked to us about nonviolence and how to handle difficult situations was totally ignored by Marion, Gail Vavasseur and me. We never really heard what the speaker was saying because every time he came up with a nonviolent way to resolve an issue, we were in the back thinking of violent ways to respond to each example. We heard about all the things that might happen to us and how hard the isolation was going to be, but we'd heard the stories before and they all just went in one ear and came out the other. We had each other. They couldn't really bother us as long as it wasn't physical. There was no way that their words or isolation could hurt us. We were not looking for social life with them because we (Blacks) really had nothing in common with them. None of us wanted to talk or walk or look or dress like whites. There was nothing in them that we admired. We liked our Black world and culture and intended to keep it that way. At 15 years old how could we fathom that anything detrimental could happen to us? At that age things always happened to other people, not you. So we were not going to be affected. Again, we were invincible!

I knew that I was so smart that I could compete with anybody whether they were white or anything else. I never felt inferior to anyone except Marion, the genius. I knew I had traveled and done as much as most whites, if not more. I knew I dressed better. I talked better than them. I didn't even have a deep southern accent sounding country and stupid. My cousin Bernard Parks in Los Angeles made sure of that.

Every summer and every holiday when our family would visit, he'd laughed at me so badly and tease me that I worked very hard to get rid of my southern accent. I succeeded too. Most people didn't recognize that I was from the South. That was a compliment. I knew that I talked better than any student I'd meet at Lee High. I didn't walk dumb like them, slew footed or on my toes looking silly. I just could not envision that I was going to have a problem. I had even convinced myself that once the white students got to know me, they were going to be my friends. How could anyone not like me?

I believed that the people who hated Blacks were the ones who were ignorant and poor or who had never come in contact with Blacks before. If this were the case then the middle and upper-class intelligent whites would not perceive me as a threat. I would open their minds. They would at least be receptive to something new, me, which should not include hatred. I believed that the stereotypes that I thought were driving the hatred could be changed. Some of the stereotypes that I heard were "Negroes stink" or "Negroes are dumb" or "Negroes have tails" or "Negroes don't wear shoes" or "Negroes sit on the curb eating watermelon grinning." There were many other stereotypes I had heard, but I thought I could change them, and the stereotypes would vanish once they had contact with me and my friends. If they just gave us a chance, they would immediately see that we didn't fit those stereotypes and hatred would vanish. Just give us a few weeks of class to let them see that we were smart, talented, and could compete with anyone. In fact I had projected by the end of the first grading period that I was going to win over their minds and attitudes. So I felt pretty confident that I would definitely be on top of this situation. All 28 of us would break down the barriers and change the country's hatred for Blacks.

The next few weeks we continued to go to meetings and make plans for the school year. Marion and I had talked to Mrs. Herson at the Lab and she assured us that all of us who desegregated would be welcome to participate in any event at the school, including graduation. The Lab school was traditionally closed to outsiders except by invitation. Thus we would have been limited if we were not someone's date at any of the schools dances. We truly appreciated Mrs. Herson's special invitation. Fortunately the adults realized what a horrific year we were going to have, and they tried to soften the blow as much as they could. All of our Black high schools extended the courtesy of permitting us to participate in school activities including dances, athletic events, and any other special events and days to help us protect our sanity.

David Brinkley and Ed Bradley of the Huntley-Brinkley television national news show flew down and conducted an interview with the students who were going to desegregate the schools. The newsmen set up at Mount Zion Baptist Church. I thought that this was strange how Mount Zion became the focus when it had not participated in any of the other sessions. Why wasn't it at Bethel? It was also strange that only the light skinned students were called for the interview. When Daddy and I got there he immediately perceived what was going on and got on the phone to make a few phone calls. He then got back in his car and picked up some of the darker students and brought them for the interview. One in particular was Doretha Davis. David Brinkley interviewed the students. He also interviewed Rev. Jemison and John G. Lewis. Both of these men were community and national Black leaders, but neither of these men had been directly involved with the desegregation. However, white folks decided who they wanted to represent Blacks. See, they know everything, including who speaks for us, and the Blacks that they selected were the chosen ones of white society, not ours. The men who were really doing the work and had our backs were not interviewed. When the interviews finally aired on national news, I was highlighted asking the question, "What should we do if there is violence?"

Even though the world felt like it had stopped moving and there was nothing else going on but our planning for the desegregation of the schools, the world did not stop. On the same day of the desegregation article there was another article on desegregation, **"Lunch Counters Serve Negroes in Baton Rouge."** Twelve major stores in downtown Baton Rouge and the shopping mall desegregated several lunch counters. It was a coordinated effort taken mainly by national chain stores and a few local stores that decided to desegregate by a prearranged schedule. This major effort was undertaken by the merchants and the Baton Rouge Biracial Committee, which Daddy belonged and served as a leader. This article was followed the next day with, **"Negroes picketing several stores in downtown Baton Rouge**." The picket signs were protesting the lunch counters at some of the local stores that still refused Negroes service and also refused to hire Negroes.

Also, during this time, with pressure from the Bi-Racial Committee, the City of Baton Rouge began to hire Negro employees in two areas of service: garbage collection and police. Blacks were not allowed to apply for city positions, but that summer, garbage collection jobs became available on a limited basis along with the positions at the police department. Blacks in Baton Rouge were breaking barriers that had previously been considered impossible because of segregation. Historically, the excuse that the city had given was that Blacks were not qualified. What would be the qualifications for trash collection? Maybe two considerations would be that he could walk and lift. The whites were telling our community that they could not find a qualified Black in all of Baton Rouge that could walk, lift, and empty a trash can. I can't imagine the humiliation that Black men felt when they were told they were not qualified to be hired as a garbage man when some of these men had not only high school diplomas but also college degrees. They had to feel worthless as men and as human beings. Daily their self-concept was being stomped on and even buried with the trash as they went home full of anger and hatred not being able to vent anger at the whites. Many times that anger became self-deprecating through violence or drugs and leaving or just walking out on their families. Another reason that Black men left their families is because the family could be more financially secure without a man in the house. One of the rules for welfare payments was to not have a man in the house. Sorry for that tirade, but we need to understand all of the environmental factors that made me persevere. Discrimination affected everything.

When the barrier was broken for trash collectors, the newly hired Black collectors became celebrities. We would wait to hear the trucks coming down the street, and then people would come out and wave or offer them water. Blacks would walk to the street to say hello and wish them well. They'd smile and wave back and greet their well-wishers. The Black police officers were treated the same. They were not allowed to police the white areas or give whites tickets, but they were in the Black neighborhoods and we were proud of it. They were treated as celebrities also with waves and greetings and offers of food or cool lemonade. Even though they could not go looking for whites, they told Daddy and me that if whites ever bothered us, they would stop them and arrest them. They did carry a gun and were allowed to use it if necessary. After all, they were real policemen!

I was quite happy to have Black policemen on the force that summer because Daddy had bought Mama a new aqua convertible Rambler that I took for myself. The public knew that I was a transfer student, and the threats and harassment continued in all forms and at all times, day and night. Several times I was followed that summer and once even run off the road. I became very cautious and always looked to see if anyone was following me. When I'd see someone, I drove to East Washington Street to Marcelle's Gas Station. I knew I could count on finding a Black policeman in that area or if not there would be a dependable group of Black men at the gas station who would have my back. Once I'd drive into the gas station, whoever was following me went away. I had to stop Uncle Earl (Mr. Marcelle) from getting in his car to chase the white boy who blew his horn and gave me the finger as he drove away. Not only was I in danger, but those crazy white boys put many Black families who tried to protect us in danger. Uncle Earl could have gone to jail if he had done anything to that boy, but the white boy would have been exonerated for his actions.

The white police officers harassed me as much as the white thugs. Daddy and I were on their list. Sometimes they'd follow me for miles trying to catch me doing something wrong. When they continued to follow me, I'd lead them to Uncle Earl's gas station. They, too, would keep driving once I stopped.

Since they couldn't catch me with any driving errors, they tried to arrest me for walking. On one occasion, my friends Cynthia Davis and Anna Jean Howard had come to spend the day with me, and as usual, we ended up walking around the lakes. It was early August and of course the weather was steaming hot in Baton Rouge with 99+ degrees and 99+ humidity. We were wearing shorts and crop tops and of course we thought we were quite "fine."

We walked to the end of Christian Street and then to Bet-R-Store to buy bubblegum. We left the store and walked down Ellisade and picked honeysuckles growing wild on the fences on the white side of the street. One side was white and the side that backed Christian Street was Black. The white side was the back of their houses with fences and garages. After a few minutes of pulling the strings off the honeysuckle and licking the sweetness, we then walked to Morning Glory Street and turned right to go down by the lakes. At the end of Morning Glory, we made a right turn on Lakeshore Drive where we were going to walk by my favorite gazebo. We were walking three abreast, but there was no traffic so we felt safe and secure. When we encountered a car, we'd move to the side of the road to make sure the car had room to pass without any difficulty. This was 1963 and there was not a traffic problem, especially around the lakes. As we began to pass the first house on the left, two white police officers in a patrol car drove by. As they passed us they turned and looked back at us—even the driver turned backwards! Still looking back they ran up on a lawn and hit the garbage cans in front of the house on the right. Naturally, we laughed at them for being so stupid. Ugly rednecks being foolish, looking at young girls had run aground. They didn't like us laughing at them for their accident. So, they turned the car around and came back. Driving up on the side of us they stopped and began the harassment.

Black parents had/have frequent conversations with their children on what to do "if." They knew/know that their children are always in danger. Mama had warned me to be careful whenever police stopped me because young Black girls had been known to have been raped and beaten by the police. When the girl/s were let go it was their word against a white police officer's. The police never had to deny any charges because the young girls were always too afraid to press charges if they were alive. Sometimes the girls were never seen again. They just came up missing. Keeping that in mind I tried to answer the questions without sarcasm or ridicule, but I answered through clenched teeth and locked jaws with deep-set steel eyes looking straight through them. They had no right to stop us, but I also realized I had no power to fight right there. I memorized their badge numbers and the car number. The first question from them was, "What are y'all doing?"

My response was, "We are walking around the lake. Is it against the law?"

"Where do you live?"

"I live at 2135 Christian Street. Why are you stopping us?"

"What is your mother's name?"

"My father's name is Dr. Dupuy H. Anderson and he's in the office now at 3615 North Street, phone number 344-1754."

"I ast you your mother's name."

"I told you my father's name."

With that the policeman on the right side of the car jumped out of the car and opened the back door. He then said, "You're trying to be smart. I'll take you to the Day Tang Shun home (meaning the detention home)."

I replied, "On what charges?"

"Girl, don't you have no respect? Don't you know how to say sir?"

I became belligerent, "'Sir' went out with slavery exactly 100 years ago."

The police officer turn deep red, put his hand on his holster, walked to me and put his hand on my arm. All I could think of was that he was going to throw me in the car and kill me, but I couldn't let him see that I was afraid or he would have done so without hesitation. I turned to Cynthia and Anna Jean and said, "If they put me in this car, walk home, call my father and tell him this badge number, this car number, and to meet me at the chief of police at the downtown station. Also tell him we weren't doing anything but walking." The police officer let my arm go and stepped back. He looked at me and said, "Y'all need to mind your manners and learn to respect authority." He got back in the car and they drove off. I was ready to faint. For a brief moment I was petrified, unable to move or even shake from my fear. I was so very glad that they left and didn't put me in that car. It didn't matter who I was. I could have never been seen again. Cynthia, Jean, and I ran home.

As soon as I got in the house I told Mama, and she called Daddy, and Daddy called the chief of police. Within the next hour the chief returned Daddy's call. Daddy came home and picked me up from the house. He took me to the police station. Mama had me change clothes and this time I was dressed up. Once we entered the chief's office, Daddy proceeded to cuss and fuss and berate the chief up one side and down the other even before the chief was allowed to say good evening. The chief was apologizing and saying he was sorry and that he would get to the bottom of this. I had never seen white folks back down like this, but he knew Daddy, and I guess he knew he would end up in his own jail if he didn't do something. Daddy had already taken a case to the Supreme Court, and everyone knew he had no problem filing suits.

Daddy told the chief that he had been harassed by his officers and that some had followed me before where I had to drive to Marcelle's station for protection. Daddy warned the chief, by putting his finger in the chief's face, "It's one thing for me to be threatened, but I will not stand for you or anyone else to intimidate my children." Daddy continued, "The Black community has worked well with the white community albeit slow and laborious and has not had any major violent racial issues. However, if our (Black) children are now on the chopping block, then we will respond and it won't be pretty." The chief began to stutter and sweat. He promised Daddy that this need not go any further and that he would get to the bottom of this situation and resolve it.

White folks took Daddy seriously. They knew he did not shuffle and smile. He had organized Blacks in the city and registered them to vote. He was a leader in the bus boycott. He was leading the business desegregation. He had run for Mayor and the School Board. He had taken cases to court and won in spite of the racist Louisiana judges. He had gotten an injunction against electioneering too close to the polls, and he went all the way to the Supreme Court and eliminated race on the ballot. In fact the news of the case was published in the Weekly Reader news report for schools. My civics teacher, Mr. Harrison, from Crowley, Louisiana was so proud that he had me read it to my Junior class, and he posted it on the bulletin board. Daddy was a legend in Baton Rouge. Blacks and whites knew him, and whites had to respect him whether they liked him or not.

The chief called in his secretary who wrote all the information, and the chief apologized again. He told Daddy he would find out who and why by tomorrow morning. Daddy drove back home rather solemnly. I think he was thinking about what could have happened to me. I could tell by the look on his face. Occasionally I'd catch him looking out of the corner of his eyes at me. When he saw me looking back, he gave me that big Anderson grin that meant everything was okay. It's called an Anderson grin because when we smile with our hereditary long chins and big wide mouths, it is distinctively Anderson. If you cut off our faces from the nose up, one can tell all the Andersons by their smiles. That smile is comforting when you're facing trouble.

I sat there silently and smiled back, but I was waiting for the storm. I knew I had handled the situation fine, but the first rule was that I should not have been around the lakes. The lakes have always been off limits for that very reason. The lakes were white territory. I guess I had just been lucky that no one ever bothered me before. Yet Daddy never said, "I told you so." I did stop going around the lakes after that, for a while anyway. The second rule was that I was told to not answer back if ever confronted by the police, just memorize the badge and car number and try to get away alive without any trouble, but I had talked back. Daddy didn't say anything about how I handled that situation either. I think he was just relieved that I was not harmed.

The next morning the chief called Daddy and told him he found the officers and the reason they gave for stopping us was that we were walking three abreast blocking traffic. There was no traffic on the street. The officers were the only car that passed us on Lakeshore Drive. The chief sent the officers to Daddy's office to apologize. I wanted to go, and Mama wanted to go too, but Daddy told us to stay home. He said he would take care of it, and he wanted to take care of it. I think he did not want us around in case the situation got ugly and deteriorated into him being arrested and going to jail or worse being shot for his aggressiveness. He talked to the officers alone. His receptionist called us as soon as the officers left. She told Mama that Daddy blessed those officers (told them off, cursed them, threatened them) so badly that she began to feel sorry for them. She said he told them not to ever stop Black youngsters again and harass them like they did us. He told them it was strictly harassment and racism and they never would have stopped white girls for walking. He then told them that he taught his children manners, but he didn't teach us to be smiling, bowing, feet shuffling, or sir answering to anybody, and he'd be damned if any one of us would ever say sir to the likes of them. He then gave them a Black History and Civil Rights lecture that kept them there for over an hour. I wish I could have been there just to see the looks on their faces. I wanted to rub it in some more. Mama was furious. She's always been like a mother lion protecting her cubs. She never had to defend Daddy because she figured he could handle himself, but her hair stood up and her fangs came out when her children were threatened.

Her strength emerged when Robert was ill and when she decided to go back to school. I had seen it all my life in her sarcasm when people thought she was white, but today I saw her anger. If she would have been at that office, she would have torn those white officers apart limb from limb. The night before, she told Daddy what he should say. She really did not want me to desegregate, but she stood behind my decision. She knew I didn't have a choice even though she kept saying if I didn't want to go I didn't have to. She never trusted white folks. Daddy always found some whites that he could work with and believe in, and he did believe that some were decent and honest and that the only way the world would be better is for all people to come together in unity. Mama's response would always be, "But a cracker is a cracker and always will be a cracker so don't ever turn your back." I heard these exact words a year later from a Southern High alumnus, Rap Brown, as he explained to me how he could work with whites in SNCC (Student Non-Violent Coordinating Committee). He warned me that, "When the line is drawn, whites will stay with whites and you'll be left alone to fend for yourself."

The incident with the police officers should have been an indication of what was to come. As more city, state, and national institutions desegregated, the EBRP School Board continued to fight every way possible. They tried to undermine the application process by sending out card assignments to all the Black families in East Baton Rouge Parish. It was a trick to get parents to sign these cards that basically indicated that they were willing to stay at their home school and not desegregate. As soon as this information was known, many Black organizations worked together and sent out flyers in all of the Black communities asking them not to sign the cards. Once the card was signed, parents would face a very difficult and maybe impossible problem of having the child enrolled in another school. Plus, signing would also legitimize the board by showing that Blacks did not want desegregation.

The effort to send a flyer to residents asking them not to sign took money away from other resources that the committee needed for the coming school year. The Black organizations that signed the flyer were the Federated Organization for the Cause of Unlimited Self-Development, Raymond Scott, Chairman; United Campaign Committee, Dr. Dupuy Anderson, Chairman; Commission on Christian Social Concerns, Mrs. Antoinette Fisher, Chairman; Bethel AME Church, Rev. John de Leon Walker, Pastor; East Baton Rouge Parish Medical Association, Dr. Leo S. Butler, President; Second Ward Voters League, Acie Belton, President; St. Mark Methodist Church, Rev. W. T. Handy, Pastor; Wesley Methodist Church, Rev. L. L. Haynes, Pastor; Mount Zion Baptist Church, Reverend T. J. Jemison, Pastor; Capital City Dental Society, Dr. Joseph Dyer, President; Baton Rouge Chapter of the NAACP, Reverend Arthur Jelks, Sr., President.

The meetings continued at Bethel AME Church with the students who applied for transfers to desegregate. Naturally, Daddy, Raymond Scott, and Wade Mackie, the committee, were still the ones making most of the decisions. I'm sure there were other adults present, but those are the ones I remember, excluding the parents of the students. They met with us (the students) to reiterate the difficulties we might face and to give us tactics for strength and support. The meetings gave all of us a chance to meet each other and to discuss what we thought about the coming year. I remember each of us introducing ourselves by name, school, hopes for college, and our major interests in high school. Of course, I was Freya Anderson from Southern High, honor student, and president of the band. I hadn't selected a college yet as long as it was a Black school away from Baton Rouge, preferably Howard or Fisk. Most of us knew each other because there were twelve of us from Southern High. All of the students were Honor Society students from their schools because GPA was one of the criteria for selection. Two of the boys from McKinley High school would have been the Valedictorian and Salutatorian of their class.

Across the state school boards were up in arms protesting the involvement of the federal government in "States Rights" issues especially as it involved local education. The Louisiana School Boards Association directed its leader, Ballard, to ask Louisiana Congressmen to vigorously protest the extension of executive power. They did not want presidential or attorney general interference in local issues. The closer the time came to the March on Washington and the beginning of school, the more racial violence occurred across the country.

On August 14th the local newspaper reported that a white woman in Walnut, California was tarred and feathered because she had associated with a Negro man. In Lake Charles, Louisiana, the klan was burning crosses, and Blacks were being arrested in Plaquemines Parish, about 13 miles southwest of Baton Rouge, for demonstrating under the leadership of James Farmer, head of the Congress of Racial Equality (CORE). Over 150 Blacks were arrested for entering white restaurants and washeterias. The mayor said that Plaquemines is now "reaping seeds planted by the Kennedy boys," and local government was being taken away from the people. A local Black activist Bertrand Tyson responded that Plaquemine would become a ghost town if Blacks refused to patronize the white businesses and went elsewhere.

During these confrontations in Plaquemines Parish, Thurgood Marshall came down to offer advice and encouragement. Blacks had been forbidden to gather in groups. Whites used the "inciting a riot" law for enforcement, but Blacks met under many disguises. When Thurgood came down, they met in a church one night for a "wake." However, the sheriff found out that there was a meeting, and they rode through the church on horseback beating those who were still in the sanctuary with whips and electric cattle prods. There were only a few Blacks left inside when the deputies arrived because word had reached the meeting that the sheriff was coming. As soon as the leaders were notified, Thurgood was smuggled out in a casket and everyone started to leave. When Daddy came home that night, he was almost as white as a klansman's sheet. He told us what happened and that he was afraid, not only when they got Thurgood out, but more so when the deputies arrived. He feared that they were going to lynch the people that had been at the meeting if they had been caught. I think if Daddy could have killed those deputies that night, he would have. I had never seen him that upset.

1963 brought all kinds of protests and change. There was no peace or harmony or calm anywhere. Every time the newspapers came out in the morning and evening, there was always unrest and commotion. We had racial killings, demonstrations, picketing, Black policemen and garbage collectors and now Blacks were beginning another campaign to register to vote. The news reported that nine Blacks registered on August 20th along with 11 whites. We were determined to get more. There were literacy tests to pass that involved knowledge of the Constitution, but worse was a subjective response by the registrar of voters as to the correctness of the response. Many Blacks were denied when they had answered the questions correctly and were proven literate, but there was no appeal process. The bottom line was that blatant racism allowed the registrar to determine who was eligible to register and to refuse the right to vote to Black citizens.

On August 20th I found out that 28 Black students who applied for transfer had passed the screening test. Ten of the original group had not been accepted. I was secretly hoping again that I was one of the ones not accepted, but I knew that would never be the case since Daddy was leading the charge. The school board may have been crazy, but not that crazy. No way would they not admit me. On August 21st, a registered, return receipt requested letter dated August 20th, addressed to Dr. and Mrs. D. H. Anderson was received from the East Baton Rouge Parish School Board Superintendent, Lloyd L. Lindsey. It stated:

> *This is to advise you that the application of your child for transfer from the Southern University Laboratory School to Robert E. Lee High School has been approved.*
>
> *You will report to the office of the Assistant Superintendent on Friday, August 23, 1963, between 9:00 A.M. and 12:00 noon to receive instructions on registration procedures.*

August 22nd the "Tentative Assignments" were made with 14 Black students going to Baton Rouge High, six to Glen Oaks, and four each to Istrouma and Robert E. Lee. The assignments were tentative until we formally accepted the assignment on August 23rd. There was another meeting called at Bethel AME for the 28 students who accepted, with their parents and the core group of people spearheading the implementation, Daddy, Raymond, and Wade. They wanted to make sure that everyone had received their letters and school assignments. I did not want to be the only girl at Lee High and asked for a special transfer, but of course it was denied. I guess Lindsey hoped that I would decline to enroll. I wished I had that option, I did not. So, I was assigned to Lee High with Louis Morgan, Melvin Patrick, and Murphy Bell. The students at Glen Oaks were Merrill Patin, Carmen Williams, and Paula Waller from Southern High and Grace Henley, Yolanda Laws and Winnie Posey from Capitol. The students at Istrouma were Rosa Lee Bowie, Freddie Engles, Rita Guidroz and Gloria Dean Holloway. At Baton Rouge High from Southern High there were Betta Bowman, Elaine Boyle, Charles Burchell, Velma Jean Hunter, Bettye Jemison, Marion Greenup, Aurelius Martinez and Clara Kay Patin. Some of my former classmates from St. Francis Xavier were Elaine Chustz, and Gail Vavasseur. Attending Baton Rouge High from McKinley were Doretha Davis, Irma Harrison, Patricia Wells and Sharon LeDuff.

Daddy and I met with Assistant Superintendent Robert Aertker on the assigned date of August 23rd. He informed us of the process that had taken place for transfer. He reported that I had passed all the criteria as if there was any doubt that I would not. He also told us that the schedule for registration at the school for class schedules would be August 28th.

DAMN! They did it again. They scheduled registration the same day as the March on Washington! Daddy and I had planned to go. He made me a promise that we would be there, but those damn crackers screwed up everything. I know it was done on purpose because registration for all other students in the district was on August 30th. Only the Black transfer students were to register on August 28th. If we had the regular registration date, Daddy and I could have attended the March on Washington and been back in time to register, but I know the whites selected that date to insure that Daddy and other prominent Blacks in Baton Rouge could not attend the march.

The tensions were so high in the community that the newspaper reported an appeal for order made by ministers of the Baton Rouge Ministerial Association. They asked "that there be no congregation of crowds around schools and that all citizens cooperate with law enforcement officers" when high schools opened on an "integrated" basis. This statement was issued on the Sunday prior to the March on Washington and a week before school opened. Newspapers and TV reporters kept referring to this as integration; it was not. It was desegregation and very limited desegregation at that. Integration is to bring together parts into a whole. This, whatever it was, threw a few Blacks into a hostile white environment for slaughter. It allowed a few Blacks to penetrate a previously all white environment in a screened, structured, minimalist, secured arena. By no means was this integration. No one worked freely together in harmony.

On the morning of August 28th, Daddy and I drove to Robert E. Lee. Lee High was a very impressive school with its domed auditorium as the focal point of the campus on the right with ramps and bridges crossing the entrance driveway with long individual classroom buildings that spread out like fingers on an open hand to the left. We drove down the entrance under the ramps to the left side of the dome auditorium. Daddy parked the car, looked at me and smiled. Then he asked, "Are you ready?" I smiled back, "As ready as I'll ever be," but deep inside every organ in my body was trembling. I looked around and thought, "Damn Lee High rebels. I hate you and I hate this place and I hate that I have to be here!" Daddy got out of the car. He walked around to open the door. Usually I would have just jumped out but today I needed the extra security of Daddy taking care of me. As he held the door I stepped out and we walked up the sidewalk to the office on the far side of the auditorium.

Entering the office, a little white lady with fuzzy blonde almost white hair and a big smile said, "Hi, I'm Miss Grant and you must be Free-uh Anderson." I replied, "No, my name is Freya with a long "a." She tried to pronounce it correctly and continued with, "We were waiting for you. Let me get Mr. McGhee, the principal and Mrs. Whitey the guidance counselor." Daddy and I sat in the office and waited for about five minutes. Miss Grant walked back into the office. Then she showed us in to the principal's office. Mr. McGhee was seated behind his desk, and Mrs. Whitey was seated at a small round table to the right of the room.

Mr. McGhee was a short man about 5'5", kind of stubby with graying black hair. He had chubby cheeks and deep dark eyes. He looked like he should've been a big man and someone cut him off at the knees. There was a scowl on his face, and he did not extend his hand for Daddy to shake. Without the offer, Daddy did not extend his hand either. McGhee began literally without a greeting of any kind. He began with, "Mrs. Whitey will help you with the schedule. You need to report to school at 9 AM on the first day. We want to prepare the faculty and students for all this. We hope there will not be any problems."

He motioned us to Mrs. Whitey. She offered a painful smile that was more of a grimace as she waved us to be seated at the table. I wanted to say, "I'm not hearing impaired. You can talk!" I held my tongue and followed their hand signals to the table. No need in making this any worse than it was or prolonging the morning. I already knew the classes I wanted to take, but I didn't know if they would fit in the school's schedule. I had to have a college curriculum complete with English Literature, Trigonometry and American History. PE was also a requirement and the rest of the courses were electives. Of course band would be one of my choices. If I had been at the Lab, physics and French would have been in my schedule, but I decided not to take anything at the white school that may cause me pain and neither of those was my strongest class.

We decided on sociology first semester, economics second semester, physical education, band, trigonometry, English, and American History. Mrs. Whitey explained the layout of the buildings and the schedule of classes with room numbers. She reiterated to report to the office at 9 AM on the first day; I would be escorted to my first class. With the registration completed in less than a half hour and the additional information on school times and where to report on the first day, Daddy and I immediately left the office as Miss Grant smiled and waved good-bye. We hurriedly drove home to watch the March.

My jaws locked. My teeth were clinched. My eyes were like spears that could have stabbed Mr. McGhee and Mr. Aertker's hearts. I was so angry that they made me miss my trip to Washington for that mess that I had completed in 15 minutes. All summer I had planned to be in Washington the day of the March, but instead I had to be at Lee High for 15 minutes of wasted time that literally could have been done by phone or at any time other than this day.

Mama already had the TV on as we ran into the room. The people in DC were still coming, and it looked as if it was going to be larger than expected. Hundreds of thousands of people, Blacks and whites, were there holding hands, smiling, singing and sweating together in the hot sun. There were whites and Blacks together with signs filling the Lincoln Memorial, the reflecting pool, and all the surrounding areas. I swallowed the tears that were burning inside trying to get out. I just kept thinking, "I should have been there!" Daddy was pointing out all the dignitaries that he personally knew or had previously met or that he knew of from Black newspapers and magazines. He was so very proud as he reached out and hugged both me and Mama. There were 200,000 people or more. Blacks had come from everywhere, calm and dignified, on a mission to let the world know that we will not be deterred in our quest for freedom and equality.

Tears filled my eyes. I fought back by not letting them fall. If I had blinked there would've been a flood. Look at all the people. I should have been there. Goosebumps quickly cascaded down my arms. I began to rub the bumps while holding my arms across my chest trying not to explode. The climax of the day was the speech by the Reverend Doctor Martin Luther King, Jr. As he stood there with Congressman Adam Clayton Powell, Baynard Rustin, Roy Wilkins, and others in the background, his melodious voice rang out in beautiful rhythms and verse. Most people remember the "I had a dream" part, but the part that stuck with me was,

> *one hundred years later, the Negro still is not free. One hundred years later, the life of the Negro is still sadly crippled by the manacles of segregation and the chains of discrimination. One hundred years later, the Negro lives on a lonely island of poverty in the midst of a vast ocean of material prosperity. One hundred years later, the Negro is still languished in the corners of American society and finds himself an exile in his own land.*

Yes, he spoke to me….a hundred years later and we're still an exile in our own land in poverty, chained and oppressed. He continued with,

> *we've come to our nation's capital to cash a check. When the architects of our republic wrote the magnificent words of the Constitution and the Declaration of Independence, they were signing a promissory note to which every American was to fall heir. This note was a promise that all men, yes, black men as well as white men, would be guaranteed the "unalienable Rights" of "Life, Liberty and the pursuit of Happiness." It is obvious today that America has defaulted on this promissory note, insofar as her citizens of color are concerned. Instead of honoring this sacred obligation, America has given the Negro people a bad check, a check which has come back marked "insufficient funds."*

I jumped up and hollered, "Preach, Doctor, Preach! Yeah, you're so right! We were given a NSF check and we have no rights of life, liberty or the pursuit of happiness!" I could not guarantee him his points of not *satisfying my thirst with bitterness and hatred* or not *degenerating into physical violence.* My soul force was not that great. I was starting this school year with getting revenge for making me miss my senior year at Southern High. I would try to maintain a high plane of dignity and discipline, but only if the white folks let me. I believed an "eye for an eye." By the time Dr. King got to the dream part, I was exhausted from jumping up and down and hollering like I was smitten by the Holy Spirit in a sanctified church.

You could feel the pride of being there, of being a part of history, of having seen and heard an event of Negro history that would never die. Just watching the people of this country walking together, smiling, holding signs and finally holding hands singing "We Shall Overcome" was a source of strength. Mama, Daddy, Aunt Phine, and I held hands and sang together. Tears slowly dropped from all of our faces as we sang,

> *We shall overcome*
> *We shall overcome*
> *We shall overcome someday, someway*
> *Oh, deep in our hearts I do believe that*
> *We shall overcome someday*
> *We'll walk hand-in-hand*
> *We'll walk hand-in-hand*
> *We'll walk hand-in-hand someday, someway*
> *Oh, deep in our hearts I do believe*
> *that we shall overcome someday*

Almost 50 years later every time the song is sung, I still swallow the tears. Most times I can't even sing it for fear of crying. I just hold someone's hand and sway. The memory of that day in Washington, DC and having to go to Lee High overcomes my body as if I have a loaf of bread rising inside me choking off the breath of life. That day will forever be embedded in my memory. If we had been in a theater, I would have been thrown out because I was talking back, jumping up and down, clapping and yelling. King was wonderful, and I was exhausted. He was representing Blacks across the diaspora, and he was magnificent, but none of that changed anything in Baton Rouge.

We watched television until they stopped the broadcast. We watched the people leave and listened to the comments about the day. Everyone was so full of emotion. We did it! We were unstoppable now. The march gave me renewed strength and power. I had the support of Lincoln, Martin, and Kennedy. I would persevere and succeed.

That feeling did not last for long. Another kink in the desegregation plan was caused by me scheduling band as an elective. Assistant Superintendent Aertker called Daddy and told him I could not be in the band because the band traveled to other school districts and EBR could not guarantee my safety out of the city. Daddy argued that he would take me wherever I needed to go. The final decision was that I could play in the band at the home football games in East Baton Rouge Parish but if the band traveled to outside parish games, I could not go. I did not want to play in the marching band anyway, but I would play in the concert band. I could not envision me in any band other than the Kittens with Mr. Freeman. Whites didn't even march. They walked and only played march songs, not the latest hits and dance routines that I was accustomed to at Southern High. I could not join mediocrity after greatness. My wish was granted. I would only play in the concert band. With that concluded, another crisis was averted.

Labor Day weekend, the weekend before school began I had a party at my house. It was our last fling before school, and we found an excuse to celebrate. It was Anna Jean Howard and Helen Hedgemon's birthday. Jean and Marion were at my house all day. We cooked and baked a cake for the party. We made green icing for Southern High's colors. It looked strange being green, but we didn't have time to make another one. I had learned not to rush while in the kitchen from the incident when I was younger blowing up the oven and having to live with no eyebrows. The thought of maybe repeating this gave me a deep respect for having patience in the kitchen. So we just settled for the green cake and hoped that our guests would at least taste it because it definitely should taste better than it looked. Just about everyone we knew came to that party. There may have been 60 students in the living and dining room. Choo Choo and PaHoo and friends came from McKinley High School in the bottom, the Beauchamps from Scotlandville, my cousin Charles Hightower from Capital High School, and naturally the senior class of the "Mighty Kittens."

I stayed at the door all night saying, "Hi, you're welcome to come in but just don't start any SHIT!" I prayed hard that it would go smoothly without any problems. I had never had any problems with my house parties, but with guys from all the Black schools represented, there was always the possibility of trouble, and Daddy did not need a riot in his living room the weekend before the desegregation. The worst thing that happened was a group of Southern High boys stole the green cake off the table and actually ate it. They said it was good. We laughed until we cried. We really didn't want to eat it because it looked so strange. All we wanted to do was blow out candles and sing Happy Birthday to Jean. That's when we realized the cake was missing, when we got ready to sing and light the candles. All they had to do was ask; we would've given it to them. After we finished laughing, we sang to her without a cake.

As usual Daddy kept coming in the party turning on the lights. He walked through the living room to the dining room and out of the swinging door to the kitchen. As soon as he entered the kitchen door from the living room we turned the lights off again. That was one of the best parties ever. It was more like a reunion, like we knew we were going to be separated and feared losing each other. We talked and laughed and danced and sang and held on as long as we could before Daddy turned on lights and announced, "Good night." With the lights on we continued to talk about the good old times before he came back and finally said, "Good morning." When everyone left Marion, Jean, and I cleaned up and sat up the rest of the night talking. This would be the last time we were all Kittens. On Tuesday only Jean would be a Kitten. Marion was going to Baton Rouge High, and I would be going to Robert E. Lee, home of the fucking rebels.

That damn Lee High would not go away. I did not believe MLK's dream was possible. I didn't want to sit down at a table of brotherhood with white folks or join hands with white girls and boys as sisters and brothers. I just wanted my own table with my own friends, but the same kind of table and opportunities as whites. No way did I believe that Mississippi or Louisiana would ever be transformed into an oasis of freedom and justice for Blacks or that Black children would ever be judged by the content of their character anywhere or anyhow. My stone of hope was in the struggle to get through this year without having to kill someone and end up in jail, alone without anyone praying for me except my Daddy and Mama.

I had decided that I was not going to say the pledge, sing the anthem, or "My Country Tis of Thee," and definitely forget about fucking "Dixie," Lee High's School song. These symbols did not represent me or my people. This country did nothing but oppress Blacks. I owed it no allegiance. It represented white people's lies of freedom and liberty for all. The Constitution was not meant for me and mine. The Declaration was garbage for Blacks. Fight for whom? What? This country did not claim me and I sure as hell was not going to claim it and definitely not fight for it.

On August 29th the paper reported that 28 Negro students registered for classes at their assigned schools the previous day and were expected to begin classes the following Tuesday, the day after Labor Day. Another appeal for cooperation by parents and the public was issued by the school superintendent. Parents were asked not to visit classrooms as Lindsey tried to assure them that all "precautionary steps are being taken to insure the safety of your children." On Monday, September 2nd, Catholic and Protestant churches appealed once more in the news for peace and public tranquility.

Bishop Tracy of the Catholic Diocese prayed for the smooth transition while stating that the Catholic Schools would begin the process in the following school year. If the Catholic Church had such great concern, they should have started prior to the public schools to set an example. Worse was that the Catholic Churches were segregated with Blacks having to sit in the back of a white church if they decided to attend mass rather than staying in their place by attending a Black church (St. Francis Xavier or Immaculate Conception in Scotlandville off the campus of Southern University). Even God discriminated.

On Labor Day, the day before schools opened, an effigy of a Negro was hung from one of the oak trees in front of Baton Rouge High School. The klan burned a cross at Glen Oaks High School, and I did not sleep that Labor Day night. As long as I can remember I have had difficulty sleeping when there was something on my mind. I remember as far back as second grade when I was afraid of not being able to borrow in math; and fifth grade when I planned how I was going to run away; or the two nights I was reading *Gone With the Wind*; or the night I had to plan how to get Mr. Freeman back on the field for practice. Those are specific times, but many nights the mental stress was just an idea that needed to be resolved or a plan to make the world better. I just had a hard time sleeping when there was something on my mind, which occurred often, and these sleepless nights occasionally lasted for days. There were times when I felt manic and obsessed. Those were the times when I needed to ride my bike around the lakes and meditate, but I couldn't do that in the middle of the night. So, I just lay awake and suffered through the torment of not being able to clear my mind.

Labor Day night 1963 was one of the most difficult nights to try to sleep even though I wanted to, desperately. I didn't want bags under my eyes in the morning or to feel stressed and edgy, but I could not sleep. I wasn't afraid but I kept planning the "what ifs." What if there were a mob of racists waiting? What if the students tried to fight? What if the teachers ignored us or called us names? What was I going to do if any of these things occurred? What was I going to wear? After the million questions with no firm answers, I got up and looked in my closet for the right outfit. Settling on one I ironed it and got all the accessories that went with it. I double checked my notebooks, pens, pencils to make sure I wasn't forgetting anything I needed because I knew there was no one to borrow from if I didn't have all the supplies. Finally, when I thought that it wasn't too early to disturb anyone, I went into the bathroom to begin my morning rituals.

With only one bathroom in the house, time was rationed, and I didn't want to be rushed, especially this morning. I had become an early riser since attending Southern High because the bus picked me up at 6:50AM every morning for the hour ride to Scotlandville. I didn't mind because there were always people I knew and cared about, and the destination of Southern High was my favorite place, but the half hour ride to Lee High would be an eternity waiting for hell. As I exited from the bathroom, Mama was waiting. I could tell that she was concerned asking, "How are you feeling? You know it's still not too late to change your mind. Whatever you decide I'm here for you. Do you need anything? What do you want for breakfast?" I don't even remember her giving me time to answer any of those questions. She just kept asking. After all these years, she had acquiesced and allowed me to eat cold cereal, and that's all I wanted. Not wanting to offend her, I just could not bear one of her infamous hot meals this morning.

The shower rejuvenated me. Breakfast gave me a chance to relax. I didn't taste it at all. Mama sat next to me talking and talking. I don't know what she said or even if I responded. Just her being there was reassuring, and I knew she needed to be there with me. I walked to my room to get dressed. I had decided to wear a gray A-line skirt and a gray and white striped shirt with the matching silver gray belt. I put on the standard white bobby socks and gray Golo suede shoes. I felt like I looked pretty good. I was still not wearing makeup or jewelry, just a natural look for a 16 year old. Almost all of my clothes were new from our last California trip. If I had been at Southern High I would have been embarrassed to walk out in all new clothes whether it was the first or last day of school. My friends would have sounded me from one end of the hall to the other (sound means that someone talks about you loudly). Wesley Bean would have begun with, "New shoes! New skirt and blouse! Flashy new belt! Somebody is all new, but I'm not calling any names!" I could hear him sounding me from homeroom to our first class. It would have been embarrassing, but thinking about it that morning made me smile and wish I was at Southern with him.

At Lee High white folks didn't know our customs, so I could wear all new clothes without any fear of harassment. The weather was hot and steamy as usual, which caused me to worry about my hair. The humidity made it wave and curl no matter how large the rollers were or how hot the dryer was or how good the perm was. It may have started out straight and bouncy in the air conditioning but as soon as the door opened and the heat and humidity engulfed it, curls and waves began to move like ripples on a stream. All I could think of was how was it going to look about noon? Mama reassured me that most people Blacks or whites wanted hair like mine, naturally curly. It was pretty and soft, and if it were 1920 with the Marcel Curl style, I would have been "All that," but it was 1963 and waves were not the style. All I knew was that it wasn't straight which was a flaw before becoming "Black and Proud" in the late 1960's. I had to be perfect. I couldn't have my hair "go back" around white folks. They wouldn't understand. I had eaten, dressed, and gathered all my supplies. I was ready to leave my home for hell. Mama made the boys, my brothers, wish me well and give me a hug.

Lee High Rebels

A hug from my brothers was a sign that I was headed for something really scary. Mama had tears in her eyes, but the lateness of the taxi took my mind off of everything, and I began to worry. Daddy was calling the taxi company to find out where it was and what the problem was. The principal, McGhee, had asked us to report an hour later to give him a chance to have an assembly with the student body to prepare them. "Prepare them?" For what? Whaaaat? Were we from out of space or something? What did he expect us to do? He should have prepared us to meet with them!

The taxi finally arrived after two phone calls with Daddy pacing back and forth, nervously anticipating that he might have to drive us. Charlie's Cabs arrived with this big black greasy man smoking a cigar. He was nice, but his cigar was disgusting. Daddy asked him to try to be on time every day because we could not accumulate tardies. The driver, smoking his cigar, smiled and began to describe his morning of car trouble but promised to check the car the night before to make sure everything was fine for the next morning.

His first stop had been to pick up Murphy Bell on Ellisade, the street behind us, then me on Christian Street. I couldn't believe that all these years Murphy lived on Ellisade and I never knew him. After picking up Murphy and me, he drove down Perkins Road to Staring Lane and picked up Melvin Patrick. Melvin lived in a small wood frame home set back off Staring Lane. His home was the poorest of all of us. Last we went to Mayfair Park to get Louis Morgan who lived in this very nice newly built brick home in the new Black subdivision where Daddy had purchased a lot but not yet started building. With all four of us in the taxi we rode back down Perkins Road to Lee Drive. Daddy followed our taxi the entire time. Raymond Scott and other Black leaders followed each taxi to the other schools. I didn't learn until later that federal marshals had been assigned for the orderly desegregation of schools and Daddy, Raymond, and the others were to stay in touch in the event of any trouble.

The four of us sat nervously in the car with very little talking. I tried to think optimistically that the year was not going to be as bad as everyone had predicted. Maybe, after the students got to know us, they'd realize that we were human beings like them. How in the world could anyone hate me after they got to know me? I was cute, smart, well dressed; I smelled good; I was very talented and quite friendly. All of the preconceived notions about Blacks being dumb and lazy, and having tails and a stench were lies. I kept trying to make myself believe that once the white students saw us and worked with us in class, they would know that their ideas about us were lies, and the hatred would cease. What other reason would they hate if it weren't just ignorance? I began to toss the idea around that they would just need a little time to change their perspectives. After all, they had been reared all their lives to believe Blacks were inferior, so change was going to take a little time. As the taxi drove closer to the school I had second thoughts about my great rationalization.

About one block before the school, we could see the crowd. The police were holding the demonstrators across the street from the school. The jeering crowd was not allowed on the same side of the street as the school, but they were lined up the width of the school three to four deep across the street. I could see their white faces and hear the hatred in their voices. I saw only one sign. There were others but I only focused on the one that said, "Niggers go home!" All I could think of was that these were ignorant people. They didn't even know me so how could they hate me so much. I tuned out the noise so I couldn't hear the chants, but I could see the red in their angry white faces. White people were focusing on us, but I had tuned out their hateful words. Their mouths were moving, but nothing was coming out.

Murphy, Melvin, Louis, and I slowly got out of the taxi. Daddy walked over and I hugged him. I asked him not to come in because I did not want any special privileges. I wanted to be treated as all the rest of the Black students who were desegregating that day. I knew he was waiting out front with the taxi, and I really wanted him with me, but I walked alone with the three other guys around the dome-shaped auditorium to the office. It was a long walk; it seemed as if we'd never make it to the office. Murphy was talking about some of the signs. He said they were, "We hate Niggers," "Go back to Africa," "Niggers go Home!" We all kept walking until we reached the office where Miss Grant was smiling and bubbly as ever with a cheerful, "Good morning." Her gracious welcome made me smile whether I wanted to or not. I felt like I could depend on her, one person at least, to be nice in hell.

Mrs. Whitey and Mr. McGhee were waiting for us and took the four of us to our classes. We walked out of the office and across the ramp to the first building. Someone in the crowd started yelling, "Go home Niggers!" Then the crowd began to chant, "Go home Niggers!" The four of us kept walking trying to ignore the yelling. We looked at each other and said nothing. We kept walking looking ahead at the building before us. My jaws locked and I tried to get my head together to get through the day. Mrs. Whitey took Melvin and Louis to their class and Mr. McGhee took Murphy and me. We stopped by the first room on the left of the first building and McGhee told us that this was our homeroom. He left us in the hall as he walked into the room motioning for the instructor to come to the door. He walked out into the hall and McGhee introduced Murphy and me to Coach Cracker, our sociology teacher. He was about six feet tall, sandy or ruddy complexion with a crew cut, his hair standing straight up like he had been electrocuted. He wore khakis, loafers, and white socks, which was typical white boy attire. There was no smile or greeting. He nodded and held the door for us to go in.

Murphy and I walked in the door, which was the rear door of the class. Cracker stayed in the hall with Mr. McGhee looking through the door. We sat down in the last two seats on the last row that were closest to the door. As soon as we sat down the students who were seated in front of us got up and moved to the other side of the room. There were no students in front of us and one entire empty row to the left between us and the other students. Some of the white students begin fanning their hands in front of their faces like they smelled something while others were laughing. Cracker then walked back in the room and sat down and said nothing and acted as if nothing had happened.

Cracker didn't introduce or welcome us or acknowledge us in any way. In fact he didn't even look in our direction. He addressed the students who all moved away from us and began his lecture on sociological terminology. Throughout the lecture he often digressed on several tangents. The students knew his weakness and led him into discussions on cars and the basketball team, which both appeared to be far more interesting to him than sociology. I gathered immediately that he was a know-it-all. He was an authority on every subject asked. I guessed being a coach made him omnipotent. What seemed like an eternity ended, and the class was over. We had been ignored the entire time. Murphy and I sat there looking at each other and saying nothing. When class ended Murphy and I had to split up to go to different classes.

My next class was physical education in the gym with teachers Ms. Sugar and Ms. Spice. Since it was the first day, the teachers discussed the dress code and regulations. All the girls sat on the bleachers. I sat on the first row alone and all the other girls sat above me. We were assigned lockers and I was informed that since I was a senior there was no need to buy a new gym uniform, but that I could wear my Southern High uniform. I told Ms. Sugar that we wore white shorts with a white shirt at Southern High, and she told me that was acceptable. Ms. Sugar spoke to me and told me if I had any questions just come to her. I thanked her. She seemed to be a nice person. Ms. Spice was a short, stocky, muscular lady. She smiled in my direction but Ms. Sugar addressed the class. I don't remember Spice saying anything.

After PE there was a daily 10- or 15-minute recess. Murphy, Louis, Melvin, and I found each other, which was not difficult, and staked out a bench at the end of the walkway from the gym. That space pretty much gave us a view of the entire area with each of us watching every direction for safety. We tried to stay together whenever we could. The first week the students stayed away from us acting as if we didn't exist. They gave us space in the hallways and classrooms by moving far away to make sure they didn't touch us. I felt like we had a deadly plague that was severely contagious, but as long as they were not touching me, I was comfortable.

After recess I went to band. The classroom was across the bridge that went over the entrance drive to the domed auditorium. The director was Mr. Bowen. We auditioned for section chairs, and he placed me as second chair clarinet. Reverb was first chair only because of seniority—and she was white. She was pretty good, but I was definitely better. She stayed in first chair all year. The band room was circular since it was one of the rooms in the dome. No one moved away from me because Mr. Bowen assigned seats. However, no one spoke to me in band either even though I had people on both sides of me. The students talked around me and across me but never to me. I was invisible. After I played for my chair position, Mr. Bowen moved on to other students and that was band class.

From band my next class was trigonometry with Ms. Giesel. I think she was single. The students liked her and she engaged them while maintaining a professional attitude. She was quite competent in math and pressed to challenge students throughout class. She didn't call on me to answer any question even though I raised my hand, and I wondered if she was trying to ignore me or thinking I might not know the answer, be kind to me. I would find out what her motives were later, but she was pleasant, not overtly so. She was a muscular woman with huge calves. I couldn't help but notice how large her legs were and wondered if something might be wrong, but I wasn't there to diagnose or prescribe. She did welcome me to her class as a new student and for the first time that day, I felt like maybe I am in school and I will belong.

Lunchtime! It was so nice to go to the lunchroom. I was hoping that I'd see the guys. Yes, I wanted to see those same guys that I didn't know and didn't want to be with because I didn't know them. They were my refuge and solace now, and I had no one else. As I found my way to the cafeteria, the four of us caught each other's eye and got in line together. We found Black cafeteria workers who spoke to us, smiled at as, and asked us what we wanted to eat. They let us know indirectly to just to let them know what we wanted and we could have more than what was allowed. We always had a nice plate of food. They were so supportive. Just their smiles when we entered the room and their greeting of "Good morning, how are you?" helped us survive. They were the first people that spoke to us, smiled at us, and approved of us being there. They were proud of us, and we were equally proud to have them there supporting us. Their smiles helped to get us through each day. Murphy, Melvin, Louis, and I sat together at the first table on the left as we exited the line at the back of the cafeteria. There were students in the cafeteria when we entered and that was the only table left where no one was seated. We all sat together because we didn't know anyone else, because we needed each other, and because we knew if we tried to sit with someone what would happen. No matter how good the food was, it didn't make a difference because the tension was so strong that my stomach was in knots and all I could do was chew and swallow and swallow and swallow to try to get it to stay down. In the lunchroom there was a table or two of students pointing at us and laughing and talking and turning around and going back to pointing and laughing. I knew they were taunting us, so I tried to ignore them. All I could think of was the mantra, "Sticks and stones may break my bones but words will never harm me." Whoever said that did not understand the power of words. No, words may not break bones, but they bruise and shatter emotions, egos, self-esteem and can ultimately lead to a mental breakdown.

I swallowed hard and tried to prepare myself for the next class, English Literature with Mrs. Helene B. Church. Murphy and I were together again for this class. Mrs. Church was quite rigid in her procedures, but I could tell that she was an excellent teacher. She had planned every minute with precision. When we left her first class we all knew what was expected from now until the end of the school year. She, like Ms. Geisel, welcomed new students, but she went further and asked us to introduce ourselves. She introduced herself and told us where she went to school, that she was married and that she had a dog that she was training to respond to commands in French. There was no disrespect in her class. No one moved away from us. No one made noises or gestures or anything else that may be construed as racist. I could tell by her stern eyes that she did not play and would not tolerate any racism. She offered her assistance to every student in the class and with a nod of her head I knew that Murphy and I were included in the offer. I left that class feeling refreshed and hopeful for the first time that day.

The last class of the day was American History with Mrs. Klan. Just listening to her slow southern draaawl and looking at her extended midriff, I knew she was going to be a pain in the butt. She didn't say anything derogatory, and the students didn't do anything threatening in the class other than move away leaving one seat vacant to my left and right and two in back as I sat in the middle of the first row, but I felt the hairs rise on my arms as goose bumps began to emerge. There was a current of racism emitted from her being that caused me to become very cautious of this woman. She reminded me of a witch with her long fingers and black hair and pointed nose. All she needed was pointed-toe shoes and a broom. Her voice had a whiny tone that seduced you into her spell of hell by pretense of concern. She gave me chills. An hour ago I had hope, but it was quickly dispelled in American History.

This first day three students actually spoke to me. Brownie, the daughter of a prominent real estate agent in the city and a member of the biracial committee with Daddy, walked up to me when I was standing in the cafeteria line. She introduced herself and said if I needed anything she would help me. She said our fathers were friends. I thanked her and told her I really appreciated her assistance and that I'd be sure to find her if need be. Daddy told me about Brownie who was going to be in my class at Lee High and that she would openly befriend me. She was a senior at Lee, but she was not in any of my classes. Thank God I didn't need her because after that day she became invisible until the last week of school. As Mama always said, "A cracker is a cracker is a cracker. They never change."

Another person that spoke to me the first day was Ginny Ralph. She walked up to me after Brownie left and introduced herself. She welcomed me to the school and hoped that I wouldn't have any troubles. I think she was a freshman; she was not a senior. She repeated to us what the principal, Mr. McGhee, told the student body assembly before we arrived. She said he told them that he didn't want these Niggras at the school any more than the rest of them but they would just have to make the best of it. Ginny tried to reassure me that everyone didn't feel that way and to give them time. She was really very nice. Every time she'd see me in the hallways she'd smile and speak. Her smile always said, "Hang in there. I'm with you."

The last person that spoke on the first day was Win. He was in band, Trig and English with me. He didn't hold a conversation but said, "Hi" as we were passing through the hall at the end of the day. First day down and three people had spoken, one teacher was really nice, Mrs. Church, and the cafeteria workers were great. I wasn't feeling too bad. The isolation of people moving away and not talking would come in time. The day was better than expected. Maybe there was hope. Just give it time. That's all we needed. Time to move from hate toward acceptance.

After seven years of fighting the inevitable, East Baton Rouge Parish Schools opened on Tuesday, September 3, 1963 with 28 Negro students enrolled in the 12th grade at four previously all white high schools. The afternoon paper, *State Times* (Tuesday, September 3, 1963, Capital City Press, Baton Rouge, LA), offered a few new details in the **article "BR Schools Admit Negroes Without Serious Incident."**

> *Four East Baton Rouge previously all white high schools were peacefully desegregated today as 27 Negro transfer students attended integrated classes. Of the 28 Negroes approved for transfer to the white schools one was disqualified shortly after she entered Istrouma High School, but she will be replaced by another Negro girl tomorrow. There were minor picketing incidents at Istrouma and Baton Rouge High and a disgruntled Glen Oaks High bus driver was sent home for the day as the*

first Louisiana white public high schools were integrated almost without incident. Istrouma principal Ellis Fuzzy Brown reported a bomb threat at midmorning, but said he ignored the call. He reported to the school board office that a man called with a warning a bomb had been placed in the school, set to go off at 10:30 AM, but he said he knew there was not any way anyone could have gotten to the school to plant such a bomb and the decision was made to ignore the call and label it the work of crank. There was an official report from Lee High and Istrouma that two of the Negro students ate in the school cafeterias with white students. School and law enforcement officials of the parish and city said conditions of the schools were about the same as any normal opening day of a new school year. The Negro girl student at Istrouma, one of four entering that school, was sent to the school board office early this morning when it was discovered she lacked a half credit of being a qualified Senior. The school board office said after the girl met with superintendent Lloyd Lindsey that the girl had failed physical education courses for two years and therefore had not earned the credits needed to make her a full-fledged senior. The school board office said the girl had been advised not to report to Istrouma today but apparently there was a misunderstanding. They blamed it on a clerical error which caused her card to be placed in the file with the other 27 Negro students approved for transfer to the formerly white high schools. The school board office verified the other 27 Negro students showed up for classes today. Three Negro students entered Istrouma, six went to Glen Oaks, four went to Lee High and 14 to Baton Rouge High. The groups at Lee, Istrouma and Baton Rouge arrived in Negro taxicabs. There was only one official report of withdrawal from classes by a white student. It was reported one girl refused to attend classes today at Istrouma, and stood outside the school with her parents. The school board office said attendance at all the integrated schools was normal. Lindsey declined to make a formal statement on the opening of schools today. The Mayor president Jack Christian said he was very well satisfied with the way things turned out. Sheriff Clemens who spent most of the morning at Glen Oaks said, "I want to thank the majority of the parents for cooperating with units of the Sheriff's office in maintaining law and order at Glen Oaks High School. We were there in cooperation with school officials and the East Baton Rouge Parish School Board.

We were not there for the purpose of escorting students in and out of school. We will not escort students in or out of school. I sincerely hope that the same attitude will be maintained in the future as it was demonstrated here today." Police chief Wingate White said he assigned nine officers to direct school traffic at the three integrated schools within the city limits. He said there was one extra officer at each of the three schools in an observatory capacity. However there were reports of considerably more police officers at the school than officially reported. Reportedly FBI agents were seen around each of the four integrated schools. Chief White said, "Everything went off as smoothly as any normal school opening day and nothing out of the ordinary happened." The Negro girl ruled ineligible to enter Istrouma conferred at the school board office late this morning with Dr. Dupuy Anderson and Raymond Scott, members of the biracial committee. Before they left Dr. Anderson said he would have to check the records before making a statement. Meanwhile the school board announced officially she would not be admitted to Istrouma and would be replaced with another Negro girl tomorrow. The only serious picketing was at Istrouma some 45 minutes before a general assembly at 8:30 AM. A man showed up on the 38th St. side of Istrouma just across the street from the auditorium, carrying a sign saying: "Don't go in the school" and "Students do not let those Negroes stay." City police confiscated the sign and asked the unidentified white man to leave. He later left in a red car. A small group of students who had gathered around the picket were dispersed by principal Brown. Across the front entrance from Istrouma several high school aged students stood on the front porch of a private home next to a sign reading, "Token today – taken tomorrow." However they removed the sign and went inside the home when approached by a newsman. At Glen Oaks Mrs. Ethel Falconer of 5035 Prescott Road, a school bus driver since 1946, stopped her bus in front of the school and announced to no one in particular she would say what she wanted to say whenever she wanted to say it. Principal Pat Roberts asked the Sheriff's deputy to ask bus drivers to move their vehicles away from the school entrance. Mrs. Falconer moved the bus a short distance away, and returned to talk with another driver. At this point Superintendent of schools Lindsey instructed Roberts to have the bus drivers take their vehicles away from the school. Later Lindsey ordered Mrs.

Falconer home for the remainder of the day. This is a report on the entrance to each of the four formerly all-white high schools by Negroes for the first time.

*   **Lee High School.** Three Negro boys and one girl arrived in the Negro taxicab at 9 AM accompanied by one Negro man. They disembarked at the front of the school went directly to Principal C. G. McGhee's office for a briefing on school routine before being taken to home rooms by the principal. Some 975 white students met in assembly before the Negro students arrived and heard McGhee say, "We have always had cooperation here. We appreciate that fact. I expect it will continue." Then all students except seniors were asked to leave the meeting and McGhee told the seniors: "The people we have coming here for the first time are all seniors. You'll be in class with them. What you do is what the others are going to do. We've been together for a long time and this is just another problem we have to face. We are soliciting your cooperation." The seniors showed no visible reaction to the talk. **Baton Rouge High School.** Twelve Negro girls and two boys arrived in three Negro taxicabs at 9:00AM without incident. With only a small group of onlookers across Government Street they walked to the school entrance with a Negro man and went into the school. Principal Dennis F. Byrd said the Negro students will leave school this afternoon at the same time as white students, but have been asked to arrive tomorrow morning just as the bell rings for school. Byrd said he planned to, "Play it by ear" regarding school dances and other school activities at the school in the coming year. But he added, this did not mean there were any plans to cancel any school activities. **Istrouma High School.** Four Negro girls arrived in a Negro taxicab at 8:25 AM, entered the auditorium for general assembly and took seats on the back row virtually unnoticed by white students. Principal Brown told students he expected them to handle any problems that arise with "Dignity." The students then dispersed without incident to home rooms. **Glen Oaks High School.** One Negro boy and five girls arrived at 8:55 AM and were taken into the library for orientation and assignment of lockers. At the same time white students were holding a student body assembly in the auditorium. Principal Robert asked the six Negroes not attend today's assembly. The students later scattered to classes without incident. At Glen Oaks parents parked some 20 to 40 cars in front of the school but were*

persuaded to disperse at 9:30 AM by Sheriff's deputies led by Sheriff Brian Clemens. Integration of the four schools here today culminates an eight year campaign by the NAACP for opening of East Baton Rouge Public Schools to Negroes. School officials today declined to release names of the Negro students, contending it would serve no useful purpose and that normally names of transfer students are confidential until they are settled in a new school. Educators here expressed students will accept the Negro students without incident, but asked parents to help preserve order by staying away from school for at least the first week of the new term. James Winfree, chairman of the local biracial committee, the first in Louisiana, today said in a prepared statement: "The citizenry of Baton Rouge is proud of their community and their heritage and certainly they are law-abiding, peace-loving and God-fearing. Aside from this they are an educated people. They realize that ideas and principles are constantly undergoing revolution." Catholic Church officials of the new Baton Rouge diocese said recently Catholic schools will be integrated next year. New Orleans diocese Catholic schools are already integrated.

The next day the *Morning Advocate's* (Wednesday, September 4, 1963, Capital City Press, Baton Rouge, LA) front page article was, **"No Major Incidents As Negroes Attend BR High Schools."** The four high schools were guarded by police and FBI. The paper reported that "the white students completely ignored the Negroes during classes and in school cafeterias at lunch hours." A telephone bomb threat was received at Istrouma High School but it did not disrupt classes for the day. The news was almost identical to the State Times article the evening before.

Baton Rouge High School

Approximately a dozen spectators were on hand as 12 Negro girls and two Negro boys arriving in three taxicabs entered Baton Rouge High School at exactly 9 AM. Some of the spectators were obviously from outside the Baton Rouge High School district, but practically all were gone from around the school two hours later. At noon the Negro children marched to the cafeteria with the white students then sat at separate tables. At one point a Negro student reportedly sat at a table with a white youth, but the latter left at once. Generally speaking the white students ignored the presence of the Negroes. At 3 PM when school was dismissed, the 14 Negroes walked out the front door with the rest of the pupils and entered waiting taxis. Their presence aroused not even a ripple. One white boy boarding a bus wanted to know why he could not have a taxi, but otherwise there were no remarks pass. At Baton Rouge High School police officers kept spectators off the school grounds.

Lee high school

No spectators were present at Lee when three Negro boys and one Negro girl arrived in a taxicab accompanied by Dr. Dupuy Anderson, a Negro member of the city's biracial committee. Anderson left with the cab and did not enter the school. The arrival of the four was completely unnoticed by students and passing motorists. At his office, Principal C. G. McGhee briefed the Negroes on their school routine and then took them to their home rooms. Before the start of classes McGhee said to the seniors, who were kept behind when the other students were dismissed, "The people we have coming here for the first time are all seniors. You'll be in class with them. What you do is what others are going to do." He added, "We have been together a long time. This is another problem we have to face. We are soliciting your cooperation." There was no visible reaction to the talk. During the day the white students generally ignored the Negroes who ate in the cafeteria with the student body that sat at separate tables. One of the Negro students reported later he had been struck on the leg by a small piece of brick at the gymnasium class, but that it did not injure him. He said he did not report the incident to the principal. The four left the school by taxi with Dr. Anderson as a passenger.

Glen Oaks High School

One Negro boy and five Negro girls arrived at Glen Oaks by 8:55 AM. They were taken to the library for briefing before being sent to their classes. At the same time, the white students were assembled for a brief talk from their principal. A group of white parents parked near the school to watch the proceedings from their cars. They moved readily, however when requested by deputies. Sheriff Clemens also addressed the group, urging parents to stay at their homes. Inside the school normal routine was reported being carried out. As at other schools, the white students paid little attention to the Negroes. All six Negro students sat together in the cafeteria for lunch, but there was no incident. Principal Pat C. Robert said later that opening day was one of the smoothest in the history of the school. He commended the Glen Oaks students for exemplary behavior.

Istrouma High School

School authorities asked students to assemble in the audito-rium after the unidentified picket appeared at the school. While they were assembled, four Negro girl students quietly entered the auditorium and sat on the back row. They were virtually un-noticed during the assembly. Principal Brown told the student body he expected them to handle any problem that might arise "with dignity." At lunchtime two of the Negro girls entered the cafeteria and went through the line. They sat opposite each other at one of the long cafeteria tables. Two white girls were seated at the other end of the table. Two white boys set near the Negro girls in the middle of the table, but there were no incidents.

Lee High Principal McGhee said in the newspaper on September 4th that "Everything is lovely here." I don't know what world these reporters or the principal lived in, but it was not mine. They made me think I was crazy. Did it really happen the way it was reported? Did I imagine that I saw people that really weren't there? Was the reception from the students and teachers lovely? Were they reporting on Baton Rouge deseg or Mars? To test my sanity, I actually had to call some of the other students to see if they felt the same as I did and if the news reports were correct. I don't know where the Lee High reporter was but it wasn't at the same place or city or planet where I was. With both newspapers reporting the same thing, if you weren't there, you'd think that we were all one big family of friends and there were no angry crowds yelling, "Go home Niggers!" "Go back to Africa."

The first week continued the same as the first day with students moving away in Cracker's class because he allowed them to do so and refused to acknowledge our existence. In American History there was one chair vacant on three sides and not four because I sat on the first row. One student in band said hello. His name was Jeter. Verbal taunts of nigger, coon, and baboon became more frequently in open areas. I didn't see Brownie, but Ginny and Win spoke at least two more times that week. On Friday, I saw Win coming towards me in the hall as I was going to American History, and I spoke to him first, but to my surprise, he looked around to see if anyone saw me speaking to him and quickly turned his head. Well, that put me in my place. I'd never speak first to him or anyone else for that matter ever again at that school. If no one spoke to me, then I wasn't going to speak to them.

On Monday of the second week, I was in Cracker's homeroom, and he was on one of his tangents. This time he was talking about basketball, one of his specialties since he was the basketball coach. He and the guys on the front row of the class were talking about the team, and I heard another student say something about Sin, who was on the team. During the discussion someone said something about Win, his identical twin, and the difficulty they had in telling them apart. Coach had it figured out and tried to explain the differences. Then it struck me. Evidently I had spoken to Sin and not Win on Friday. I still didn't speak to anyone first, even though I had made a mistake, for fear that there might be additional twins lurking. The second week followed the first and I was beginning to feel that the environment was at least bearable.

On Saturday, most of the group of 28 met at the "Y" to debrief. We talked about all the incidents that happened at the school, discussed the teachers and administrators and who was nice, who wasn't, and who was downright racist to the core. Missing old classmates and teachers was a major topic and sometimes schoolwork entered the conversations. Marion and I talked every night. Spending an entire day at school with no one to talk to and being ostracized was torture, especially for young people who were the leaders at their previous schools. Even teachers didn't call on you in class, which would have at least given you a chance to open your mouth. I kept peppermints in my purse to suck on in class just to keep my mouth from getting dry.

Two weeks of school had passed then Sunday, September 15th, there was a church bombing in Birmingham, Alabama. Birmingham had just desegregated their schools, and the Governor, George Wallace, had done everything he could to make the situation as nasty as possible. In fact, he made the statement, "Alabama needs a few first-class funerals." Well, he got them. The klan put dynamite under the steps of the Sixteenth Street Baptist Church that exploded Sunday morning killing four young Black girls, Denise McNair (11), Addie Mae Collins (14), Carole Robertson (14), and Cynthia Wesley (14). The four girls had been attending Sunday school classes at the church. No place was off limits to the cowards who hid behind their white hats and masks. Nothing was sacred. Their hatred consumed them to the degree that children were fair game for their viciousness.

We sat in front of the television watching the news and hoping they wouldn't find any more bodies. The expressions on the faces at the scene ranged from shock and horror to anger and hatred. You could see red eyes and clinched jaws. People were crying and in a daze. Others were trying to help, but the emergency personnel kept moving them back. We sat glued to the TV. Mama had tears in her eyes and Daddy was cursing. I could only wonder what was next.

Blacks across the country were enraged. Anger permeated every conversation. All anyone could think of was getting even along with the thought of who or what or where might be next for an attack. We were at war with racists terrorists. This was a war that was almost impossible to defend or counter with an offense. Terrorists succeeded by making people afraid to do anything or go anywhere, but even these terrorist tactics of the klan could not deter us from our greater mission. We were willing to give our lives. We just didn't think that other humans would be so cruel as to prey on children. Mama again broached the subject of not going back to Lee High, but I knew that I couldn't let those white folks think they scared me or us away. If we quit, then they had won, and there would be no stopping them from doing anything else that they wanted. Daddy, Raymond, Wade, and other leaders followed the taxis the next morning to make sure there was not going to be a problem. We didn't know what to expect. We were relieved to see that there were few protestors and not mobs, and that the schools had not received any bomb threats.

Once inside the school the environment was different. We could feel the agitation in the air. Students were talking loudly in the halls about the killing of the four girls and what might happen to us if we stayed. One remark was, "Four gone and four to go!" If I could have killed four of them that morning, that would have satisfied the next four, and I would have been more than pleased to avenge the little girls of Birmingham. As we walked through the halls some students bumped into us, knocking us around, forcing us to bump into other students who pushed back. They bumped me into the wall and laughed. I was 5'8" and 104 pounds. Tall, but no weight to fight back. They started throwing things at us and Cracker gave them free reign by walking out of the class. This was what I had expected the first week, but the bombing empowered them to let go and do whatever they felt with no repercussions from staff or administration.

We endured hell that week. Day after day the taunting and name calling went on and the bumping in the halls. I held tightly to my books because I did not want to drop them and have to try to pick them up. I knew that if I bent down I would not be able to get up. There would probably be someone over me kicking me while I was down, and there would also be no one to come to my rescue. With only four of us there, and I only had class with Murphy twice a day, most of the times I was alone. I walked the halls with my head held high trying to stay alert to all around me. Rarely did anyone look me in the eye. They glanced away as they approached. They were truly cowards because the bumping came from the back or sides where I couldn't see them. Let me see you coming so I can prepare and defend myself. I was not practicing non-violence. I would have punched the shit out of the person bumping me if I could have caught them, but with those cowards, after I was bumped, it was impossible to figure out who did it. Later in the week I guessed that a group of them were working together. I needed a plan to fight back.

When we met for the weekend at the "Y" all of us had experienced the same kinds of things. Some talked of quitting, but instead we came up with ways to fight back. I had been trying to think of a way to fight and win. On Friday night I could not sleep again because I was not going back until I could defend myself. Then the light went off in my head. I got up in the middle of the night and searched until I found two safety pins. I opened them giving me enough of an end to hold while also having enough of an end protruding from my hand that would stick someone. Then I practiced holding my books wrapped with my arms in front and the pins in my hands. If someone bumped me, they would bump into the pins on either side. I didn't sleep at all that night because I could not wait to tell the 28 a way to fight back. At the meeting that Saturday, I suggested the safety pin trick as a way of fighting back against those who were bumping us in the halls. The plan was before you walked out of the class into the hall, you would open two large safety pins and cross your arms with the endpoints of the pins aimed outward while carrying your books and looking innocent, minding your own business. When someone bumped you, they would be stuck with the pins, not knowing what happened or how. You would just hear a loud ouch or yell depending on how hard they bumped. That was the plan.

I couldn't believe how compassionate Black people were! There were a couple in our group who were concerned about the innocent people who might get stuck just for walking near us. I had to remind them that no one got close to us unless they were trying to do us harm. Anyway, the decision was theirs to make, but I was going to fight back. The most difficult part of the plan was trying to keep a straight face knowing that you had just won another round when you heard the expletive after someone bumped you. This was one way to get back, and it was quite enjoyable. After a couple of weeks, out of nowhere, the bumping stopped. Some dummy must have finally figured out that I was doing something that hurt them. Maybe it was the "Nigger voodoo!" When they stopped trying to bump me, I regretted it because I was really enjoying hurting them. I anxiously awaited someone coming near so I could stick them with the pins, but they finally got smart and stopped.

By October the students in Cracker's class decided that needing their space trumped sitting next to us. So, they began to move closer and closer. Eventually, there was only one chair between us and them. I'd have preferred if they would have kept their distance because whether they knew it or not, we were prejudiced also, and I didn't like being close to them either because they smelled like wet dogs especially with the heat and humidity of Baton Rouge. I not only showered every morning, but I had a ritual of lotion, powder, and cologne so I always smelled good. The other problem with them moving close to us is that I heard their conversations about boyfriends and who came over when their parents weren't home and what they did and how the boy had to sneak out of the window or where they went on the weekend in the car and who got drunk. I couldn't imagine that they were doing all these things. They talked constantly while Cracker was talking, so I was stuck between listening to them and Cracker. Neither was a good option. While the girls were talking, they were putting on make-up or combing hair. One girl who sat in front of me had red hair that turned up in a flip; she was constantly chewing gum and popping it with passion. Another girl who sat in the row next to her had short hair, but it was teased high into a beehive and dyed blond. She looked like a beehive. That hair always frightened me because I kept waiting for something to crawl out. It looked like a haystack. Occasionally, Murphy would just look at me and shake his head, and we'd smile.

The students moved closer, but they still managed to totally ignore us unless Cracker walked out of the room, then spitballs were thrown. It was only a couple of people who did it, but no one else said or did anything about it, and Cracker knew what was happening. I resolved that issue by walking out whenever he did. He asked me, once, why I was standing in the hall, and I told him what the students were doing when he walked out. He didn't respond and kept walking. From that time on whenever he walked out, so did I. Murphy stayed in, but I was not going to solicit abuse. It was extremely hard to avoid in that class.

Cracker began talking about race as part of the sociology class and of course he found the most racist theorists and philosophers of the time. He spent the entire semester trying to humiliate Murphy and me. We had to sit and listen to the inferiority of the Negro race with their small brains, no accomplishments, the barbarism of Africa and its people, and their lack of intelligence. Murphy and I had to take notes on kinky hair, broad noses, thick lips, and athletic ability. With any questioning from either of us challenging what he said, his response was that he would have to look it up. He always had photographs that he passed around the class to prove his point and to get laughter going. He went from one topic to the other espousing the inferiority of the Negro quoting any character who had ever said something negative from brain size to culture to morals and values. He talked about the uncivilized cannibals of Africa. Daily, he mentioned the Hottentots and their hair that he described as one strand of straight and the next strand nappy. He'd laugh and get his boys in front to do the same. I couldn't find any documentation for his lies, but I had to take notes or fail the test, which was not a choice because I wasn't going to repeat his course ever again in life. I'd rather not graduate. Cracker justified those Blacks who had pulled themselves up from cannibalism and ignorance were of mixed descent and should therefore be thankful to the whites who raped their ancestors on the plantations.

One thing that I knew for certain was that I would not take his economics class the next semester. It was an elective and not mandatory for college

academic requirements. Therefore, I went to Mrs. Whitey and dropped econ
for second semester. That was the one bright spot that drove me to get through
Cracker's class. When I passed this semester, I would never have to sit in
one of his classes again. Day after day Murphy and I tried to fight back,
but Cracker wouldn't even call on us or recognize our hands when we tried
to participate. Many times I would just speak out without recognition and
he'd ignore me like I had said nothing. When he began the classifications of
races into Negroid, Caucasoid, and Mongoloid, I asked who developed these
classifications and why, because few people fit into those molds. I showed him
a picture of my mother, and he identified her as white. I said she was not.
She was Black. And my mother. He then began a tirade about why the races
should stay pure because all other races were inferior to the Caucasian and
mixing would destroy their excellence. He became Hitler and I had to sit in
this class every morning. I didn't know enough to refute him because we had
never been taught Negro History even at the Black schools. It was not allowed.
I felt so ignorant. If I could have found a way to poison him, I would have.
He needed a slow painful death like burying him alive with only his head
covered in honey protruding from the ground and the red ants of Louisiana
in the hole with him. I had read about this torture and could only think of
him as worthy of it. That's how I spent my time in his class, trying to block
out him and the girls around me. I'd daydream about ways to kill him in a
slow painful way, the way that he was torturing me.

If only I had the knowledge to refute him I would not have had to be
denigrated day after day. I knew I was not inferior to anyone, especially them.
I knew that Blacks were not inherently or genetically inferior. I knew that if
given a chance and an education, we could do anything we desired but what
facts did I have to combat this idiot? What books or references could I use?
Never before had I felt so defenseless. I am glad that I did have to experience
him and his un-fact-filled class because it made me a stronger person, one
determined to find out all the information about Black people that existed.
That became my quest. I made a conscious decision that I would begin
the study of Blacks and my African heritage. Self-knowledge became my
educational goal in the struggle against racism, and I have Coach Cracker to
thank for being such a jackass trying to show off and be a friend to the racists
in the class. Without his constant degradation, I never would have found out
about my heritage and the great contributions of Africa, Africans, and all
the Black peoples of the diaspora who are literally the fathers and mothers of
human beings (homo sapiens sapiens) and civilization.

Daddy was the major source of information and my resource for
suggestions. He told me about World War II and the Black regiments who
made major contributions. Whenever there was a book or movie about Blacks,

I was interested. Once I saw a movie called the *Red Ball Express* or at least I think that was the name. Anyway, it was about black soldiers who brought gasoline to Patton whose tanks had run out of fuel. Without the Black troops, who drove the tankers of gasoline through enemy lines at night under fire when no one else would, Patton would have not have succeeded. The Blacks took the risk and saved another white man and the country without ever getting respect or acknowledgement.

Daddy told me about the Tuskegee Airman and their flights. He admitted that he never flew under the bridge, but he was proud of the men at Tuskegee who were fliers. He knew about Eleanor Roosevelt coming to Tuskegee and flying with a Black pilot. He said that was one story that will live forever. He knew of other Black units during the war, but no one gave them credit.

Daddy named several talented Blacks like Joe Louis, who won the heavyweight championship beating that white man while the whole world listened on the radio to prove Hitler wrong. He told me about Althea Gibson and reminded me about Muhammad Ali. Daddy reminded me of the jazz greats like Louis Armstrong, Count Basie, Duke Ellington, and Lionel Hampton and my favorite singers like Dinah Washington, Billie Holiday, Sarah Vaughn, and Nina Simone. He told me of the great Negro leaders including DuBois of the NAACP, Booker T. Washington, Mary McLeod Bethune, and Paul Robeson. He showed me books about the continent of Africa and some of its great leaders and countries like Haile Selassie of Ethiopia and who defeated the Italians and Gamal Nasser of Egypt. People often told Daddy that he looked like him. He told me that Black people were all over the world and had made contributions wherever they were. I began to feel better having begun to accumulate some knowledge of self, but I wanted more, so my quest continued.

Yes, Mama was right. She used to tell us that we were the best because only the strongest and best people were kidnapped from Africa and only the best of that best survived the Middle Passage and only the best of that best survived enslavement and only the best of that best survived Jim Crow and we are the best of that best who are alive today. She proposed that our demise came with being mixed with whites, who diluted our strength and perseverance. They ruined everything.

Needless to say, starting every day with Cracker was nothing that I desired. I left that class with my jaws hurting, from being locked so long and a headache. That's probably how I developed TMJ. Following Cracker to jump start each morning was PE. From day one I knew there was no hope of being accepted here. All the girls wore blue gym suits except me. The teachers insisted that I wear whatever I had worn at Southern High because I was a senior and there was no need to order a uniform for one year. I requested that one be ordered for me. Every time I asked a different reason was given as to why it could not be done. First, they were changing colors; then, they were changing companies; at one point, they were considering not using uniforms anymore. So, on top of being the only Black in class, I was also the only one dressed in white shorts and shirt while everyone else wore blue. Peer mimicking is important. No one wants to be totally different. Even at the Lab, whatever was in was it. You just didn't deviate, but at Lee, being Black wearing white while everyone else was white wearing blue added to my self-consciousness. Of course, thinking back, if they had required me to wear blue, I probably would have protested. I didn't like their uniform anyway because it looked like bloomers.

The colors I wore were not the determining factor of why the girls never selected me for a team in PE. The teachers would select the team captains and allow them to pick their team members with alternating selections. The first captain called a name, then the second captain chose, then back to the first followed by the second. They called every girl in the class until no one was left standing but me, and then neither called any more names. I was always left alone at the end with the teacher deciding which team I had to play on. Ms Sugar would ask, "Who called last?" Then there would be an argument as if they didn't remember. Finally, Ms. Sugar would just say, "Freya, go to this team." And she would point to the end of one of the lines. How humiliating to know that in every class you would be left standing alone, with no one wanting you on the team. Maybe one of the teachers one time might assign all members of the team. Maybe one of the teachers one time might be a team captain and select me. Both of the teachers knew the result each time, but they never changed the protocol. The actions of the teachers let me know where they stood. They aligned themselves with their captains keeping me in my place, last standing, never selected, deeply humiliated.

Every now and then when we were playing a game, one of the girls would forget and mistake me for a human. Caught up in the moment, they'd actually call my name or throw a ball to me. When that happened, they immediately realized the mistake and turned to their peers to see if anyone saw or heard them speak to the Niggra. One day while playing touch football, I caught a pass and ran for the touchdown. My team actually cheered. I was shocked. I turned around to see if there was something else happening for surely it couldn't have been me that they were cheering. They evidently chastised themselves for that slip and it never happened again.

Recess following PE gave me a chance to open my mouth and unclench my jaws. Murphy, Melvin, Louis, and I found each other at our bench and talked about what had happened to us that day. The guys actually had people that spoke to them and participated with them in class. They even liked most of their teachers, especially their math teacher, Mr. Wood. We never failed to watch our backs while we talked as we stood in a circle protecting all fronts and sides and backs. Even though we met by the bench, rarely did one of us ever sit on the bench. It would have made us too vulnerable. We had to be on guard against everything especially the "bull pen."

This was an outside area near the basketball court where boys who had parental permission could smoke. Yes, boys could smoke at school in 1963. Yes, you can imagine the type of boys that had permission to do this and imagine their parents too. They were the sleezy, bad asses who were bullies. They looked disgusting and nasty with greasy hair, crew cuts, bad teeth and dirty fingernails. When I was being bumped in the hall, I believed it was a few of these guys that were doing it. I couldn't swear to it because they all look alike, but I got them with the pins whoever they were. They were the most disgusting group of people at the school and really shouldn't have been in school. They were the ones that should have been in a "day tang shun center." As long as they kept their distance or we could see them, I felt comfortable. So, we always watched their comings and goings.

I couldn't even go to the restroom. I walked in one to wash my hands and quickly realized that this was unsafe territory. The girls stopped talking and started staring. I don't know if there were girls in the stalls but the room was crowded with girls putting on make-up, doing hair and a few smoking. One asked, "Nigger, what are you doing in here? You're not allowed." I did not respond. I just washed my hands and tried to leave. I was no fool and knew that there was no one here that had my back. I needed to retreat. One girl stood by the door to block it but no one else stepped up to help carry her bluff. I stood there and looked at her straight in the eye staring her down without blinking and she eventually moved aside. What if she hadn't moved? What if they decided to jump me? I was unprepared and had not considered the "What ifs." That became an area off limits for me because I was totally unprotected. Unless I carried a grenade there was no way to win in that situation. Thank goodness segregation had taught me to hold necessary bodily functions until I got home. Many times I stayed home if I were bleeding heavily on my period because there was no place to change. I was grateful that I didn't develop stomach issues until later in life. I never could have survived the cramping and diarrhea.

By October the students began spitting on us in the halls. In all the schools we were facing the same things. We, the 28, met to discuss what the white kids were doing and how they were going to harass us next. So, we had to come up with a plan to fight back just like we had done for the hallway bumping. Even though the whites liked to spit, one thing they would surely not stand for was us spitting on them. So how could we get it accomplished?

Most of the girls could not projectile spit and did not want to. Who wanted to go around spitting like those nasty bastards? But something had to be done. I tried practicing in the bathroom at home, but the spit never projected. It only dribbled. I was pathetic, and anyway I didn't want to lower myself to act like them. They were just lucky as hell that no one spit in my face; it only landed on my clothes. I didn't care how small I was or how much anyone preached non-violence. If someone had spit in my face, I was going to beat the living hell out of them or die trying. That has to be the nastiest thing someone can do.

So, Plan B. Get a miniature water-gun that fits in the palm of your hand. Again, make sure that the gun is prepared before you get to school and get it out without being seen when the bell rings to change class. Keep the gun in the palm of your hand and when someone spits, you put your hand to your mouth and give a real loud, "Hark!" like you're spitting but instead you're shooting the water-gun. They don't know that you're shooting them with water. They think you're spitting. Problem was that the small gun was good for only a couple of shoots, which meant that your aim had to be perfect. We hoped the word would circulate among the white students to prevent having to use the gun more than once or twice a day. Plan B worked so well that the spitting stopped within the week, but I began to use it offensively against the known terrorists. I'd strike first and eventually they started to avoid me. "YEAH! Mission accomplished." I passed that trick on to the other 28 since we all shared tactics.

Wow! This is getting to be fun. Don't speak to me. Ignore me. I don't give a shit. This is war and I'm getting you back. A big problem that I faced was that most times I could never identify who the culprits were because they all looked alike. Now I could understand when white folks said that, "All them Niggers look alike." Yup, we probably do because white folks do too. At that time white boys were wearing crew cuts with their hair sticking up on top of their heads, white socks, and penny loafers. They all looked the same—crazy. So, half the time I didn't recognize the enemy. However, most of them came from the "bullpen" or at least they looked like those guys.

The bullpen should never have been allowed in a school, but from what I understood, all the white schools had one. The dummies, racists, and incorrigibles (with parents of the same description who allowed them to smoke) stayed in trouble. There were no such areas in Black schools. Our parents had too much sense to allow us to smoke. Not that a few boys weren't smoking, but it was definitely without parents' knowledge. The bullpen at Lee High should have had electrified fences around them to help protect them from themselves and protect civilized society. In fact, bulls should have been insulted because they have more sense and respect for others than the idiots confined in an area named after bulls. These were the boys I targeted in the halls with the water guns. I had gotten accustomed to the isolation, the space between me and the rest of the class, and no one speaking, but I refused to let anyone physically abuse me. So, I took the offensive against the bull pen guys.

Things that we take for granted are monumental issues in a war zone, and I was at war. That school taught me a lesson, "Be Prepared!" the old Girl Scout motto. My purse became an artillery garrison with safety pins, water guns, and a knife. It was one of those souvenir curved knives in a case, but it was sharp as hell. I almost lost half my pointer finger while holding onto the case hidden in my purse. I grasped the case with the left hand but had not cleared the halfway opening which meant that when I pulled it out with my right hand the pointer finger was across the line and it got cut, deeply. So much for Ninja me, but I did learn to not hold the case, just pull. That incident didn't happen at Lee High, but it prepared me in the use of my knife if needed. The restroom experience made me revisit the knife and add it to my arsenal. I may not have been successful in hurting every girl in that restroom, but I would have hurt a few and maybe drawing blood would get them to back off. If not, I just wasn't going to be the only hurt person. My other weapon was the purse itself.

Most of the girls of the 28 carried large shoulder bags for a purse with a strap over the shoulder. The purpose was to use it as a weapon when necessary. If you carried it by the strap, it could be used to clip a person on the legs and cause them to fall. It could be swung to hit someone on the head because it was always heavy. It could be used as a buffer against someone trying to push you. Just carry it and figure out new ways. One day I was crossing one of the ramps to go to band and this guy from the bullpen was coming towards me. He looked at me and called me a Nigger. I said, "Your Mama." As he neared me, I slowed up to wait for him to reach the steps at the end of the ramp. I looked him straight in the eyes and swung my purse catching one leg and causing him to fall flat on his face down the steps. Too bad there were only two steps and not twenty. He was too embarrassed to tell anyone, so I got away with it. They were learning not to mess with me. I was taking no prisoners.

Band and trigonometry were just no-incident classes. In band we played our instruments, and no one really bothered me except the time when someone started throwing spitballs when Mr. Bowen walked out. I walked out and remained outside until he returned. I told Mr. Bowen what happened, and he threatened to put any student harassing me out of the band. I was quite proud of him. Since I couldn't play in the marching band, when they practiced on the field for football season, I just sat on the bleachers and watched them kick a leg and walk the 8 to 5 while I smugly laughed at them and did homework or read a book. The white kids in the band looked spastic compared to

Blacks. The right leg kick always made it look like they had been shocked by something and the kick was a reflex to the shock. Then they started walking all stiff and turning or walking backwards and sideways looking lost. That band was not my cup of tea, and I was so happy that I did not have to play on the field with them. After Mr. Freeman, Lee High was not an option.

I did enjoy the concert band. It wasn't Mr. Freeman, but I liked music, and Mr. Bowen was nice even if he didn't give me first chair. Lee High had a pretty decent concert band. They didn't play songs like "Overture of 1812," but the sound was good and what they played, they played well. I think Mr. Bowen knew I was better than Reverb but why upset the apple cart when things are going well? I didn't blame him for it, and I didn't need the aggravation. If memory serves me correctly, there was one time that he did give me first chair and Reverb turned blood red. She got it back after a week or two, but she was furious. I really didn't give a shit. They could have put me in last chair. I was just serving time and hoping for the year to end quickly.

Ms. Giesel in trig had begun to call on me to answer questions and realized that I was no dummy. She'd have me go to the board and explain problems just like everyone else. Win was in the class and he occasionally spoke, but he generally withheld acknowledgement until the halls. That was ok, too. I think many of the students wanted to talk to us but were afraid of the repercussions from their peers. Trig was a challenge and I thanked God for our tutors. Mr. Williams, Carmen Williams' father, my tutor for math, helped me when Lulu and Daddy couldn't. One night Carmen and I were stuck on some homework problems and I refused to go to school not knowing my work. After we couldn't resolve it by phone, I had Daddy take me to Carmen's house in Southern Heights at about 9 PM. We worked until almost midnight with her father until we fully understood what we were doing. The next day I was the only one in the class with the right answer, and I had to explain it at the board. Ms. Giesel was impressed, and so were the other students. A couple of them smiled and nodded at me. I wasn't part of the crowd that she kept around her desk or a shining star, but at least I was recognized and respected for what I knew. No one called me names or moved away in that class. I almost felt like I belonged there. If I had been at the Lab when I was the only one with the right answer, my classmates would have given me "DAP!" There are moments when you feel the need to be appreciated.

Lunch was the second chance for all four of us to be together. After talking to the lunchroom workers and smiling and reassuring them that we were all right, we sat down to eat at our table. No one ever sat there but us. I guess we contaminated it. From what I overheard from some of the white students in other classes, no one even sat at our table on the second lunch shift because the "Niggers sat there." Melvin decided to sit at a table with one of the guys that spoke to him in class, but as soon as he sat down everyone else got up and moved. Melvin came back to our table and joined us. That was the third time any one of us ever tried that— first, last, and never again. All three at one time. Usually the students didn't bother us during lunch, but every now and then someone would have to pass and say Nigger or coon. We just expected some fool to say something, but we ignored them like they ignored us.

There were times that I would not be ignored and started stuff just to get back. Almost every Friday was spirit day with an assembly/pep rally during football season. We reported to the gym with our classes, but once in the gym, Murphy, Melvin, Louis, and I found each other and sat together. Our first shock was the cheerleaders. We knew it was a pep rally but where were the cheerleaders. We saw these girls on stage dancing and another group doing acrobatics but where were the cheerleaders. I asked the guys if they knew, and we decided that one of those groups must be cheerleaders, but it was nothing that we had seen before.

At the Black schools, the cheerleaders sang cheers to beats and danced with hips swaying while we responded to their call and response. The whites didn't have a "Sister Lucy" or a "Mr Lee." We finally figured out who the cheerleaders were when they called, "2-4-6-8, Who do we appreciate?" Those cheerleaders were the strangest creatures that we had ever seen! We had to go back and tell the group to see if their schools were the same. That next weekend of our gathering at the "Y" we had to do our Black cheers, to reminisce, and the white cheers, to laugh about with our straight arms and robotic movements and southern drawls. We laughed until we cried.

One spirit day was flag day. Homerooms and school organizations competed to bring the largest rebel flag since the mascot was the Lee High Rebels of the old confederate south. This was one insult that I could not let slide. I went shopping to find the smallest flag that I could find. I found one at TG&Y. The flag I found was on a match stick barely an inch. I knew that was perfect. Near the end of the pep rally, the student body was standing and singing some southern song that I don't remember, could have been "Dixie" or "Old Black Joe," I don't remember, but I do remember holding up that damn match stick flag and lighting it with a Bic lighter. The flag was so small that it burned instantly in a poof, but I held it up for those around me to see it go up in smoke.

I hadn't told Melvin, Murphy, and Louis what I had planned because I knew they would be afraid to let me do it. When they saw me light that flag, they grabbed me and rushed me out of the auditorium as fast as they could. Only a few students around us saw what I did but the word traveled quickly. Melvin and Louis' math teacher stood next to us to protect us from the few students that thought they might teach me a lesson. Murphy, Melvin and

Louis were so angry with me that I think they would have tarred and feathered me if they could. Their math teacher was also angry and threatened that if I did anything like that again to incite a riot, he would see that I be suspended, and he didn't care whose daughter I was. Well, needless to say, that incident sparked another whole round of threats, name calling and abuse. I didn't care. I just wanted to hurt them like they had been hurting me. Suspend me? That would have been a privilege, an honor, a "Red Badge of Courage."

The person that never hurt me was Mrs. Church. I absolutely loved her class. She taught Shakespeare the first semester and we read *Julius Caesar* and *Macbeth* along with several sonnets, which had to be memorized, along with memorizing most of Caesar and Macbeth! There were great class discussions of the plays and sonnets and mandatory participation in the critiques and presentations. I could almost quote verbatim both plays and my favorite sonnet,

Sonnet 116

Let me not to the marriage of true minds
Admit impediments. Love is not love
Which alters when it alteration finds,
Or bends with the remover to remove:
O no; it is an ever-fixed mark,
That looks on tempests, and is never shaken;
It is the star to every wandering bark,
Whose worth's unknown, although his height be taken.
Love's not Time's fool, though rosy lips and cheeks
Within his bending sickle's compass come;
Love alters not with his brief hours and weeks,
But bears it out even to the edge of doom.
If this be error, and upon me prov'd,
I never writ, nor no man ever lov'd.

With knees shaking, I had to recite this in front of the class. The romantic that I was gave it my all as I had done at Southern High with Poe's "Tell-Tale Heart." Mrs. Church applauded and so did some in the class. This was one place that I felt really comfortable and could let down my guard and be an ordinary person. Mrs. Church made us feel welcome from the first day. She treated us as she did all her students and never once doubted our competence. She challenged me to offer the best, and I did. I would actually smile in her class and freely participate. She was quite eccentric, training her dog to respond in French, but kind.

Mrs. Church gave me the strength to end the day with American History. The American History teacher only called on me when she thought I didn't know an answer. She never called on me when I raised my hand. She finally realized that I had done my work and always stayed ahead of where she was in the book to be totally prepared. She could not catch me and had to remark many times that I was correct but that was in the next chapter and we hadn't gotten to it yet. "Then why did you call on me to answer when you knew you hadn't taught it?" were my thoughts that I kept to myself. Her racism was much more subtle than Cracker's, but I knew it was there. I just stopped raising my hand because I knew when no one knew the answer, she would call me.

I couldn't wait to get home each evening. I didn't bother to bring my clarinet home because I could just sight read the music and get by since I knew there wasn't a chance in hell to move to first chair. I settled for second and got by without practice. As soon as I got home I went to my room and called Marion to see what her day was like. I never told Mama about the things we went through each day. Besides, both she and Daddy would have had a stroke if they knew I was carrying a knife. It was just too much. I think Mama would have pulled me out if she had known all the details. I know she knew I was suffering, but I tried to keep most of it away from her. I couldn't stand to see her worrying about me, but there were days when I just couldn't make it.

Every time the students at least settled down to make life bearable, which means that they stopped bumping, spitting, moving aisles away and throwing spitballs, something would happen locally or nationally that would set them off again, and we would have to begin fighting all over as if it were the first week. At the end of September the Huntley-Brinkley news aired the taped show of us done at Mt. Zion in August. Of all the Black students there for the interview, I was spotlighted asking the question about what we should do if there were violence. Needless to say, the next day at school and the following week, we had to bring out our total arsenal of tricks to fight back the abuse and harassment.

October was a good month for me and all of us who desegregated. Not that the white students had gotten any better, but we actively participated in our Black schools. Mr. Freeman invited Charles Burchell and me to play with the band at half-time at one of the home games. I could barely play a note because my embouchure couldn't hold the mouthpiece tightly as I fought the big grin on my face. The warmth of my fellow band members and seeing our team (with real cheerleaders!) was overwhelming. We also attended homecoming activities, including the dance. What a great evening dancing, talking, and singing along with Bobby Powell, the fantastic live band that played for the dance. They played "You really got a hold on me" by Smokey Robinson and the Miracles and it became the theme of the night as we sang along with them. Every time we went back to the Lab made returning to Lee High harder and harder. I felt like I was being sent to prison.

By November there were weeks that were off and on again with no letting up. They didn't want us at "their" schools, and, hell, we really didn't want to be there. We would have preferred to be in our Black schools with our friends and teachers that cared about us. As far as we were concerned, we had proven our point that we could succeed at white schools. There was really no need for us to continue. The majority of us were fed up and talked about stopping this madness. We met as usual at the "Y" on the weekend of November 16th and decided that we were going to quit! Yes, all of us were going back to our Black schools. To hell with trying to desegregate. We really didn't care what people thought. Our schools taught us better than the white ones, even with inferior buildings, materials, and supplies. What our Black schools lacked, the teachers made up with their knowledge, understanding, respect, expectations, and nurturing. We decided that all Black children would be better off remaining in Black schools. Returning to Lee High the week of the 18th was joyous because we knew it was going to be our last week in hell.

HELL and Beyond

The week of November 17, 1963 began as a normal week of isolation, name calling, and abuse, but I didn't care what they did or tried to do to me that week. I took it all with a smile. I told Mama that we had decided to quit after this week because we felt Black students were better off in Black schools, and she agreed. Daddy protested but said he understood and again left the decision to me. I knew he was disappointed because he felt it was a project started that should be finished. He didn't press the point but I could see the wind had been knocked out of him, his face bloodless. His drive halted. I couldn't face him without knowing that I had let him down, but with everyone else quitting, I was not going to be left alone in the mob of hatred that existed at Lee High. Hurting my father was beyond comprehension. He could barely talk to me and really tried to avoid looking directly at me. He respected my wishes even though he didn't agree. His life's work of equality, justice, and freedom was going down the drain, and his very own daughter was part of the dream's destruction. He was disappointed beyond description. There was no way I could explain to him how I felt being at Lee High. There was no way to justify quitting to him. I had made the sacrifice initially for him, but at some point I had to rescue my sanity, and each day I was losing more and more of it. Daddy just didn't understand. All I could do was hope that in time he would forgive me.

I had one day left. Just make it through today, Friday, November 22nd and all the torment would be over. The day began as any other day at Lee High, but the euphoria of this being my last day was overwhelming. All schools in East Baton Rouge Parish School District would be out of school the following week for Thanksgiving Break. Teachers had their annual conference before the holiday and that closed schools for the week. Blacks had their meetings and whites had theirs. We were not coming back after today. As I walked around the gym to Cracker's class a smile beamed across my face. I almost skipped across the ramp to his homeroom. Oblivious to everything he said, all I could do was think of the fun next week at the Lab. Southern High would be in school on Monday and Tuesday because it was not part of the District. Rather, it was part of the University, so I was going to spend my first days back at the Lab. I sat in Cracker's class not hearing a word he said or anyone else. I barely heard the bell ring to change class. I started to give Cracker a piece of my mind and tell him that he was racist and ignorant and the worst teacher I had ever encountered, but I didn't want to break my mood of euphoria.

Walking to gym for PE I was glad that I hadn't bought that blue romper. It was not going to be of any use to me anymore when I returned to "MY" school. I didn't notice that I was the last one standing and the teacher had to place me on a team. I didn't even care. This would be the last day that I would be left standing alone. Why did I bother to participate when no one wanted me on a team? I knew my grade depended on my skills that were demonstrated when placed on a team, but I didn't want to assist either side win. However, I had always given 100% at any task undertaken and I could not do less than my best. Daddy had instilled that in me to the core. I wanted to yell at the girls that I wasn't going to be there the next week for them and the teachers to ostracize. I was going to my school where people fought to have me on their teams, where we were so good we beat the boys in track, but again I held back. I just smiled inside knowing that this was my last day of PE.

Recess flew by with the four of us talking around our bench. We watched our backs as usual but we played a mock "Taps" to the bench actually laughing for a change. The guys in the bullpen were looking at us trying to figure out what we were doing, but they had no clue that this was our last day. Even a couple of students walking by turned back to look at us when they saw us laughing. I found their interest in us amazing because the white students were actually noticing that we were happy. Then they must have also noticed that until that day we had been unhappy, and it never bothered them. Imagine being around people for two and a half months knowing they are in pain and not trying to help. A dog would have been offered assistance, but I guess we did not rank as high as animals. Chattel slavery at least gave us the value of horses and other farm animals, but after emancipation, if Blacks were not working at almost free labor, we had no worth. All I knew was that this country would have no worth if it hadn't been for Blacks, but I was going to be worth a million on Monday morning at Southern High. When recess ended the four of us hugged each other as a salute to the last recess, and we walked to our next class.

I crossed the ramp to the auditorium and actually enjoyed looking at the entire campus of Lee High. If it had been a Black school I would have enjoyed the setting of the dome auditorium, ramps over the entrance drive and the buildings that looked like spokes emanating from the dome. I didn't know of a comparable Black High School. Looking at the campus reminded me of why I was here. I was supposed to make a difference in the lives of Black children for the future. Now I was being selfish, thinking only of myself and as Daddy said, "Good Times." Yes, I did want the return of good times at the Lab. I was 16 years old, and this was my senior year. Was that asking too much? I found myself still trying to justify leaving. Could I live with this decision or would I forever chastise myself for quitting? Daddy had fought all his life. He put his life in danger and risked death for our people. Why couldn't I make a sacrifice for one year? Not a lifetime, one year. I slowly completed the walk to the band room and began my last band class.

Sitting in band for the last time should have been glorious. Next week I'd be back with Mr. Freeman and the State Championship band where there would be real competition between Charles Burchell, Comie Barges, Herbert Robert Carter, and me with real marching and dance routines and contemporary music and SOUL! Isn't this what I wanted? Isn't this what I had been wishing for all year? I wanted to put on the green and gold uniforms and march with thighs parallel to the ground, real marching. I wanted to hear Mr. Freeman tease me. I wanted to go to State Competition and win first place in marching, concert band, and sight reading to show everyone that we were the champions in every area. Yet, I knew that Southern High's band could do all that without me. When I left Lee High, who would be doing what I'm doing now? Am I giving 100%? Am I being all that I can be? Am I finishing what I started?

My emotions were a mixed bag. I left band doubting my decision to leave. The Black Baton Rouge Community was depending on us to change the education and economic systems that relegated Blacks to the bottom of the ladder. The community had raised money to send all of us in taxis to school in hopes of a better day. They honored us as heroes and heroines and now we were going to let them down. Mama had always told us that wherever we were we should be on our best behavior because we represented them, our parents, and that we should not want to embarrass them. Was I representing my family if I left? Was I respecting my Daddy for all he had given? My legs were beginning to feel like steel columns that I had to drag along the ramp. I finally made the walk to trig and sat down unable to concentrate on the class.

I had planned to blurt out, "We're leaving and we won't be back! I hope that makes you happy because it makes me even happier not having to be around uncivilized, uncouth, uncaring, hate-filled animals like you," but the students in trig never did anything to me. No, they didn't speak or acknowledge my presence but they never called me names, or moved away or threw things at me. Sometimes, I even felt like they cared a little when they gave me a nod of approval for a right answer. Didn't I tell myself at the beginning that I could win over whites in time once they realized the stereotypes were untrue? Had I really given them enough time? When class ended I held my announcement and didn't say anything. I was just not going to show up on Monday, December 2nd. Or was I? Could I give them the satisfaction of knowing that they accomplished their mission to get rid of us? Leaving trig, I solemnly walked to the lunchroom, joined Murphy, Melvin, and Louis and sat at "our" table.

As we began eating our lunch and before I could ask the guys if we were making the right decision, the cafeteria began to slowly erupt with students whispering, looking at us and moving quickly from table to table. The noise level was increasing and more and more heads were turning to and from us, as other tables joined. The wave of emotions quickly moved from the door to us. We heard a joyous eruption of, "Hey, have you heard? Kennedy's been shot!" Murphy, Melvin, Louis, and I looked at each other in disbelief. Then, to reassure ourselves, decided that this was another ploy aimed to upset us. The cacophony of students rejoicing over Kennedy being shot had to be a ploy. There was no way that even these monsters could rejoice if the president had been shot. Someone said loudly, "We killed Lincoln and now we got another Nigger lover."

The four of us couldn't say anything. We knew Kennedy was going to be in Dallas today. We knew that whenever he was in public, there was a risk, but could this really be true? Could these students be telling the truth? Could they really be so heartless as to laugh and rejoice if the president had been shot? As we left the lunchroom for our next hour classes, Murphy and I had to stand in the hallway to wait for Mrs. Church to unlock the door. Students were running around disorderly and a little unruly. This was strange standing in the hall waiting for Mrs. Church because she'd never been late, and we never had to wait before. We only waited for a short time but during those brief minutes, several students felt empowered again to bump into us, hurl racial insults, laugh and brag, "'We' shot Kennedy!"

Once Mrs. Church opened the door and we began walking to our seats, the school intercom was turned on throughout the school with the news broadcast. The president had been shot and there was still no news as to his condition but it was thought to be grave. I was in shock. Those uncaring, ignorant, racist bastards were telling the truth. They had the audacity to laugh. Someone in our class laughed aloud and said, "Yeah!" If there was any redeeming feature of that day, it was that I heard the news in Mrs. Church's class. Before I could stand or look around to find out who said it and curse them out while trying to beat the shit out of him, Mrs. Church was jolted by the remark to take center stage with a soliloquy on ethics and humaneness. She emphatically admonished the class, "I don't care what your political views are or how you feel about anybody. If you are human, you should at least think of what this means for the country. It's a sad state when we, who consider ourselves a democratic society, shoot a president because his philosophy doesn't agree with ours. That's why we vote! That's what makes us a democracy." I truly respected her for having the courage to stand up and say something to those idiots. However, she made one mistake. She assumed they were human.

Before she could finish telling the class off, the radio announcer said, "We have just learned that the President of the United States is dead. President Kennedy died at 1 PM Central Standard Time." Instantly two large white men appeared in the doorway, talked to Mrs. Church, then approached Murphy and me. We were told to get our things and leave with these men. Murphy said he needed to go to his locker. As we reached the locker, Melvin and Louis were there with two other large white men that I had not seen before, and Louis and Melvin's math teacher. Before the guys could get to their lockers, a crowd of students started forming around us chanting, "We killed Lincoln, we killed Kennedy, and we'll kill anyone else who tries to help Niggers!" The men, who I later learned were Federal Marshalls, and the math teacher surrounded us by linking their arms around us and violently yelling, "Move it!" as they pushed us towards the door. They realized that we could not make it to the lockers. Louis and Melvin had already been to their lockers under the protection of their teacher, but as Murphy and I met them, the crowd around us had increased and was becoming violent, shouting and pushing and throwing punches at the men surrounding us. The math teacher and the Marshalls stayed with us. They wrapped us tightly in the center of them and began to push us into the corridor and across the ramp to the front of the auditorium. Everywhere that I could see, there were groups of students rallying, yelling insults, laughing and taunting us. I felt as if I couldn't breathe wrapped so tightly. We were being suffocated from being held so tightly. I kept lifting my head for air while trying to maintain my balance in the huddle. I just moved with the group not knowing where we were going.

To my surprise the taxi was waiting. How did he get there so fast? How did he know we were leaving? But there was no time for questions; we just kept moving. The Marshalls were able to get us to the waiting taxi unharmed. They remained around us as they literally pushed us into the car. Slamming the door, one screamed, "Get them out of here! Get them out of here!" as a bucket of something was thrown on them and the car but missed us. Whatever it was smelled like shit. The drift of toxic air permeated the car as the door closed. (Some time later, after having cleaned the car, the taxi driver told us that it was urine and feces.) For the first time that year, I felt fear. I don't know who called the Marshalls or where they came from so quickly or who called the taxi, but I am thankful that they did. Without the help of the Marshalls and the help of that one teacher, we would have been injured, to say the least. I had never heard such vitriol or seen such vicious hatred. They wanted blood. They wanted Black blood. They wanted my blood.

When I got home Mama was nervous and visibly shaken anxiously awaiting the taxi's arrival. She had tried to watch the news but was unable to concentrate wondering what was happening to me. She grabbed me in a big hug and just held on tightly as if she never expected to see me again, but here I was delivered safe and sound. When she finally let go, we watched the news unfolding. Daddy was still out trying to make sure that all of us in all of the schools had been picked up safely. He called Mama to make sure I was home. As I sat, stood, paced all at once and all together my anger grew exponentially. My head felt as if it were going to explode. All I could think of was, "We killed Lincoln. We killed Kennedy, and we'll kill anyone else that helps niggers!" I wanted to kill, too. I wanted to just go out and shoot, hang, and murder anything white that moved. I wanted to burn their city down. I couldn't be still, but I couldn't stop listening to the news. We saw the swearing in of Lyndon Johnson on Air Force One, and my heart stopped. I could not believe that this southern cracker would replace Kennedy. All was lost. He was a southern democrat and he'd never back Civil Rights. Jackie Kennedy looked like a zombie as she watched him being sworn in, and the nation joined her in shock. The 6 PM local news in Baton Rouge continued with national coverage as the reports came in from around the world of countries in mourning and heads of state sending their condolences. We also heard that in spite of the death of the president and worldwide events being cancelled, Lee High continued with their planned hootenanny after school. That school needed to be bombed off the face of the earth!

Daddy, Mama, and I were glued to the television the entire weekend watching every move and re-watching every event. From the swearing in of President Johnson on Air Force One to watching Jackie walk with the flag draped coffin as it emerged from the plane to seeing the hundreds of thousand visitors showing respect as President Kennedy lay in state in the East Room of the White House and the Rotunda of the Capitol. We silently paid our respects through the TV. On Monday, we saw the caisson pass in front of the family as John John (Kennedy's son) gave his father a salute.

I never told Mama or Daddy what happened to us at Lee High. The events were too painful and scary. I just said that we were glad the Marshalls showed up. I didn't go to Southern High on Monday because school closed for the funeral of the president, but Monday night, the Southern High students who desegregated planned to meet at the Lab on Tuesday. We almost said simultaneously, "I'm not quitting!" We each talked about what happened at our schools on Friday and how the hatred of the white students was not going to stop us. We realized that we had been acting liking spoiled brats and should have known that desegregating was not going to be easy. What made us think that we could change over 500 years of racial hatred and white superiority in a little over six weeks? Each of us had our own stories to tell about how we felt when we heard the news of Kennedy's assassination. Then we stacked hands in a one-for-all and pledged not to quit even if it meant our death. Too many people had given their lives for the cause of equality, justice, and freedom and we were willing to become martyrs for the cause if necessary.

I had not slept the entire weekend after Thanksgiving. Before I met with the other students I knew I could not quit. Too many people had died and were still dying in the fight for justice and equality: Martin Luther King, Jr. had been jailed, Fannie Lou Hamer savagely beaten, Medgar Evers killed, the four little girls in Birmingham bombed and killed, not to mention the previous lynchings, beatings and deaths, including Emmitt Till, and then there was the lynching of my own grandmother's brother. Who could quit now? From the kidnapping and enslavement of African people until the present, over a hundred million lives had been lost. The history books only counted the lives lost during the Middle Passage, and even those numbers were incorrect. They still are!

The entire African Holocaust includes the African people who were slaughtered in the villages where the kidnappings occurred. The entire African Holocaust includes the lives lost on the way to the slave dungeons and while in the dungeons. The entire African Holocaust includes the lives lost during the Middle Passage. The entire African Holocaust includes the lives lost during enslavement, during the Civil War, after the Civil War through Reconstruction and through Jim Crow. The African Holocaust is on-going whenever Blacks are killed through oppression and institutionalized racism. Having read *Exodus* in middle school, I remembered feeling sorry for the Jews, but what about us? Is there no one who values Black life? Is there no one who thinks that what happened to Africa is a crime? Why can't we talk about our history? Why can't we mourn those who died for our survival and freedom? When will the United States apologize for their terrorist actions in the European enslavement of African people for profit? When will they apologize for the horrendous violation of human rights during the middle passage, enslavement, and Jim Crow? When will Blacks be compensated for building this country with free labor? That labor allowed this country to become a world power. Without "US," the United States would not be what it is today.

We built the skyscrapers of New York and the Capitol, the White House and monuments of DC. We grew the cotton, tobacco, and sugar for the factories of the north creating wealth for both regions. We fought in every war for this country in all of the most vulnerable positions of safety to defend rights and privileges that we could not enjoy. We are still on the front lines today risking our lives and forfeiting our dreams "in order to form a more perfect union." Even though the words of the Constitution were never meant for us, those words were and still are the most profound philosophy for freedom.

No, I was not going to quit. Yes, I was going back and going back with a vengeance. I had to apologize to Daddy for causing him such heartache. Just to think that after all he had gone through that I had considered walking away and leaving hundreds of dreams unfulfilled and martyred lives having died in vain. I could not believe that I had been so selfish. Kennedy's assassination had been a wake-up call. I was not going back to avenge his death. I was going back to avenge all the Black people that had died to get me in that damn school. And I was going back for my Daddy. I was going back for all the Black children who would be able to go to better schools, and schools in their neighborhoods, and schools with new books and supplies. I was going back to pave the way for Black teachers to receive the same pay as white teachers for the same work. I was going back. I was going back. I was going back for Daddy, for me, for my people. No one would live to say that they conquered me. I really would be invincible and crazy as hell.

Thanksgiving was a very solemn day at our household. Grandmother, Lulu, Tony, Bobby, Lillie, Uncle Helvius, Uncle Bernie, Aunt Wilma, Daddy, Mama, Dupuy Jr., Ralph, Robert, and I sat around the table together to eat the traditional dinner of turkey, dressing, macaroni and cheese, sweet potatoes, green beans, rolls, and cakes and pies. Grandmother cooked most of the dinner with Mama's help. Lulu cooked the peas twice because she burnt them the first time. Tony led us in the 23rd Psalm and grandmother prayed for the world. We each gave thanks for something special to us, especially in this time of turmoil, as grandmother put it. Mama gave thanks, "I want to thank God for all my children, the health of Robert, and I pray for the safety of Freya as she continues her fight to desegregate Lee High." I gave thanks for all my family that was gathered that day and those who could not be with us but who we had talked to on the phone. I even thanked God for my brothers. Daddy gave a sermon on hate and love and ended hoping that the world would one day have peace built on love for all people.

On Monday morning as the four of us departed the taxi, we walked around the auditorium at Lee High with a new assertiveness. The students could see that we were not trying to be nice or be their friends. They could see that there was no more humble pie. They could see we were not taking any of their shit. I was hoping that someone would say or do anything that might increase my anger and hatred. I kept looking for trouble, but for some strange reason, all was quiet on the western front of racism. Even Cracker didn't try to provoke me. "What the hell? Provoke me! Bump me! Spit on me! Move away! Cracker, say something mean! Give me a reason to attack!" I needed to beat the shit out of someone or curse them the hell out. I couldn't find any reason to vent, but other schools had action.

The Black students in the other schools were not taking any shit either. A boy passed by the "Negro" table at Baton Rouge High and threw some food on the Black students sitting at a lunch table. Velma Jean Hunter got up with her tray and broke the tray with all her food on it across his head.

Merrill Patin, at Glen Oaks, was suspended for fighting when he was merely defending himself. However, the principal told Merrill that he incited the fight because he chose to attend the white school. We never knew what to expect from the students, teachers, or administrators but whatever happened, we were not standing idly by and taking it. Non-violence was dead in Baton Rouge School desegregation. We were not a non-violent group. We gave back what we received. That's called reciprocity.

Until Christmas Holidays the school remained stable. I sat on the row closest to the wall in Cracker's class and there was always a vacant chair in front of me and Murphy, who sat on my left side, a vacant chair behind him and me, and one vacant on Murphy's left side. No one talked to us, but no one bothered us either. Cracker talked to the few boys in the front of the class who sat in front of his desk while he sat on his desk mainly talking about basketball. The girls who sat in front of us brushed and combed their hair in different styles, talked of make-up and who went out with whom. I couldn't wait until next semester when I would not be in that class any longer.

PE continued the same with team captains selecting their players and me left standing until placed by the teacher. I wore my white outfit and proud of it now because I wanted to stand out and let people know that I was there and not going anywhere. I caught passes in football, made shots and defended in basketball, and hit spikes in volleyball. I even overheard a girl comment once that they should ask me to be on the volleyball team, but that was quickly frowned upon and she apologized for suggesting it.

Recess remained the same. We had our bench, and we stood and talked each day about our weekends and our old schools and how much we missed them. Rarely did we discuss our classwork at Lee High because most of us were in different classes, but sometimes we did offer help to each other when we could. I was disappointed that the boys weren't doing as well as I thought they should, and they didn't use the tutors offered by our support group. I told them about Mr. Williams and the other students that were utilizing the tutors, but they would not try them. Sometimes, I felt that they were more alone than me even though it was three of them because they never participated in any of the activities at the Y or other socialization provided by the committee. None of them came to the Saturday meetings. Murphy started with us in the beginning but quit. Melvin and Louis never came. They did go to events at their home school, McKinley, but they pretty much stayed by themselves except for when they were talking to me. No matter what I did, they always had my back, and for that I was thankful.

One day at recess after Thanksgiving, the weather was cold and dreary, and it had just finished raining. Out of the gray sky a large rock about the size of my fist flew by my shoulder barely missing Murphy and slicing the space between him and me. It came from the area of the bullpen. I looked back and saw this skinny guy with blonde hair standing straight up on his head grinning and the boys around him laughing and patting him on the back. Even though the rock missed both Murphy and me, I was not going to let that act of aggression go unnoticed. I picked up the rock, rubbed a little of the mud on my right sleeve near the shoulder and went to the office. I showed the assistant principal Mr. Trailtrash, who truly hated us, the spot on my coat and lied and told him that the rock hit me. He asked if I could identify the boy that threw the rock, and I told him I could. He asked how I could be positive when my back was turned. I told him Murphy saw him, and when I turned the boys in the bullpen were patting him on the back. Murphy backed me up. Trailtrash took me to the bullpen area and asked me to identify him, and I did. The boy said he did throw the rock, but it didn't hit me. I told him that he must not be able to see because surely there was a mark on my coat. (He didn't see me put it there because I rubbed it on the coat sleeve while I was crossing the ramp as I was going to the office.) He was suspended for a few days and when he returned, I threatened him that if he or any of his boys thought of doing anything, I'd have his butt in jail because I had the full protection of the Federal Marshalls. They believed me after seeing the Marshalls come in after the assassination of the president. With that incident we were never bothered again by the bullpen.

Football season was over, and the band commenced (that's grandmother's word I love) practicing for the spring concert and the State Festival. Each year there was a state festival of academic and performing arts competition, one for Blacks and one for whites. I had participated the previous year at Southern University, representing our band and received a superior award for clarinet. So, I planned to participate again, but this time I would be competing against whites. Mr. Bowen asked us to select the piece that we wanted to play for the festival during the holidays and give it to him for approval when we returned. There were no problems in band; just every now and then I'd get irked having to sit next to Reverb listening to her wavering flow of notes that sounded like a reverberation, but no one bothered me. Jeter began to faithfully speak to me every time he saw me. He was really nice and even tried to talk making small comments here and there. Thanks, Jeter. Sometimes, you have to be careful what you ask for because I got to the place that I tried to avoid seeing him. He was just too happy to be at Lee High and most of the time I did not want to smile at white folks. I actually didn't want white friends. I didn't want them to speak to me or be nice. I just wanted to be left alone.

Trig was coming along well, and I kept doing well with the help of Mr. Williams. Most times I could figure the problems out on my own and sometimes Carmen and I could figure them out together on the phone, but when all of that failed, Mr. Williams was our back-up, and he always came through. Ms. Geisel announced that she was applying for the school to become a chapter in Mu Alpha Theta, a national math honor society. She said that our class would be the charter members if accepted. All of the students in the class were excited. I didn't give a shit, but my name was submitted as part of the class. I remember Win asking me to sign the application as a charter member. This was the first time that anyone had spoken to me in the class and actually asked me to do something. Win occasionally spoke in the hallway but never in class. The shocking part was that he came over and talked like we were old friends. Just out of the blue, "Freya, will you sign the application here? You are part of the class and will be a charter member." I signed and said nothing because I think I was in shock.

The lunchroom workers were consistently there to be our comfort. They spoke to us and smiled and gave us nice plates of food. One student asked them why we always got such a big plate, and they kept smiling at us but ignored him and placed the same amount as always on his plate while staring him down. The look they gave him meant he better shut the fuck up! The "f" word was not part of my regular profane vocabulary of shit, damn, hell, jackass and an occasional bastard, but rare moments needed that adjective. If he had continued protesting he may not have gotten any food. He finished the line declaring, "Maybe if I were a 'Negro' I could get some food around here." Yes, that's exactly what it would take for him to get more food. Be Black! I'm sure he wouldn't want to trade places with us for a few more morsels of food or anything else including money.

I shouldn't say just being Black because an amazing thing was that the hatred was not color based. It was because we had been defined as Negroes. There was an Indian (from India) boy at Lee High who was much darker than I was and had hair nappier than mine, but he was accepted. He had friends. He belonged to the clubs and was surrounded by girls and boys, while we were ostracized. Go figure! I guess if I were from another country I wouldn't be hated. WOW! Racism is confusing. All the time I thought the whites did not like us because we were people of color but that was not it. I thought that the whites did not like Africans, but that was not it because they accepted people from North Africa, even dark skinned people. The whites did not know who they really hated if they had to describe the person, but they did know they did not like African Americans when they could identify them.

Being African American in Mrs. Church's class was not an issue. It was still the best class and the best part of my day that I had at the school. She treated me like a human being and after her stand when Kennedy was assassinated, I would forever be in her debt for keeping me from murdering someone that day. We actually had conversations in her class, discussions about ideas, philosophy, poetry and literature. That part of the day was always the first time of the day when I could actually open my mouth and talk to another human, except at recess and lunch with the guys. In all the other classes I was ignored, with the exception of Ms. Geisel calling on me to explain a problem at the board.

American History remained the most boring. She didn't know what she was teaching and frequently had to refer back to the book to answer questions from students. She had us read and she'd read along with us. She asked questions from the book and expected answers verbatim from the book. She still only called on me when she thought I might not know an answer, never when I raised my hand, so I stopped raising my hand. I sat on the front row right in her face looking her straight in her eyes defying her to say anything wrong or disrespectful. I knew the day was coming when we would have a confrontation, but so far she managed to keep her southern drawl and racism inbounds.

Christmas couldn't come fast enough. The holidays didn't mean anything to me but time away from that school. Marion and I were again with our friends from Southern High. We had parties all through the holidays. Wanda Cage had the most memorable party where we played Charles Brown's "Please Come Home for Christmas" almost all night. I went to a party at my cousin Maryella's, and one at Donald Ray's (Aunt Phine's grandson) house. Daddy or Mama still escorted me and picked me up from all the parties. We were seniors in high school and still not permitted to date. I couldn't even drive myself to parties for fear of being out at night with all that was going on with the schools and Daddy's Civil Rights activism.

The night of Donald Ray's party, a few of the guys and girls wanted to go across the river to Plaquemine to a nightclub to see James Brown. Now, I would take risks and do things that I wasn't supposed to do, but something told me that I'd better not go. My friends promised that they would be back before the party ended and no one would ever know that we had left. HA! There was a shooting at the club. No one got shot, but some of my classmates were held for their parents to pick them up for being under-age in a bar. If I had been with them and Dupuy H. Anderson had been called to pick me up, I would have preferred to have had the klan tar, feather and burn me, chop off my head and impale my body for all to see. For once I listened to my inner conscious voice and did not go. I remembered what Mama said, and that was everywhere I went I represented my family. I knew that if I were at a nightclub as a minor I would not be representing my family, but the bottom line was also my fear of my father. Every now and then I did what was right. Children need to fear something in life to keep them safe from themselves.

Another memorable night during the holidays, Marion and I were babysitting my brothers while Mama and Daddy went out to the Bonanza Dance. The Bonanza was a social club of Black men that gave a white tie formal the day after Christmas every year. Daddy was a member and he and Mama looked regal, like a king and queen each year. I loved to see them before they left, Mama in her long gown and Daddy in his tails complaining every year that he couldn't stand being dressed up like a penguin. I thought he was cute. They were a beautiful couple. They were going to be gone all night and part of the morning because there was a breakfast following the dance. My brothers were asleep when Mama and Daddy left, which meant Marion and I were alone.

Feeling grown and independent, we sat in my room with the window up smoking a cigarette blowing the smoke out of the window. I don't remember where the one cigarette came from, but we shared it trying to act grown in our state of being blue. After we finished we flushed the butt and ashes down the toilet and washed the ashtray. There could be no signs left in the house that we had smoked. We then retreated to the living room to listen to music and have a drink. We poured a small shot of Chivas Regal. We had never drunk any liquor before and just a few days earlier at a party at Anna Jean's house some of the guys in our class had a bottle and were passing it around. I took someone's glass to taste it, but Wesley took the glass out of my hand and would not let me try it. That's what I appreciated about our classmates. The guys looked out for us and protected us. They would not let us get into trouble nor do something that might ruin our reputation.

This night Marion and I were going to take our chances and let our worries of the world, our schools, and Civil Rights go. Tonight was going to be an escape from reality. Adults drank. We figured that we were going through so much that we were adults. So, we drank Chivas that night. We truly sipped it because it burned as it went down. Our first sip made us both cough, but we were determined to drink it and like it. We listened to Nina Simone, Dinah Washington, Dakota Staton, Earl Grant, Miles Davis and more. Once we were sufficiently blue listening to our favorite jazz artists, we played 45's until we got to Garnet Mimms. Then we played his "Cry Baby," looked at each other, and began crying our hearts out. We've always been like that. We don't have to say anything. We just look at each other and feel and do the same thing. We say each other's sentences at the same time. I don't remember how many times we played it, but we played it over and over and over and just cried and cried and talked about Southern High. The hard façade we wore every day was broken and we were two young women missing our friends, our adolescence, and our school.

We talked about our loneliness at the white school which hurt worse than the overt violence and aggression. We talked about how not being able to talk to a classmate when a teacher or student said something dumb or not being able to laugh when something was utterly silly made us choke from holding in our emotions. We knew we had to make the sacrifice of our senior year, but that did not mean we had to like it. After crying profusely, we regrouped and began to talk about the white kids at our schools. We talked about their dumb elephant jokes that no one found funny except them. We talked and laughed at the white socks that the boys wore with any and everything, and we concluded they probably wore them with tuxedos. We mimicked them singing and dancing, their stupid hootenanny music, and their tooo southern drawls. We mimicked their dumb walking on their toes, their conversations of hair and dates. We tried to mimic their clapping off beat and their spastic dancing but concluded that it's really hard for us to clap and dance off beat. We laughed at their cheap clothes and their way over the top make-up that made them look like they were 60 years old! The teased hair looking like a haystack and how we hoped something crawly would actually get in that hair. We laughed until we cried again. Turning our noses up at the boy's flat behinds and their flat tops that looked like they had stuck their finger in an electric socket reminded us that the klan never had to worry about us inter-marrying. We agreed with the klan on that point. There was no way we could marry white. After we finished laughing we made a pact to never wear white socks with penny loafers. We also promised each other to strive for excellence to show those white students we were the best so that they'd never forget "THESE NIGGERS!"

We went back to fight the racist terrorists after Christmas. They must have missed us because they started acting like they did the first week of school, calling names, bumping, throwing spitballs. I had to pull out my arsenal and remind them that I was taking no prisoners; I was going to give someone a real good ass-kicking if they bothered me. There were some guys that I knew were trouble, so I bumped them first so hard that they were apologizing to the other students that they bumped when they lost their balance and accidentally hit someone. Not only did I bump, but I also had my pins in my hands to hurt. They never figured out what I was doing. I used my purse to clip people on the legs and make them fall. I spoke out in class without being called on just to let them know I was there and not going away. The hatred for me only increased and I didn't give a damn. I didn't want them to like me, but they were going to know that I was there and not forget me.

After a few weeks, calm returned again and Lee High went back to normal with them just ignoring us and keeping their distance. That was fine with me. Leave me alone and I'll leave you alone. It was my new mantra. However, activity at our homes picked up. Now those hooligans knew where we lived. They started drive-bys at night and on the weekends. Again, we could not be in the front of the house for fear of being hit with rotten fruit or eggs. Dead animals were hung from the front porch again, even another cat. The klan burned another cross on the lot across the street from us. Some of the men on our street got together and formed a watch committee. They took turns at night to try to catch some of the terrorists who were wreaking havoc in our community. I was hoping that they'd catch the klan because my plan was to burn one of those suckers up. I just wanted to light one of those sheets and see how fast it would take that cracker to come out when he was on fire. One night Uncle Helvius and the man that lived across the street from him heard a car coming and saw that it did not have on its headlights. The car threw stuff in the yard and sped off down the street. Uncle Helvius and the neighbor were waiting in their car. They chased the car without lights down Christian Street and followed them making a right turn onto Morning Glory. With Uncle Helvius on their tails, with his bright lights shining in their window, they kept speeding trying to get away, but they lost control. Going too fast to maneuver the left turn on to Lakeshore Drive, they ran into the lake. Uncle Helvius came back and told us the story. It was in the paper the next day that a car drove in the lake, but the news didn't explain what happened or how it got there. Being prepared and fighting back helped to alleviate some of the attacks.

I was followed more often when I was driving, but I went to Marcelle's Gas Station for protection. The persons who followed me, including the white police, turned away when they saw I was heading in that direction. They knew who they could threaten and who they couldn't or should I say who wasn't going to take their shit. They were cowards and would not fight out in the open with equal opponents. When pushed, Blacks in Baton Rouge did fight back.

Finally, the semester ended and I didn't have to go to Cracker any more. This made my mornings a lot better. Both Murphy and I had study hall where we could be together to talk and relax while supposedly doing homework. I always finished my homework the night before because I never wanted any surprises. Therefore, I had nothing to do but relax. I didn't take any chances that there might be something I might not know and would need help with, and there would be no help for me in study hall. I couldn't imagine asking Mrs. Whitey for assistance. First of all, she could probably not answer a question if asked one. Second, I was not going to let anyone know that I didn't know something. I had a reputation to uphold which was "Miss Know-It-All."

No more Cracker. One down. In PE I also got a reprieve. The next few weeks were tumbling. I had asthma and had gone through all the allergy tests and shots but could still have a severe attack that would send me to the emergency room for a shot. Black doctors were still not allowed to practice in the hospitals, and Uncle Doc, Judy and Nan's Daddy, would contact the white physician on duty and prescribe the medication I needed. I was allergic to everything: household dust, mold, pollen, wheat, corn, soy, bananas, oranges, eggplant and who remembers what else. The allergies gave me an excuse not to tumble. The mats were old and dusty and could trigger an attack. So, I had a medical excuse not to take gym for the next few weeks. I think I could have managed, but I wasn't that good and was not going to let anyone know that. I kept all my frailties hidden. It would have been ok had I been at the Lab because my friends and I would have laughed it off if I couldn't turn over without rolling to the side and coming off the mat or if I was afraid to go over backwards. Friends gave you the courage to try and not feel humiliated. Lee High didn't.

Many days on the ride to school in the taxi even though the three guys were with me, I'd feel alone, rejected, and I hated every minute of being alive. The ride seemed like an eternity waiting to descend into hell or prison. By the time we'd arrive at school, I was so depressed I could barely walk across the ramp to class. I knew I was just feeling sorry for myself but at those times I could feel my insides swelling. I could taste bile in my mouth. I could feel my legs trembling and my skin becoming damp. My head would throb, and I could feel my chest tightening making my breathing harder, almost wheezing. Sometimes, I had to hold onto the railing of the ramp and stop walking to try to gain my composure. I had to talk to myself when I stopped, and I would close my eyes to meditate. I'd take deep breaths to try to relax to recall pleasant visions of how I could conquer the day. Most times the meditation worked, but sometimes it didn't.

This day it didn't. All of my tactics failed me. As I walked across the ramp I felt my jaws tighten and the bile rising until I tasted it strongly. Having to take deep breaths to keep it down and not spewing out vomit like a sick puppy, I swallowed hard and breathed quicker, but my cheeks were weakening and I felt tears coming. I closed my eyes grabbing the rail while digging my fingernails into my palm trying not to faint or fall or vomit or cry. I could not take another step. Murphy asked me if I were all right and I could not answer. I just clung harder to the rail. He held my arm and told me I didn't look good and said that maybe I should go home. I nodded in agreement, and he walked me back to the office. Miss Grant took one look and said she would call home to have someone come and get me. Mama came and picked me up. I got in the car and went home. I don't remember what she said, but I do remember not talking, just nodding. Mama didn't try to talk to me anymore. She could see my pain. We rode home in silence. At home I immediately went to my room, closed my door, laid my head on my pillow, and stared at the ceiling. Mama brought me hot tea and asked if I needed anything else. She told me she was there whenever I wanted to talk. When the nausea passed, my head stopped throbbing, and I could breathe easier, I found Mama and told her that I was better and that she didn't have to worry. Her response was, "Freya, you don't have to do this. It's too much. You can quit!"

She knew my pain even though I could not talk about it. I felt so close to her that year. More than at any other time in my life my mother and I shared our pain and emotions without speaking because we understood what we had to do. We both did it. We hurt together. We comforted each other in silence. I had to bear it alone because Mama would have suffered so much more if she knew all that we had to endure, but she instinctively knew and felt my pain. She already carried the stress of Robert's epilepsy. I could not put more on her plate. Grandmother used to say that the Lord never gives you more than you can handle, but I think Mama had enough. She worried about all of us from Daddy to Robert. I did not want to burden her more. I talked to her about how depressed I was, not about Lee High, but about missing Southern High. I told her how much I hurt by not being able to march for graduation with my Southern High class, by not being there during class night, and the major thing I was going to miss more than anything else was our senior class trip. She told me she understood how much my class meant to me and she was sorry that this had happened my senior year. She asked me if there were anything that she could do and I shook my head, "No." Somehow, I'd just have to get over it.

The battles continued each day and I welcomed the solitude of no one speaking. Over the months of no one speaking and being treated as an invisible person I gradually learned to like and appreciate being alone left to my inner thoughts and meditations. I could lose myself as I walked through the halls thinking of my travels and friends and my weekend plans. I could plan dream cities and modules for learning, remembering Mrs. Wooten. I practiced speeches that I would be called to make about Civil Rights and the injustices of racism. I created schools of excellence where every child achieved their maximum potential, where learning was fun, where all children were respected and appreciated and could be unique. Many times I became lost in thought and missed almost the entire class while I was sitting there totally oblivious to everything around me.

The two class exceptions were Ms. Geisel in trig because I never knew when she'd decide to call on me to work a problem, and Mrs. Church who I utterly enjoyed. Her class was an escape all its own as we delved into Shakespeare and critiqued other literature. However, we were nearing the end of the year and I had a major research project to complete, which meant that I had to stop daydreaming and get my work done. I was going to maintain

my honor status whether they recognized me or not. Win inquired once as
we were passing in the hall, "I just saw the honor roll posted in the library
and I didn't see your name. I know you must be an honor student. Why
aren't you a member of the honor society?" My only response was, "I am but
no one recognizes me here." He said he would check into it, but he never
said anymore. He was different. Just out of the blue he would speak or ask
a question. He, Jeter, and Ginny gave me hope that all white people weren't
devils who were sent here to terrorize Blacks.

The first end of the year project due was the State Music Festival. My song,
"Concertino," had been approved by Mr. Bowen with the comment, "This is a
difficult piece. Don't you want to do something easier for the competition?" I
told him no. "Concertino" was my selection and my mother would accompany
me on the piano. About a week or two before the competition, he informed
me that I could not participate. When I asked why not, I was informed that
when Mr. Bowen submitted my name and race, he was told that Blacks were
not allowed. I smiled and said nothing because I knew he did not have the
power to change anything. He told me he thought it wasn't fair, but there was
nothing he could do. There may not have been anything he could do, but I
knew who could and would, Daddy.

When I repeated what Mr. Bowen told me, Daddy immediately picked
up the phone and called the Superintendent demanding that this be resolved
before he had to go to court and issue an injunction to stop the entire state
festival. A day later, Assistant Superintendent Aertker called us to ask if we
could see him that afternoon. When we arrived, he apologetically explained
that it was a state festival, and if it had been in another district that had
not "integrated," I would not have been allowed to play and he would not
have had any jurisdiction. However, this year the festival was going to be
held at Istrouma High, and that was in our district, which was under court
ordered desegregation and that meant I could play. Daddy thanked him for
responding so quickly and we walked out smiling at each other knowing
that wherever the festival would have been held, I would have played or there
would not have been a festival.

When the time came for the festival Mama and I went to Istrouma High
School. We sat in the audience listening to the others in the competition.
When my name was called, Mama and I walked up to the stage. Mama
started playing and the audience became loud with name calling and throwing
spitballs. Some on the front row were sucking lemons to try to distract me and
cause my mouth to pucker and water. It had no effect, but I was not going
to play in the noise. So, I stood there and Mama stopped playing. A judge
stood up and asked the audience to be quiet. The audience became silent and
Mama started playing again. As I raised my clarinet up to play, the noise

started again. I looked at the students who had filled the room and tightened my jaws. I was not going to play in the noise even if we had to be there all day. I would wait.

The judge stood up a second time and asked for silence. Mama started playing as the room became quiet. I began playing and the noise started and I stopped. Someone in the audience yelled, "Disqualified!" "Go home Nigger." The judge stood up and finally said that if there were any more interruptions, he would have the room emptied. He asked those who did not want to listen quietly to get up and leave. A few people left but most stayed. The ones on the front row continued to suck on lemons hiding them from the judges but that didn't matter because the lemons didn't bother me. I played "Concertino" just as I had the previous year for the Southern High Concert band performance. My lento section was beautiful as ever. The lower octave tones slowly resonated throughout the room filling it with deep soul searing sounds of music that brought tears to eyes. I had a Selmer clarinet that was made of real wood, not plastic. That horn was far superior to that of anyone else's horn that played in the competition. Daddy always made sure that we had the best of everything, and he bought me one of the best horns. It cost almost $400 in those times. By the end of my solo I knew that I had better receive a Superior award since no one topped the difficulty of "Concertino" or the skill and emotion with which I played. I had to wait until Monday when the results would be announced at school. The judges were going to announce them later that day, but Mama and I decided we did not want to just hang around in that toxic environment of hatred.

Monday all of the superior awards were announced over the intercom, but my name was not called. I went to the office during recess and inquired about the results. Mrs. Whitey apologized and said that I did receive a superior award and that it was a mistake that my name was not called. I told her that I wanted my name called over the intercom like all of the other students. That afternoon before dismissal she softly said that a mistake had been made and there was another superior award for solo clarinet presentation, Freya Anderson. Naturally, there were some boos, but who the hell cared.

I had also inquired that day about why my name was not on the honor roll and why I was not a member of the Honor Society. She informed me that not having my name listed on the honor roll must have been an oversight, but I could not be a member of the Honor Society since I had not been at the school for two years or more. After that my name was listed on the honor roll for the last grading period and it was too late to argue the point of the Honor Society, but she told me that I would be an honor graduate.

Ok! Another feat accomplished, the music festival was over and all that was left was the concert band performance. I don't remember a thing about it, but I know if they had one, I played. There are a few moments that are completely blocked from my memory. With band out of the way the next project in school was a modern dance project for PE. I was not a great dancer, but I knew that in a pinch I could do something to get me over. Again, no one wanted to have me in their dance routine so I did a solo performance. I danced to Killer Joe with a routine I pulled from my memory of something that Mackie Jenkins had done at Southern High. The girls in my class were mesmerized, and they actually applauded at the end. All I could do was laugh inside because I had no creativity in dance. It was all Mackie and I don't know if I ever told her that she got me through the last grading period of PE at Lee High.

Trig was coming along great, and I was keeping my "A." Robert E. Lee received national recognition and was awarded a charter in Mu Alpha Theta, international high school and junior college mathematics club, and I was a charter member in Dorothy Geisel's trigonometry class. My name was included in the *Morning Advocate* and *State Times* newspapers with all the other students. Naturally, that sparked another round of name calling and insults at the school about the "Uppity Nigger." That brought another day of incidents with, "This nigger thinks she's smart." "She only got nominated because she's in that class." "She's not that good and she doesn't deserve it." My picture was in the local Black newspaper, *The Newsleader* and the community responded with congratulations and well wishes. They were proud that I was doing a great job. I couldn't thank Mr. Williams enough. He got me through Trig with A's.

Mrs. Church assigned a major research paper for the culminating project. She assigned each student an author and we had to come up with a research project. My author was John P. Marquand. This was another author that I did not find interesting. I tried to read his novels, but the white thing about high society and trying to get in or live up to it was not my priority, and it did nothing but bore me. Second, I had no clue about writing a research paper. The information that we were given in class assumed that I had done this before, which I had not. I had written critiques and essays but not major research. Fortunately, I called our support group and got Dr. Faggett as my tutor.

He was an English professor at Southern University, and he walked me through the process step by step. First, he told me, "If you're doing research, there must be a problem to solve." I did not understand a problem in Marquand's novels. They just seemed silly to me. So, Dr. Faggett and I had discussions on what I had read. We discussed the biography of Marquand and how it might relate to his writings. Dr. Faggett asked me to read more of Marquand's novels and try to identify a theme. The next week we talked about the bio and the connections that I saw running through Marquand's books. From our discussions we had a title, "Vindictiveness in the Writings of John Marquand." The next week Dr. Faggett told me to begin my writing from the note cards and in the order that Mrs. Church wanted the paper. He gave me a couple of weeks before we went over the completed project. Mrs. Church only allowed a few mistakes. With each couple of errors a grade level dropped. I was terrified. If we missed a comma or a period or a quotation mark or an entire reference, I could have ended up with an "F." I had never been under such pressure for a grade. This paper had to be perfect. Staying awake nights was the beginning. I was staying awake weekends, and the last week I may have gotten only a few hours of sleep; I ate peppermints for sustenance. Even though the paper literally drove me crazy, I enjoyed the challenge. These were the best things that happened to me at Lee High, having Mrs. Church as my literature teacher and Dr. Faggett as my tutor for the research paper. The information and training that he provided was the foundation for all my other degrees. I think Mrs. Church found two errors, one missed comma and one period. I did get an "A." Thank you Dr. Faggett.

While all of these things were in progress, American History was moving along and I did have to have that confrontation with the teacher, Mrs. Klan. She finally reached the point in history where she could not avoid discussing the "Niggras." The first time the word came out of her mouth, I cringed. She said it a couple of times during that same class period and I had to interrupt. I raised my hand but she did not call on me. So, I blurted out and interrupted her, "The word is Negro and not niggra. If you want to say Nigger, that is another word which is derogatory. The correct word in the dictionary is Nee-Grow." She responded with, "I'm sorry but that's the way I've learned to say it. I didn't mean to be offensive." From that time on whenever she said it she put emphasis on "Nee-Grow" and looked at me.

I also had to correct her on some of the mis-information in the book, especially the part that the slaves were happy. That class got to the point that I constantly interrupted with quips on the side like, "Yeah, most people like to be beat and starved and have their families broken and sold away while they are paid nothing." She ignored me and would go on as if nothing had been said. The end of the year couldn't come fast enough for either of us but I'm sure it was going to mean more for me than her. Somehow I survived and unfortunately she did also continuing to further corrupt other students with prejudice and mis-information just like Cracker. I knew they were two of a kind, but I had to keep her until the end of the year. Unfortunately, for me, because her class was required for a state graduation certificate, I could not drop it.

In the middle of all these last projects, I received the best news of my entire life. Mama and Daddy had arranged for me to go on Southern High's class trip. I did not find out until two days before we were to leave. Mama and Daddy had been working with Southern High on the details about insurance for an out of school student attending and liability issues and all the other necessities that go into planning an out of state field trip for a school. Daddy told me that I had to ask permission from Mr. McGhee to see if he would allow me to attend and miss those days from Lee High. I almost died. Was my trip really going to depend on those white folks at Lee High who didn't care what happened to me?

Daddy insisted that we talk to the principal. He went with me and we told McGhee all the details of the trip and everywhere we were going. We told him about the educational advantage and the historic places that we were going to visit. He replied that he did not have a problem but that I would have to get permission from all my teachers. I carried the paper for them to sign granting me permission. Everyone did sign and Mrs. Church remarked that the trip sounded wonderful and she hoped that I enjoyed it. Ms. Klan was so glad to be rid of me she signed quickly after seeing all the other signatures without me even explaining.

Suddenly, I was whisked into "Never Never Land." I was on the bus with my Southern High classmates going on our senior class trip. We left Baton Rouge, Sunday, April 5, 1964. That night we slept on the bus and the next day we visited a Native American reservation in the Smokey Mountains. There was still snow on the mountain and we had a snowball fight on the very top. The scenery was beautiful as we looked down below while riding a cable car across the mountain. We were fearless. On the way down the mountain the bus driver was passing a beautiful stream flowing down the mountain. Helen Hedgemon was looking at the stream and started talking about how thirsty she was. She just wouldn't stop. As we listened to Helen talking about dying of thirst, our mouths became dry and drier. She described the beautiful clear cold stream flowing right next to the bus and all of us had visions of drinking that cool sparkling spring water. We joined Helen talking about our thirst and asking the teachers and bus driver to please stop and let us touch the stream. I don't know who was crazier, us, the teachers or the bus driver, but we did stop. We rushed to the stream as if we had been in the desert without water for a month. We cupped our dirty hands and drank the unpurified mountain stream water. Once we re-boarded the bus we begin to think about what we had just drunk and all the possible contaminants in it but we shrugged it off saying, "What don't kill you will make you fat!" It was the best water I ever drank.

That night we stayed in a motel in Bristol, Virginia. The owner of the motel gave us a party. While we were attending dinner and the party, Mackie was exploring. She found a window that led to the roof ledge. We sat on the roof for most of the night watching the stars, laughing and having fun while Helen smoked a peace-pipe that she purchased from the reservation. Every moment was becoming a cherished memory that I never wanted to end. The next morning we toured the Luray Caverns, which were beautiful. The stalactites and stalagmites were the largest that I remembered, even when comparing them to Mammoth Cave. Luray was definitely more beautiful and the organ was simply amazing where a tune was played by mechanical arms hitting the stalactites. Luray advertises that you can 'Hear Rocks Sing' as you experience the haunting sounds of the world's largest musical instrument, The Great Stalacpipe Organ." All I can say is that we were completely amazed.

We left Luray and headed for Washington, DC. We toured the Jefferson, Lincoln, and Washington memorials. We also visited the Smithsonian Natural History Museum. At the Capitol we heard a debate on the Civil Rights Bill with Senator Mike Mansfield speaking. The Secretary of State, Dean Rusk, was also there. The Capitol was quite busy that day because General Douglas MacArthur's body was lying in state in the Rotunda after the procession with a rider-less horse and caisson, just as was done for President Kennedy. It brought back that dreaded day. President Johnson and Attorney General Robert Kennedy were in the procession. DC was really putting on a show for us. Of the millions of people who visited that city I'm sure few were privileged to see all that we saw and did in the few days that we were there. We saw the mint where the money was printed, and we also saw the Pentagon. Last we visited Arlington Cemetery and saw the temporary site of President John Fitzgerald Kennedy's grave. That day we happened to catch Senator Ted Kennedy visiting the grave. At some point in DC we ate at a restaurant called the China Doll. I loved it!

Thursday night we arrived at the Hotel New Yorker. My roommates were Anna Jean, Janice Lewis, and Diane Thomas. On Friday we went to China Town, Greenwich Village, Wall Street, Empire State Building, Harlem, the Cathedral of St. John Divine and took the ferry to the Statue of Liberty. That night we ate at an Italian Restaurant, and Yvonne and I ate an entire pizza. We were starving. What an adventure! Saturday we visited the Metropolitan Museum of Art and the Guggenheim. We certainly enjoyed walking in circles viewing the art. This was quite an unusual design for a museum. To end the day we visited Grant's tomb and Central Park. Our sponsors suggested dinner on our own with an early curfew.

Well, anyone can guess that we did not listen. Most of us decided to venture out on our own to Palisades Park in New Jersey. We had heard about the boardwalk and the amusement rides and did not want to come this far and miss it. So, we took the subway and bus and managed to get there.

Wesley was our leader. Fresh from the country, Baton Rougeans, alone in the big city of New York navigating our way to Jersey to Palisades for a night of fun. That was our destination and plan. What a fantastic journey. We made it and enjoyed the rides. We also got back to the hotel before curfew. Our sponsors, Mrs. Patterson, Mr. Young, and Mr. Jenkins thought we had been in the room all night.

The next morning, Sunday, we traveled to the grave and museum at Hyde Park to visit President Roosevelt's home. We were told that the house and horse stable were the same as when he left. That night back in New York we went to Anna Jean's brother's apartment for another party. We all knew Jean's family, Buddo included who was the oldest brother, and he knew us. That was the great thing about the Lab, we all knew each other, our families, parents and grands, brothers and sisters and most of the relatives if they lived in Baton Rouge.

Jean's family was renowned especially because of her Dad, Uncle Buddo. He always had a story to tell. The best one was his house fire when they lived next to Judy and Nan. Now, ordinarily a house fire would not be funny but when Uncle Buddo told it, you'd hurt yourself laughing. He said someone set a fire under his house and he called the fire department. Getting his family safely out of the house before the fire department arrived, he saw where the fire started and began to put it out just as the fireman arrived. Uncle Buddo stuttered and said, "I-I-I showed them where the fire was but they dddidn't listen. They-they put the ladder up and climbed to the rrrroof and started chopping. I-I-I kept telling them that the fire was under the house and not on top but they still dddid not listen. They they kept chopping through the roof into the house and through the floor. By the time they did all that the house was destroyed, not by the fire but by them and I had already put out the fire. Don't ever call the fire department. Sssshit, they cause more damage than the fire itself." The whole city knew the story of Uncle Buddo's fire and would constantly ask him to tell it to someone new just to hear it again. So, everyone knew the Howards, Sylvia, Buddo, Henry, Jean and Baby George who grew up to be called "Dr. Baby George" as a gastroenterologist.

Back to the class trip. Buddo had prepared spaghetti and salad for all of us, and it was delicious. We danced and ate. The Impressions' song, "I'm so Proud," played on the radio as we sang along. This song haunted us during the trip, seeming to play at our most memorable times. It began our journey as we left the school in Baton Rouge. We adopted it as our theme song.

Leaving Buddo's the sponsors told us to go to bed because we had an early morning. We didn't go out, but we did continue the party in our room, which was prohibited. First, several girls came and we began playing cards. Mackie called some of the guys and they came over. We played cards and listened to songs on the radio, danced, and continued the fun. Suddenly, we heard a knock on the door. It was Mrs. Patterson. We hid guys under the beds, in the bathtub, pulling the shower curtain, and in the closet. When she came in she told us to go to bed and she started sending the other girls to their rooms. We were almost clear when someone sneezed in the bathroom. I thought we were caught but Yvonne came out of the bathroom coughing and sneezing. She was always so innocent that Mrs. Patterson didn't question her. Mrs. Patterson left without finding any of the guys. We laughed until we cried.

The next morning Endas came to the room to get his jacket that he left and Mrs. Patterson saw him. She took him to Mr. Young and Mr. Jenkins. They made him pack his clothes and threatened to send him home by bus. We were scared to death. We begged and pleaded with the sponsors to let him stay with the group and not send him back. We promised that we would follow the rules for the rest of the trip. Mrs. Patterson pulled me aside and told me how disappointed she was that I was involved because of all they had gone through to let me go on the trip. She said I should have been appreciative. I told her how grateful I really was and that this was the best thing that had ever happened to me in my life. I explained that nothing was going on in the room, that we were only playing cards and listening to music. No one was even kissing or hugged up. We could have had the door opened. She listened and finally agreed to talk to the other sponsors. The male sponsors acquiesced and allowed Endas to remain, but he had to sit with them on the bus.

Why couldn't I stay out of trouble? It just seemed to follow me where ever I'd go. I was never really doing anything bad, just a little mischievous, breaking a few rules. I promised Mrs. Patterson that I would do everything in my power to make her proud of me. I knew I could do it. Monday, we went to the United Nations and Radio City Music Hall, where we saw a show with the Radio City Rockettes. We ate at the Taj Mahal Restaurant: Yvonne, Diane, Jerome (Coon), Milton Wicks, Samuel Bell and me. We were permitted to select our restaurant that night and this was our choice to try something new like Indian food.

The girls ordered Pink Lady drinks, but they would not serve the boys. I found this unusual but the guys tasted our drinks anyway. I had had a Pink Lady before at Lawry's Restaurant in Los Angeles with Mama and Daddy, and it made me feel grown up. I think the Taj Mahal served us non-alcoholic drinks and would not serve the guys just to make us think we were drinking alcohol. Yvonne swore that she got tipsy. It was all in her imagination. As I drank the Pink Lady, I had a flashback of the conversation I had with Mrs. Patterson and remembered that one whole day had not yet passed and I was again breaking the rules. All I could hope for was that we wouldn't get caught. I could not face Mrs. Patterson and have to ask for forgiveness all over again.

Fortunately, all went well and we did not get caught. I did have to sneak Yvonne into her room and put her to sleep so she would stop giggling so loud. The drinks affected no one but her. She was just high on the trip and life. We all were in heaven.

Tuesday morning we were finally able to sleep late. Then we went shopping for souvenirs in Times Square and on 7th Avenue. The boys bought sport jackets with belts that they thought were the newest styles. They were different from the styles in Baton Rouge. They were so proud of their new buys. That night we went back to Buddo's for the last night in New York. Larry Fields remembers that his father told him not to buy from vendors on the streets of New York but he failed to listen. His cousin, Aaron Hardnett bought a radio and Larry bought an umbrella, a suit and a leather coat. Aaron tried to play the radio on the bus and it had no insides. Larry's umbrella went belly up and his suit shrank. The only thing that he had left was the leather coat that was stolen at a club. He makes us laugh saying he lost all his money in New York and has nothing to show for it.

Wednesday was spent on the bus traveling to Pittsburg. Thursday, we arrived in Mammoth Caves in Kentucky and toured. The stalagmites and stalactites were huge but not as pretty to me as Luray. We left Friday morning, traveled all day and slept on the bus that night. We arrived home Saturday, April 18th at 12:30 PM. Just as we were departing the bus, "I'm so Proud" played on the radio. We stopped unpacking and sang our theme song. We gathered for a group hug and picture and I had to say good-bye. My dream had come to an end.

I couldn't thank Mama and Daddy enough for making the arrangements for me to go on the trip. I thanked the class sponsors and Mrs. Herson, the principal. It was the most wonderful thing that happened to me that year. I was sorry that all of the students from Southern High who desegregated could not attend, but I did not find out I was able to go until the last minute. If I had known earlier, I would have tried to get us all on that bus, but this time I was truly selfish and took advantage of an opportunity of a lifetime. I was hoping that the fun and camaraderie shared would get me through the end of the year at Lee High, but I was sadly mistaken.

As I walked to my first class when I returned to Lee High, the student harassment began fast and furious. I heard stuff like, "I thought you had quit." "Oh, so now you're going to LSU." They bumped, cursed, talked about my family, called me all kinds of names. I thought I had heard them all, but they found new ones. There were new threats but these were about LSU, "No Niggers are going to go to LSU!" What were they talking about? Why were they telling me this? What had happened while I was away?

I had forgotten that a week or so before I left for the trip Daddy had me complete an application for admission to LSU for summer school undergraduate enrollment. Of course, I had done so. Who was I not to follow the dictates of Dupuy Anderson? I didn't give it a second thought because I figured that by the time this had gone through the courts like the eight years it had taken EBRP I would have graduated from a Black institution. I hadn't made up my mind yet where I was going, but I had applied to Spelman and Howard. Mama wanted me to go to Fisk, but they required an autobiography for admission, and I felt that it was too elitist. I wanted to be a regular person again with Black friends who were down to earth.

So, the application to LSU was not given a second thought. I had to do it twice because Daddy sent me to mail it and told me to send it registered with a return receipt requested. I did send it registered but forgot about the return receipt. When I got home and gave him the registered receipt without a return receipt, I had to complete another application and send it to LSU registered WITH return receipt. I got it right the second time. Unbeknownst to me, the newspaper carried an article while I was on the trip that a local Black student had applied for admission to LSU.

Aw, HELL!! I should have known that the senior trip carried a penalty. Too much fun and good times demanded payback. Only four weeks left at Lee High. I could make it. I had to pull out my arsenal of tricks again, put on my armor and fortify my soul. There was no doubt in my mind that I would make it. We had come too far to quit now. If I had to fight my way out of this prison, I would, and nothing or no one could stop me unless they killed me, and they didn't have the balls to do it. Cowards.

As I completed my course work for the end of the year, my hopes and aspirations were elevated. Daddy was following through with the enrollment for LSU and Mama was sending out graduation invitations. Meanwhile I was studying for finals. I felt confident in all my classes, but I knew Mrs. Church's final exam was going to tax every brain cell left in my head. She had prepared us by giving us snippets of information that she was going to request like having to memorize almost all of *Julius Caesar* and *Hamlet* and *Macbeth* along with sonnets and poems. I spent the next few weeks trying to re-commit to memory the passages that we had presented in class. Fortunately, I liked what I was doing and it was not an impossible task. I aced my exams and school came to an end for seniors when finals were completed.

The next week and a half I spent at Southern High waiting for the seniors to complete their exams and nudging them on. After we all finished, we partied every day. I'd go to the Lab and pick up a carful of friends. I had my convertible aqua Nash Rambler that would be overflowing with kids. There were no seatbelt rules then. We'd have kids on the back seat and on top of the back seat. We went to a different house each day and had a party. Paula served the best spiced spaghetti. Yvonne's party was probably the longest card game. The parties were daily and the fun exponentially growing to infinity. Parents were unaware but there was no need to worry because we were just having pure unadulterated fun without sex or destruction.

I practiced graduating with Southern High walking down the aisle and receiving a diploma. We knew that getting to Southern to receive those diplomas was going to be a stretch because the EBR Parish School District scheduled all the graduations from every high school on the same night, including Southern High's. Those of us from the Lab who desegregated were devastated since we wanted to graduate with our class. We vowed to try to make graduation after we completed our own at the white schools even if it meant speeding all the way to Scotlandville.

One thing that was not stopped was our participation in Class Night. We did a cheer, "2-4-6-8 We don't want to integrate! Yeah!" No one would have known that we were not part of the class if they had seen us that week out of school and on class night. All of the students from Southern High were back together again. We planned and created and participated as if we had never left. If only the entire year could have been like this, I would have been spared the heartache. We were home back at the Lab.

Lee High cancelled their senior prom because they did not want us to come. I was so glad because I would have felt obligated to go just to upset them, but fortunately the formal prom was cancelled. I heard that they had one anyway supposedly without the sanction of the school. HA! This would have been impossible. The school knew and probably participated, but I didn't care. I was glad that it didn't include me. That was one event that didn't hurt me, thankfully. I went to Southern High's prom with Victor Baham. He was the son of one of Mama and Daddy's card circle. Victor grew up with Judy, Nan and me, so he was like a close cousin. Daddy did let him pick me up in his car and take me to the prom, but Daddy followed us. I had to be home immediately following the dance and could not go to the after party. I enjoyed the prom and thanked Victor for taking me. He was a great friend who was there for support.

The final days at Lee High were nearing. I could not wait, but I had to go back for the last ceremonies. Lee High did not practice for graduation or baccalaureate. Seniors were just informed to be there at a particular time. On Sunday, May 24, 1963, we lined up outside the auditorium and were told to partner off and just walk in with the partner and be seated splitting partners one on the left and one on the right side of the aisle to be seated. Murphy and I walked together and Melvin and Louis were partners. At the conclusion of the ceremony, which I do not remember, the recession began from the back. Students walked out in partners but the pairing was different. By the time the partners got to us Melvin ended up walking with a white student. Then Murphy and Louis walked together. I walked out into the aisle and waited … and waited…. and waited….but no one walked up to walk with me.

I didn't even turn around to see if anyone was there. I just stood there with my jaws locked swallowing the tears. I stood there until there was no one left in front of me. I stood there until the aisle was clear and all before me had exited the building. Then, I held my head high with my shoulders back eyes focused on the exit sign by the door and took the center of the aisle. I walked out of the auditorium as if I were a bride with a 50-foot train following me. I didn't stop or look back. I walked straight to our car and waited for Mama, Daddy, Aunt Phine, and the boys to join me. Mama was crying as she hugged me and told me how proud she was. She cursed those racist bastards and called them all kinds of names even in front of the boys, which she never did. When we arrived home she called everyone she knew and told them the story of how elegantly I walked out of that auditorium with the stature and decorum of a queen.

All I could think of was hell was coming to an end. One more event and the year was over. Can I get back to normal? Without a practice I could not imagine graduation, but I developed all types of scenarios in my head to try to stay ahead of the game and not have to create a spontaneous response that might self-combust. As I arrived on Thursday, May 28th, 1964 the names of the honor students were being called to line up in the front of the class. We were told that we would walk in single file and sit on the first rows in the front of the class on stage. So, that meant I would walk alone with the other honor students and walk out alone but this time it was planned. I don't remember who spoke or what was said or even receiving the diploma. All I could think about was hoping that whatever was going on would be quick and that I could make it to Southern High to walk out with my real class.

When the graduation ceremony finally ended I raced to Southern High only to see my classmates walking out in the recessional. I had missed graduation. I was surprised to see that they were not in caps and gowns but rather girls in white dresses and boys in dark pants, white shirts and ties. The caps and gowns had not arrived on time. The administration at Southern High was told that all the gowns assigned in our area were used because all of the high school graduations were on the same night. Was Southern High the only one without caps and gowns? Why was it a Black school without them? Why was it always us? Some things we never forget and each reunion, we reminisce about our graduation night. We are hopeful that in 2014 our 50th Year Reunion we will be able to graduate with the Lab School in our green and gold caps and gowns for the first time.

The year of hell was over. Some of the memories I recorded in "Memories

of My School Days." The happiest moment was being able to go on the
senior trip with Southern High. The saddest moment was not playing with
Southern High's band. The luckiest moments were being out for Easter break
at Lee High and attending Southern's District Festival and getting so many
excused absences. Other happy events were being an honor student graduating
with a 3.8 average, becoming a charter member of the Mu Alpha Theta
international math club, playing with Southern High's band at a football
game, Mrs. Church complimenting me on my research paper, going to play
in a parade with Southern's band, playing at the L.E.A. Convention, the
Negro teachers' education association, with Southern High's band, receiving
a superior award at the music festival, and the final day of school. Many
social and civic organizations had dinners and programs that recognized us
with awards for our courageous efforts. I don't remember which organization
brought Thurgood Marshall to speak to us and present us with awards. We
all appreciated their recognition and thanks for our sacrifices. We were glad
to know that our year of hell was not in vain. Thank the Lord Almighty God,
Allah, Buddha, and all the angels and saints and all the transcendental beings
called by any other name. I survived!

Young Men Illinois Club

Daddy and Mama

Top: Southern High Class trip in front of the Capital in Washington, DC.
Middle: Southern High Class trip in front of bus on return.
Bottom left: Freya drinking water from the stream in Smokey Mountains.
Bottom right: Class sponsors, Mr. Young, Mrs. Patterson, Mr. Jenkins

Southern High Class Trip

Senior Week House Party

Ernest,
Yvonne,
Endas,
Freya,
Jerome,
Marion,
Helen

Best Friends Forever
Freya & Marion
Return from Ghana

Southern High Friends

Local Girl Attending Lee High School Is Named As Member of Honor Society

★ ★ ★

Robert E. Lee High School received national recognition last week when it was awarded a charter in Mu Alpha Theta, international high school and junior college mathematics club.

Freya Sandra Anderson, the daughter of Dr. and Mrs. Dupuy H. Anderson, who recently integrated Robert E. Lee High School, has earned the honor of a charter membership in this club.

To be eligible for membership, minimum requirements are that a student must have completed with distinction at leas four semesters of college preparatory mathematics and be enrolled in the fifth semester. He also must have an overall grade of at least a "B" in all of his school work.

The club is sponsored by the Mathematicl Association of America and has attracted the attention of op mathematics scholars in this country and abroad.

Freya was a former student of the Southern University Laboratory School. While attending that school she was a member of the Clark Chapter of the National Honor Society and received re-

Freya Sandra Anderson

cognition for leadership in the Lab school and. She is maintaining her high scholastic record at Lee High by having made the honor roll since she began, and by having passed the tryouts for the Varsity Concert Band of which she is a participant.

Mu Alpha Theta
National Math Honor Society

Lee High Graduation

LSU

"Oh SHIT! It's not over? LSU!" I was standing in court in front of District Judge E. Gordon West. There were a few Black students in the courtroom who had joined together for the suit to desegregate the undergraduate division at LSU. Attorney A. P. Tureaud was representing us. The judge knew that he had to issue the order to desegregate because he had no other alternative. Tureaud had LSU's representative testify that it was the policy of LSU not to admit Blacks in the undergraduate school. Even though the Law School and the Graduate School had already been desegregated and there were Blacks attending classes on campus, the board had a policy not to admit Blacks in the undergraduate section. Judge West listened and turned to Tureaud. He asked him if he had anything else to add. A. P. spoke for a few minutes as West interrupted him stating that LSU had already admitted that they were discriminating and there was no need for further testimony or witnesses. With that we thought he would render a decision to desegregate.

No! That was not the case at all. Judge West told the courtroom full of people and reporters that he would hand down his decision later. He waited until the day school opened for classes to mandate that LSU had to follow through with the court order and desegregate. Since this was the day classes began, registration was officially over. This was late registration. As soon as Daddy was called by Tureaud, we drove to the campus to the registration office. My transcripts were there which alleviated some of the drama. All I had to do was register. Several other Black students tried to register but they did not have transcripts and LSU would not accept the hand carried ones because they were not official. So, some Black students went back to their schools to retrieve official transcripts in sealed envelopes. Others just left defeated.

Once again the system was trying to deter Black students from participating. LSU acted as if they wanted us to file another suit to get them to accept the transcripts. Daddy was there at the desk with me, and he talked to the registrar finally getting him to acquiesce and accept the sealed envelopes. Daddy remained calm but I was ready to jump over that counter and grab someone and slap them silly. The whole scene was too much to bear. Would it ever end?

There was this Black guy standing at the desk who was from Shreveport; his name was Adam. He was the only person that was going to try to stay on campus. He was so naïve. He reminded me of myself on the first day at Lee High. He actually thought that he would make friends and that everything was going to be wonderful once the whites met him. HA! Adam had great plans of changing the world and people's attitudes. We were all going to get along and be friends. Well, after a couple of weeks when the word got around campus that he was staying in the dorm, it was raided. Students broke windows with bricks and stones. They set trashcans on fire, threw garbage down the hall and wrote graffiti on doors and walls demonstrating their hatred, "Nigger go home!" The police had to come and get Adam out to protect him. From that time on, when he wasn't in class, he was with Larry Fields, Aaron Hardnett, and me. When we were finished with our classes, we'd retreat to my house for food, homework, cards, and a game of pool.

During the first week, one night the klan burned a cross in front of the library. It had fallen by the time classes started the next day. The campus police or no one else thought to throw it away. Rather, the students re-erected it in front of the library for all to see as if it were a warning for us to leave. COWARDS! All they could do was burn and run, and all I could think of was, "Please let me catch one of those damn sheets and set it on fire!" I'd actually prayed to catch one. Sometimes, I'd sit at home in the dark watching through the picture windows in the front of the house, hoping that the klan would try to burn another cross across the street. I knew where Daddy kept the gasoline for the lawnmower and I had planned to sneak across the street in the dark, pour the gasoline in the front of the yard and light a match. The grass would burn quickly catching those sheets up in the flames looking like dancing spirals around the already burning cross. These were my dreams. An ancestor greater than me must have been looking out for me because once I had this plan the klan never burned another cross in the yard across the street from us again.

Baton Rouge continued to defy national and even local news. Most of what I remember was not recorded in the newspapers. The city was able to keep the dirty news quiet under the pretense that they were trying not to escalate the racial issues. Our entrance into LSU virtually went unnoticed. All across the country, Mississippi and Alabama were making headlines surrounding racial atrocities, but Baton Rouge remained silent. I think LSU is probably the only university that required three separate lawsuits to desegregate, but very few people know this because Baton Rouge keeps its dirt quiet. If I hadn't lived through the desegregation of EBRP Schools and LSU, I never would have known that it was anything other than peaceful.

I took two classes that summer, English Composition and Beginning Organ. The organ class was not a problem. There were only two other students in the class, and they didn't seem to mind me being there. Occasionally, we spoke between instructions as the instructor individualized presentations. My second class was a different story. It was Lee High revisited but a little less threatening. These college students just moved away from me in class, and naturally the teacher acted as if I didn't exist. Instead of bumping me in the halls, the college students just moved away giving me lots of room to walk. They'd end up bumping into each other trying not to touch me. I appreciated all the extra effort they took to make me comfortable. I loved the "No touchy." Isn't racism nice?

The teacher for English Composition was another story. He didn't pick on me but he was of no help whatsoever. I don't remember how he taught or what he said during class. I just remember that we had writing assignments almost every night. My first few papers were A's over F's. I was devastated. I had never received an "F" in any class except BB's in junior high, and that didn't count. The instructor commented that my content was great but my mechanics sucked. Even though that wasn't his terminology, an "F" sucks. We had one chance to correct the mistakes and bring that grade up, but I could not improve my mechanics. I went back to tutoring this time with Ms. Simmons and Dr. Faggett. They helped me resolve the major problems, dangling participles, misplaced or no commas, etc. If only computers had been invented. I know it's not a complete sentence! With a little more practice, determination, and tutoring, I managed to pass the course and developed a better grasp of writing mechanics in the process.

Between classes I'd meet the guys, Larry, Aaron, and Adam in the union, usually in the Tiger Liar, the café in the LSU student union. After the first week we went downstairs to the bowling alley to kill some time. When we wanted to shoot pool, we'd come home to my house because I had a pool table at my house and there was no need to pay for a game when it was free, and we didn't have to worry about anybody white harassing us. However, one day, between classes, during the second week we decided to shoot pool in the union. Larry and Aaron got their cue sticks. Adam was going to watch us since he wasn't that good and didn't want to embarrass himself in front of whites. When I asked for a cue, the guy refused.

"What the hell? Why can't I get a cue stick?"

He replied, "You're a female."

"Yes, I am. At least the last time I checked I was. Is there a problem?"

"You're not allowed to shoot pool. It's for men only."

I laughed, "I know how to shoot pool. I have a table at my house, and I **will** shoot pool here today."

He replied, "We don't have women shooting pool."

"I just sued to get into this school. Please don't make me file another suit to shoot pool."

He didn't know what to do because he was only a student following the policy of the union. He quickly told me to wait and he went in the back office to talk to somebody greater than he. I saw a couple of men peeking out the side of the door in the back verifying the Black female at the desk who wanted to shoot pool. Someone had a phone in his hand. I guessed he was talking to a higher authority. When the little guy returned to the desk, he returned with a cue for me. I became a bit of a celebrity. All eyes were on me and I had to show off for them. I even did my infamous behind the back straight down the side rail into the end side pocket shot, which caused a little gasp in the room. My guys, Aaron, Larry, and Adam, laughed because they knew that was my shot and that I was enjoying the spotlight.

I looked around and saw white girls beginning to gather and look as we were shooting. Eventually, one of them had the courage to ask for a cue. All the guy at the desk could do was to give her one. From then on the poolroom was open to women, and I had done it without filing a suit, only the threat of one. I was on a mission now to solve the problems of racism **and** gender discrimination. Not until that moment had I ever considered that there was discrimination against women just for being female. I had never faced that before. Being Black was the only reason I had known. This scene was entirely new. I also thought that white women were stupid for not saying or doing anything about it. I wanted to tell those female students who asked for a cue after me, "Hell no, you can't play. If you've sat around all this time allowing these men to tell you what you can't do, you don't deserve to play now." But I cherished the moment of being a hero and said nothing, even if they didn't thank me. You have to learn what battles to fight, and I was getting a bit weary.

That summer the Civil Rights Bill passed Congress. To my surprise President Lyndon Baines Johnson took up the mantle of President Kennedy's Civil Rights Bill and got it passed. He ended up being one of the greatest politicians in the Civil Rights fight. As soon as we heard we went to some of the white cafes in Tiger Town immediately off campus. They would not serve us and we were too few to protest, but we did go to Southern to gather the troops. I went to the union at Southern and told them that the white restaurants would not serve us and "Let's Get it ON!" Freddie Pitcher and others got in cars and we drove to Hopper's on Scenic Highway near the campus. The workers refused to serve us and called the police. Upon arrival the police told us that we had to leave, but we staged a sit-in and refused to move. We filled the place and no one could get served. Finally, Hopper's said they were closing for the day and we had to leave. We did, but we came back. They opened again, and we shut them down again. This went on until they eventually had to close for good. They moved to LSU's Tiger Town and when they reopened, they had to serve us. We made lots of places open up that summer, including the white theaters. It was scary sitting in the dark of a theater not knowing what might happen, but we did it and it was peaceful. I had to admit that I was pleasantly surprised that no one threw soda or popcorn on us. Maybe they couldn't see us in the dark. There may have been a couple of incidents but overall it was peaceful since no one was killed.

While all this was going on in Baton Rouge, LSU was trying to act normal by ignoring us. I really didn't mind that at all. In fact, it was great to not have people all over you trying to be your friend when you knew they were being insincere. Once while I was on the phone in the basement of the union, a huge white boy balled up a sheet of paper and threw it at me. He kept walking with another guy as if nothing happened but laughed as they walked away. I let the phone drop and followed him out of the back of the union. I ran up behind him and started beating him in the middle of his back like a madwoman. He turned around and I kept hitting him in his stomach yelling, "Don't you ever throw anything at me again." With a shocked look, seeing me as a crazy woman, the guy with him took him by the arm and they walked off. I didn't care if he were a giant or a football player or a klansman. Like Fannie Lou Hamer, I was "sick and tired of being sick and tired." I just needed to hurt someone, and I didn't give a damn about the consequences.

I was going to fight the system even if it killed me. Marion and I worked throughout the summer organizing and participating in Voting Drives in the city. We set dates and times and coerced some ministers to let us use their churches to hold the training classes. At that time we still had to take and pass a test to register to vote, which was graded by whites in the registrar's office who could decide whether an answer was right or wrong. There were a few people who came out to learn the procedures and practice the questions and answers, but every vote counted and we worked on getting people registered despite the small turn-out. Many ministers were afraid to let us use their churches. Others did not want to "embarrass" their parishioners. One of the largest congregations was just a sell-out as usual for "mo money, mo money, mo money" and denied us his church.

By the end of the summer, I was exhausted and full of hate. I could not stand to see white people and didn't even want to be in the company of the so-called "good" ones. Daddy had applied for me to go to Newcomb, the female college of Tulane. He promised me a car if I'd go and that I could come home whenever I wanted from New Orleans. My response was, "You can't pay me enough to go anywhere white. I will not desegregate another thing. If I can't go to a Black college, I will not go to school at all. If I can't go to a Black college, I'll kill someone white or maybe myself." I meant every word of it and he knew it. Enough was enough.

Marion went to Newcomb. She had a full ride. I was offered a scholarship, but I declined. She tried to convince me to come with her but I had had enough. I had given my all and had nothing left. She was not as bitter as I was and she was still open minded to make white friends. Somehow she managed to have hope that things could be different. Daddy had taken me to New Orleans to meet a Black female that had desegregated Newcomb the year before. She told me that it definitely was not as bad as what I had been through and that some of the girls were really nice. I tried to consider Newcomb, but my body would not let me go. I didn't want to let Marion down. We had been together since 7th grade, but for my own survival, I could not go. Howard University sent a letter of acceptance. Mama convinced Daddy to let me go. I let Marion down. She went to Newcomb without me. I went to Howard University, Washington DC, the real "Chocolate City!" The time had come for me to rejoin Black Society. The time had come for me to laugh and cry again with no more swallowed tears.

LSU Graduations
Me (BS), Grandmother, Lulu (Masters)

Doctor of Education

George Peabody of Vanderbilt
May 9, 1980

LSU & Vanderbilt Graduations

Epilogue

The almost 50 years to complete the writing of this book made me realize that I was not angry at Kennedy for dying. Instead, I was angry that I had to grow up and face the adult responsibility of fighting for what was right. I had to have the courage of my ancestors who had given their lives for others to survive. I had to develop the dignity and pride to stand with my father and help fulfill his life's work. I'm often asked if I would do it again and each time I have to stop to think about my answer. Yes, I'd do it if I thought it made a difference in the lives of Black children, families and communities, but I'm torn because all too often I don't know whether the difference was for better or worse. Schools are still segregated. Racism still persists and is rampant. Education is worse, especially for the poor, and that includes education for whites.

For what did Daddy fight? It was not to sit next to whites in movies and schools. It was not to go to white stores. It was not for Black men to marry white women. He wanted better education for all children for he felt that was the only way to end discrimination and oppression. He was fighting for equal and better salaries. He was fighting for equal opportunities. Daddy was fighting for equal justice and freedom for all people.

As I look around at school systems across the country, we failed. From LSU to MSU most of the universities are still racist to the degree of hanging nooses over grad students' desks. There are probably fewer Black businesses per capita now than there were then. Blacks have the highest unemployment rates and the greatest percentage of children in poverty. Our families have been destroyed and to a large extent we no longer like, help, or respect each other because as Carter G. Woodson reminds us, we are brainwashed.

Did our ancestors die in vain? Was the loss of my senior year in high school worth it? Did we accomplish anything at all? We opened doors for all people, not just Blacks but Hispanics, Asians, women, gays, lesbians, bi-sexuals, transvestites, Muslims and all other groups that are not WASPS (white Anglo-Saxon protestants). We helped lead what has become a worldwide revolution against oppression, including revolutionary stands like those at Tiananmen Square to the Arab summer that is still in its infancy but growing. I have to believe that we, the thousands of unknowns who struggled against racism, brought some good into the world.

What is the future? I don't know. I can only hope that one day racism will end. Today, 2012, we are still fighting to protect the right to vote as we watch restrictions placed on that Constitutional Right by state legislatures. We are fighting to protect women's rights to make decisions about their own bodies. We are fighting First Amendment rights of religion and speech to allow all religions freedom to practice with respect for their doctrines. We are fighting for equality and justice issues of gender, size, special needs and other differences that make us human. Regardless of race, creed, color, religion, sexual orientation, size, gender, special needs, we are all one people, human beings, who live on this earth that we need to share cooperatively. We cannot remain silent and hope racism will go away. We must teach it away loudly, with passion and a love for humanity. Daddy told me that the answer to racism is love. "Look at other human beings as yourself and try to walk in their shoes. They breathe like I breathe. They eat like I eat. Their blood flows like mine. Until we can feel each other's pain, we are not going to have peace."

I hope that people who read this memoir will retrofit their hearts to become respectful and more humane. How many more children will have to suffer racism and discrimination before this country becomes a more perfect union and live out its creed of life, liberty and the pursuit of happiness? I'm telling this story to my children and family and all people who want to preserve humanity. My hope is that all who read this memoir will make a conscious effort to bring harmony and peace into the world with no more swallowed tears.

Top: Griffin and Freya Rivers
Bottom: Southern High Class of '64 Reunion 2009
Baton Rouge, Louisiana

Griffin Rivers & Southern High Reunion

ME, Now

Each next paragraph could probably be a new book of memoirs because nothing for me has ever been easy, but I want to give a brief insight into who I am today and hopefully I'll get a chance to write the next book. With all that happened and the emotions I felt, I did not want to leave you, my readers, feeling that I still hate.

Thirteen years after the desegregation of the schools, many of the original group had a reunion. That was the first time we had been together since graduation from high school. In fact, we graduated from our separate schools and left each other. Many left the city of Baton Rouge. There was no time to say good-bye. The reunion provided us with the long needed de-briefing session that we should have had at the end of the school year. We finally talked about that horrible year and how it affected us. We also realized that we never should have been allowed to depart without some type of therapy.

All of us went to college, but most of us were unable to complete our degrees within a four-year period. We dropped out, got married, had children or joined various groups looking for love, belonging, respect, and appreciation. We didn't realize how sick with hatred we had become until 13 years later when we started talking about our experiences. The 1963-64 school year had been blocked from our thoughts and memories. We hadn't talked about it to anyone. We didn't even acknowledge it to ourselves. Some of us couldn't remember the things that happened. What we did realize was that the year was traumatic.

I had completely blocked that year from my memory. I hadn't talked about it. I didn't think about it, but I hated white people. I left Baton Rouge and went to Howard University in Washington, DC. Yes, back with beautiful Black folks all around. I had a fantastic time. The men were gorgeous. I got pregnant, married, and dropped out of Howard after two years of partying and not opening a book. My husband joined the service and through our travels, I gradually began to let my guard down and developed a friendship with two white males at Ft. Dix, New Jersey. I could say like whites did, "I have white friends."

Leaving the army with a husband and two children, I returned to Baton Rouge with my family. My brothers had been at the forefront of desegregating Catholic High. Surprisingly, they have all become fine men whom I love dearly, and forgive for all their past deeds. Dupuy Jr. is a master carpenter and creates extraordinary custom cabinets and furniture. Ralph is a retired electrical engineer, and Robert is a dentist now practicing in Daddy's office on North Street.

I returned to LSU to complete my degree in 1971 and through the dual enrollment program at Southern my therapy began. Dr. Huel Perkins was the instructor and the Black American History he taught through literature was overwhelming. The healing started immediately. The inner vacuum of self-knowledge was suddenly opened with new thoughts and ideas. This had been my quest for most of my life.

I read W. E. B. DuBois and Carter G. Woodson among many others in Dr. Perkins' class. I enrolled in six hours of independent study at LSU and studied Marcus Garvey and Frederick Douglas while re-reading James Baldwin. After graduating from LSU, I began a Master of Education program at Southern through Teacher Corps, which was the best teacher certification model that I have ever seen anywhere in this country. Immediately, I realized that these white interns, soon to be teachers, no matter how liberal and compassionate they thought they were, could not go into our Black schools without some history of African Americans and insight into our culture. Quickly, I was assigned the role of Black History consultant for our group. I also acquired more white friends and one in particular, Frank Fudesco.

Completing the program in 1972, I was transferred from Capital Elementary, an all-Black elementary school, to a white elementary school. At that time in Baton Rouge, the school board was assigning the best Black teachers to the white schools and sending inexperienced white teachers to the Black schools. I went to the white school and set up my class. Then I quit. I told Daddy, and he agreed. He assured me that he had my back. Most people don't have that kind of freedom to just walk off a job especially with two children to feed.

I applied for a buyer trainee position at Goudchaux's Department Store and was hired. I became the first Black buyer in a major department store in Baton Rouge and possibly Louisiana. There were only a few Blacks in the country as far as I could tell from the Black buyers that I saw at the major markets in Dallas, New York, Los Angeles and Miami. I loved the travel and buying clothes, but I had two young children who needed me and a buyer was on the road and working late nights which meant that something had to change.

Fortunately, Ms. T. Lois Tacneau heard I would return to teaching if I could be placed in a Black school. She called me with, "Baby, I heard you want to come back to teaching? Well, if that's the case, you have a job at Buchanan." I was teaching again with one of the best principals in the city. Ms. T, as she was called, stacked her faculty in one year with Judy, Justine Potter, Daisy Slan, and me who joined some great teachers already there. She almost forced Judy, Daisy, and me to enroll in the doctoral program in educational administration offered by George Peabody College of Nashville,

Tennessee when we told her about it. Peabody offered one of the first programs of its kind, an off-campus doctoral program. We attended Friday afternoons, all day Saturday and Sunday mornings in New Orleans and spent a summer residency in Nashville. Frank Fudesco was also enrolled and we renewed our friendship. Mr. Freeman was the first person who told us about the program, and we told Ms. T, who told us that we **would** enroll. I didn't think it would be possible because I was a divorced single parent with two children working full time teaching and financially broke. Ms. T helped us with financial aid forms and gave the three of us Friday afternoons off to attend classes in New Orleans. I completed the degree in 1980. During our tenure we were able to turn Buchanan into one of the best schools in the city. The school board then converted Buchanan into a magnet gifted and talented school, and I quit again. Whenever Black institutions excel, they are taken away from us, and that was too much to bear.

During my last year at Buchanan I found out my favorite clothing store was for sale and I went after it with a vengeance. Daddy was my security blanket and financier. I bought the store and changed the name to Freya's. It was a designer boutique in one of the exclusive shopping centers in the city. I had a great run for a while until I decided that I was not going to buy an ad with the Junior League for their Holly Days booklet. The organization was still segregated in Baton Rouge and I told them that I could not patronize a segregated organization to which they replied that they could no longer patronize me. Without their patronage, customer support dwindled which meant that I eventually had to file for bankruptcy. Racism had reared its ugly head again.

I continued my mission for self-knowledge through history and joined a Black reading group initiated by Dr. E. J. Mencer. What a journey that became! We read Dr. Asa Hilliard, Dr. Ivan van Sertima, Dr. Ben Jochanan, Dr. Cheikh Anta Diop, Dr. Charles Finch, Dr. Molefi Asante, Dr. Maulana Karenga, Dr. Harriette McAdoo, Dr. Wade Nobles, Dr. Jwanzaa Kunjufu and many more. WOW! I never felt so empowered. Mama was right. We, Black people, were the mothers and fathers of humankind, civilization, language, math, medicine, physics, architecture, astronomy, art, music, dance and so much more. We were the best of the best.

Collis Temple and I began MERG (Minority Entrepreneurs Research Group), a Black Chamber of Commerce, and held the first Black Business Expo in the city. I married Griffin Rivers, head of the Louisiana Department of Corrections. He and I started Show-Offs, A Performing Arts Studio for teens and Entrepreneur's Retail Institute, a job training facility for adults, both located on College Drive, one of the major thoroughfares in the city. We thought we were moving Black people in Baton Rouge in the right direction and we must have been doing something right because the wrath of racism came barreling down on us like an F5 tornado.

Deciding that bigotry was too deeply embedded in Baton Rouge and there was no way to change the system, we left in 1991 and moved to Lansing, Michigan where Griff decided that he would pursue his doctorate in Criminal Justice at MSU. I joined him for post-doctoral study in Family and Child Ecology. Michigan became our next journey. I began working for the Lansing School District and traveled during the summers to Africa for educational enrichment in African American History.

My first trip was with Dr. Asa Hilliard and Tony Browder to Egypt (KMT), the greatest civilization of all times. The trip was truly amazing and Dr. Hilliard was absolutely a genius. He became my mentor and friend. The next summers were spent with Dr. Molefi Asante in Egypt, Senegal, Ghana and Cote D'Ivoire. Marion joined me for a wonderful trip. I went to Nigeria for a Women of Africa and the African Diaspora Conference where I acquired the paintings that now adorn the cover of this book and saw some of the most remarkable art everywhere I turned. I convinced Marion to go to Egypt with Dr. Hilliard, and I went again. At that point I could not get enough of the continent. Just a mention of a trip to Africa and I was on board to a journey to my homeland.

Meeting Dr. Asante opened another door to my growth. He introduced me to Dr. Maulana Karenga and his beautiful wife, Tiamoya. Dr. Karenga and Dr. Theophile Obenga instructed me in the foundation of MAAT and the cosmology of ancient KMT (Egypt) which became my spiritual foundation. Through these teachings and knowledge of my history, I became whole.

Another journey was calling at Willow Elementary in Lansing. A parent volunteer, Larry Scott, began prodding me to open a charter school. He liked the work that I was doing with the children in my class and the afterschool Afrocentric program that I began. I did not like the idea of charter schools and I still don't because the majority of our children will always remain in traditional public schools while charters and cyber-schools take money away. However, the thought of finally being able to teach children my way, create my own school and write my own curriculum was one of my last goals to conquer. I could not pass this opportunity to prove that children would excel under my leadership.

Larry and I worked together and both of us eventually started charters. I began Sankofa Shule, which was acclaimed "an Educational Powerhouse" by U. S. News and World Report (April 27, 1998). The Wall Street Journal acknowledged us in an article on charter schools (Wednesday, February 7, 1996). My ultimate dream was realized. Sankofa's Afrocentric curriculum, my curriculum, worked and our children succeeded.

In the forefront again promoting African culture pressure mounted from the Black and white community, and I resigned from Sankofa. I've never been good at compromise. The board wanted to change my vision and the public wanted to change our focus. I refused to do either. When I know something is right, it's my way or no way at all for me, and I still like it that way. I'm just lucky that Daddy was able to give me the luxury of being free. Most people never enjoy this total freedom where they never have to put up with people or things that compromise their ethical principles. I hope to do the same for my children and grandchildren. I want to be there for them to help them stand up for what they believe is right and make the necessary sacrifices to do so. My children were the second part of my rehab after my submersion in African American History and spirituality. Wanting a better life for them my mission was to make the world a better place for all children and that was through education. By providing children with excellent educational opportunities and truth, they are far less likely to become pawns of racism. Education is the key to opening the mind and freeing thought.

Continuing my journey Lansing School District recruited me as the principal of Bingham Elementary where I spent my last years before retirement. The faculty was apprehensive when they heard I had been assigned because they heard many unkind rumors about me in the community but I was able to convince them that I was an excellent educator and administrator. We slowly established long term friendships as they realized I cared deeply about them and the students. I have only one rule anywhere I go and that is RESPECT. I try to model the behavior I expect from others, but I still speak my mind and rarely let anyone walk over me or else I wouldn't be me.

The irony in achieving my dream is that the desegregation of EBR Parish Schools led me on the journey to know myself. With that knowledge of self, I finally became secure in my body. Baton Rouge and LSU still bring back memories of pain, but they no longer control my emotions or life. My knowledge of self and my people allowed me to gain respect for all peoples or the world. I'm sorry Daddy did not live to see the first African American President Barack Obama elected because that would have been his dream realized, but the election has not changed racism. In fact, Obama's election has brought racism and racists to the forefront in ways that I had never imagined, from cartoons to killing Blacks again without any rational reasons other than hatred. With President Obama's brilliance and accomplishments if he had been white, he would have been heralded for saving the world from a depression and terrorism while at the same time providing health care to most citizens. Yet, racism haunts his every move. We must begin a real conversation on racism to make it extinct.

Another constant besides racism in my life remains the Southern

University Laboratory School Class of 1964. We have reunions and mini-reunions to preserve our friendships. 2009 began the mini-reunions with trips to Alaska 2011 and Washington, DC 2012 to revisit our class trip. We are family and tight as ever. We lie, tell tall tales, and laugh and dance and have fun from the moment we see each other until we leave. I am so very thankful that nothing has ever destroyed our relationships. Our last trip to DC brought back memories of our great adventures. We were hoping for one more when we visited the White House but were unable to see President Barack Obama, First Lady Michelle Obama or Bo. However, I did meet the President when he was campaigning in Grand Rapids, Michigan and had a photograph taken with him. All I could do was grin and tell him, "I never thought I'd see this day!" I know he's probably heard that a million times but I hope he understands that for those of us who sacrificed to make him a reality, he is truly a miracle. Our class took pictures at Union Station superimposed with the President in the Oval Office to lie a little when we returned home.

I returned home to my third and last rehab, family. My husband, children, grandchildren, parents, brothers, aunts, uncles, cousins, in-laws and out-laws keep me sane. People ask me how I remember so much of what has happened in my life, and my answer is family. We love each other and love being together. Just give us an excuse for a dinner or party and we're there immediately telling stories and laughing. Those stories have been passed down from generation to generation and hopefully will continue. Our family is old fashioned. We talk to each other. We love to tell stories about our lives and those of our ancestors. In the ancient African tradition of libations, when we call the names of the deceased, they never die. They live forever in the hearts and minds of the next generation.

That's why I wrote this book—to tell the story, to keep history alive, to call the name of my father, Dr. Dupuy Henry Anderson. All I can do is hope that reason, truth and harmony will ultimately prevail over hate, racism and violence. I found truth and in doing so, I found myself. I am free, free to be fully human and humane. Thank you Daddy… and Mama, too

Sara (Robert's daughter), Angela (Robert's daughter), Dupuy Jr., Ralph, Robert, Jennifer (my son Aaron's daughter), Aaron (Robert's son)

Anderson sons

Shakita (my daughter), me, Maana, Asha (my granddaughter), Robert, Jr.

Nyah (my granddaughter), Ausar & Kasi (my grandsons)

Anderson Children, grands, great-grands

**Standing: Cheryl, Sonya, Marion, Joann, Mackie, Brenda
Kneeling: Freya, Ernest**

Some of this crew:
Leonard, Ernest, Marie, Freya, Yvonne, Paul, Wesley, Lorita, Cheryl, Larry, Marion

SU Reunions

DC Reunion 2012
Amos, Matthew, Tony, Freya, Bernard, Joann, Marvin, Anna Jean, Marion, Veronica, Cynthia, Larry, Mackie, Irene, Milton, Merrill, Janice, Elaine, Yvonne, Helen

DC Reunion 2012 Peoples Congregational Church
Helen, Carmen, Marion, Mackie, Bernard, Milton, Marvin

Rev Murphy, Matthew, Cynthia, Larry, Irene, Freya, Anna Jean, Anna, Elaine, Milton

SU Reunions

Permissions

Louisiana State University Libraries

Dupuy Anderson Oral History Interview, Mss. 4700.0418, Louisiana and Lower Mississippi Valley Collections, LSU Libraries, Baton Rouge, LA

Freya Rivers Oral History Interview, Mss. 4700.0335, Louisiana and Lower Mississippi Valley Collections, LSU Libraries, Baton Rouge, LA

The Advocate

State Times, Tuesday, September 3, 1963, Capital City Press, Baton Rouge, LA

Morning Advocate, Wednesday, September 4, 1963, Capital City Press, Baton Rouge, LA

Disclaimer
Some of the names have been changed to protect heirs and relations.

About the Author

Freya Anderson Rivers is the director of The Genius Academy, an educational consulting group. She is a retired principal from Bingham Elementary of the Lansing School District and founder and creator of Sankofa Publishing Company, Sankofa Shule College Preparatory Public School Academy and Sankofa Watoto Preschool. Sankofa, an Afrocentric charter school was called an "Educational Powerhouse" under her leadership by U.S. News & World Report and was also highlighted in The Wall Street Journal. She has diversified experience as a teacher, educational consultant, publisher, retail business owner and a leader in government, economic and social issues. (www. thegeniusacademy.org)